Roy Masters coached first grade rugby league. He was St George's longest-serving coach and was named Coach of the Century. An award-winning sports journalist, he has written for *The Sydney Morning Herald* for two decades. Roy is a member of a well-known literary and media family, his mother Olga being one of Australia's foremost novelists. An inaugural member of the Australian Sports Commission (1984), Roy still serves on the board, having initiated the program of modified sports for primary school children.

Roy is married to Elaine Canty and divides his time between Sydney and Melbourne.

BAD BOYS

AFL, Rugby League, Rugby Union and Soccer

ROY MASTERS

RANDOM HOUSE AUSTRALIA

A Random House book
Published by Random House Australia Pty Ltd
Level 3, 100 Pacific Highway, North Sydney, NSW 2060
www.randomhouse.com.au

First published by Random House in 2006
This edition published in 2008

Copyright © Roy Masters 2006

The moral right of the author has been asserted.

All rights reserved. No part of this book may be reproduced or transmitted by any person or entity, including internet search engines or retailers, in any form or by any means, electronic or mechanical, including photocopying (except under the statutory exceptions provisions of the Australian Copyright Act 1968), recording, scanning or by any information storage and retrieval system without the prior written permission of Random House Australia.

Addresses for companies within the Random House Group can be found at
www.randomhouse.com.au/offices.

National Library of Australia
Cataloguing-in-Publication Entry

Masters, Roy.
Bad boys.

ISBN 978 1 74166 756 1 (pbk.)

Football players – Australia.
Football players – Australia – History.
Football – Australia.
Football – Australia – Employees.
Scandals in mass media.
Celebrities – Australia.

796.330994

Excerpt from *The Sun Also Rises* by Ernest Hemingway, published by Jonathan Cape. Reprinted by permission of The Random House Group Ltd.

African Journal from Ernest Hemingway: *True at First Light*, edited with Introduction by Patrick Hemingway id. Brooks © Hemingway Foreign Rights Trust. Originally published by *Sports Illustrated*. Reprinted by permission of Scribner, an imprint of Simon & Schuster Adult Publishing Group.

Cover Photo: Paul Harragon shows a bit of cheek at a 1994 Kangaroo team photo shoot. Harragon is not otherwise mentioned in this book and not in any way portrayed as a 'bad boy' of rugby league.

Typeset by Midland Typesetters, Australia
Printed and bound by Griffin Press, South Australia

Random House Australia uses papers that are natural, renewable and recyclable products and made from wood grown in sustainable forests. The logging and manufacturing processes are expected to conform to the environmental regulations of the country of origin.

10 9 8 7 6 5 4 3 2 1

CONTENTS

BAD BOYS, THE BRAND AND THE BLAME	1
BAD BOYS AND BAD BLOOD	37
BAD BOYS AND BIRDS	73
BAD BOYS AND THE BENCH	109
BAD BOYS, BONDING AND BUSTED BODIES	147
BAD BOYS AND BRAWLS	183
BAD BOYS AND BETTING	219
BAD BOYS AND BOARDROOM BATTLES	255
BAD BOYS AND THE BEYOND	289

BAD BOYS, THE BRAND AND THE BLAME

Their eyes are a window to where madness is born.

Some have a stare so steely and assassin-like, the eyes perform laser surgery, searing through the quivering psyches of their targets. Others have the look of a draft horse in a burning barn – their wild eyes simultaneously frightened and frightening. The bad boys of football all have their mad moments.

Sometimes you see it in a game, the dressing room, the pub or an end-of-season trip. The bad boy's personal space expands to become a dark grove, charged with menace. It begins to crackle with electricity and you wonder what the hell might happen, and how far it will go before something arrives to temper the temper? A scrum erupts; a dressing room taunt becomes a fierce exchange; a blow thrown in the local ends with a glass ashtray smashed over a head.

The public has a fascination with bad boys. Why else would film-makers cast them in roles after they retire from football?

English football player Vinnie Jones – sent off 12 times during a 12-year career with five clubs and fined for threatening to rip off an opponent's ear and 'spit in the hole' – now plays villains in the movies. In 2003 he began auditioning for 'serious' roles when he was convicted of an air rage incident for slapping a fellow passenger and threatening to have the cabin crew murdered for £3,000. He became an early inductee into England's Hall of Shame for breaking a player's leg in a tackle and being photographed applying the 'Christmas hold' to superstar Paul Gascoigne.

Carlton's captain in the 1945 'Bloodbath' Grand Final, Bob Chitty, initiated the violence in what is still considered the most brutal game in Aussie Rules history – umpires spent two hours writing reports. In 1951 Chitty played the role of Ned Kelly in a film, prompting another legendary tough man, Jack 'Captain Blood' Dyer, to say it was the 'first time Chitty ever needed armour'.

New Zealand's Keith Murdoch, sent home from an All Black tour of Great Britain in 1971–72 for punching a security guard, was back in the news 30 years later when he was a witness in a coroner's inquest into the death of a 20-year-old Aboriginal burglar thrown down a mine in the Northern Territory. He was later cleared of any wrongdoing.

Jack Gibson, rugby league's emeritus coach, believed fear motivated the bad boys. He once confronted the Tigers' giant prop Steve 'Blocker' Roach, now a radio commentator and assistant coach at Manly, and said enigmatically, 'Everybody has fear.' Blocker, a glowering and combustible personality, admits he did not understand what Gibson meant, but the great coach, who often spoke in riddles, was implying that great fear – tightly controlled – is great strength.

Fear is your best friend or your worst enemy. It's like fire. If you can control it, it can cook your food and warm you. Let it out of control, and it will incinerate you and everything that belongs to you. Controlling your fear makes you more alert, like a rabbit edging across a lawn. Legendary AFL coach John Kennedy, later to become chairman of the AFL Commission, once declared that anyone without fear was either superhuman or stupid.

Les Boyd, former Western Suburbs and Manly forward and bad-boy prototype, in full flight had the look of a man dropped on a wild stallion for the first time – all arse and elbows, angles and effort. Once during a game for the Magpies against the Roosters at Lidcombe Oval, he tackled fullback Russell Fairfax in a way I have never seen replicated. Boyd played in a special realm that day, as though he was not subject to the laws of physics.

Fairfax was running helter-skelter to the posts for a try and a standard tackle would have carried him over the line, especially with the impact of the powerful second-rower driving him. Somehow Boyd arrived behind Fairfax, as if dropped from the sky. He lifted the fullback on the spot and sent him crashing down on his shoulder, performing the entire manoeuvre in a square metre of space, a monstrous display of surprising swiftness and heart-stopping power.

Those of us only 40 metres away on the bench stared at each other, mouths agape, simultaneously turning a question into an exclamation, saying, 'Did you see that!' Despite being the best tackle you could ever hope to see, it would be banned today under the lifting convention.

The match wasn't televised, meaning the moment can only be resurrected by the fevered imaginations of those who witnessed it. Of course, other Boyd moments were captured on film, including his first-half domination of Great Britain in the deciding Test in England in 1978. Boyd played above everybody that day. He was Babe Ruth pointing to the stands in the 1932 World Series, signalling his imminent home run. He was a sight to behold: knees pumping, shoulders swaying, defenders bouncing off him as they would from a rolling boulder. This menacing mass of muscle and hustle so impressed Australian coach Frank Stanton that he walked from the bench onto the field to accompany Boyd off.

TV also captured moments that led to the 'baby-faced killer', as one newspaper called Boyd, being handed two of the longest suspensions ever. He was given 12 months for breaking the jaw of Queensland forward Darryl Brohman in a State of Origin match and three weeks after returning from this suspension – in a club match for Manly – was handed a 15 month penalty for gouging the eyes of Bulldog hooker Billy Johnstone. Yet he had an uncanny instinct for the workings of the law. He holds the record for the most number of appearances by a sportsperson before a Supreme Court, some of them instigated himself because of his inherent grasp of what is meant by denial of natural justice.

He suffered white line fever from an early age, his hair-trigger temper turning his mood violent when provoked. Yet he also possessed a looking-glass self: he could see himself as others saw him.

Les once rang me, chuckling about a visit he made back to Nyngan, the small central western NSW town where he was raised. Nyngan had organised a gathering of all the town's former sports stars, and it seems the local kids had heard of one of Les's adolescent exploits: biting off a piece of a 14-year-old opponent's ear.

'Their parents must have told them about it,' he said by way of explaining what came next. 'When I pulled up out the front of the function, the kids were there waiting. "What's an ear taste like, Mr Boyd?", they said.'

He was always tolerant with children, and his job as a schools development officer with the now defunct *Sun* newspaper dictated this behaviour. But the occasional comment, via a parent, ate at his heart.

We attended a clinic for primary school kids once, teaching them passing, handling, tackling and kicking skills. 'My mother hates you,' one youngster told him.

I shot Les a sympathetic glance before he mumbled to me, 'I don't give a fuck – she's probably a slut anyway.'

A decade after he'd retired, I spent one Christmas with Les, his wife, Judy, and their two children at their Cootamundra home. I watched him throw an extra spoonful of butter into a saucepan as Judy prepared dinner, which offered a clue as to why his body looked like a third helping of mashed potatoes. Of course, arthritis has also reaped its devastating harvest, and he has artificial hips and so many knee operations that it would have been easier to sew zippers on either side of both legs. Yet weight and crepitation were irrelevant Christmas morning when his son, Grant, then 8 years old, stood drenched on the doorstep. He had been given a new pushbike for Christmas, a top-of-the-range model, all gears and lights and chrome.

A heavy rain squall overnight had flooded the creek that bisected the road past their home, only 200 metres from the historic cottage where Don Bradman was born. Grant, anxious to try out his new bike, sped along the road towards a concrete culvert, then swamped with the swift-moving floodwater. The current picked up Grant and the bike, cascading them off the culvert and into the creek running two metres above its usual level.

An adult neighbour seized Grant's hand just before the current sucked him into a huge concrete pipe that channelled water under the length of the town. The neighbour walked him to the porch where Grant now stood, a younger version of the teenager who stands penitent before his father after he has wrecked the family car. The entire neighbourhood buzzed with the chatter of kids who had seen the best present in the street disappear before breakfast and the son of the town's best-known citizen almost drown.

Two days later when the water subsided, Les walked to the creek and stood on the culvert, testing the speed of the stream, then up to his knees as it eddied in murky swirls around his tree-trunk sized legs. Confident he could stand, he then stepped off the concrete into the creek bed, the water now slapping against his back. He felt for the bike with his toes, occasionally leaning down and scooping up a drowned relic, such as an old pram.

The neighbourhood kids had assembled for the rescue mission, and the look of wonder on their little faces when he actually found an old rusted bike, devoid of any attachments, endures. You could see their little minds whirring: had Grant's bike suffered all that rust in so short a time?

A few moments later, Les's stubby toes located the bike with its seat savagely cut. Lifting it from the creek bed, he handed the bike to his son, patted him on the head and told him all that mattered was he hadn't drowned. The lesson was learned, without the long lecture the father himself had faced from a legion of disciplinarians.

Other bad boys have a look so steely, you'd swear they could smelt iron ore with their eyes. Malcolm Reilly, the Manly icon, Great Britain international and Newcastle premiership coach, studies people with the wariness of one who trusts nothing but his own eyesight. His vaporising glare so terrified opponents that some tried to gouge out his eyes.

Most bad boys have card-counting eyes. Eyes of a bird of prey. Phil Franks, who played for five clubs, has a look of cold, frank appraisal as he examines his subject, head tilted to one side as if he is studying a painting hanging slightly askew. His is an explosive, volcanic personality, as newspaper photographs of his confrontations with council inspectors, valuers and policemen attest.

Now a millionaire property developer living in a $4 million apartment in The Rocks that overlooks the Opera House, Phil has lived with a cape of suspected villainy slung around his shoulders for 40 years, the whispered accusation he killed former team-mate George Piper. He told me the full story recently (related in the final chapter), emotions rolling over his sharp features like cold fronts on a weatherman's map.

Nicknamed 'Filthy Phil' by some ex-footballers, the file of stories on him appears ever expanding – threatening to 'glass' people in pubs, producing a hand gun to threaten others, or waiting for Dallas Donnelly to get drunk in order to king-hit him. Phil's volatility is such that having a meal with him is like picnicking on the slopes of a smouldering volcano. Yet when he invited a group of his friends to dinner on the Gold Coast to celebrate a significant birthday, some of the code's biggest names accepted, including Ken Arthurson and Colin Love – the past and current chairmen of the Australian Rugby League.

He moved the guests with his welcoming speech. 'This is the only party I have ever had,' he said, explaining he had been raised in orphanages and reformatories. Franks is a man with a short temper but a long memory, and the guests were those who had treated him fairly.

The measure of any man, certainly any sportsperson, should no more be his worst moments than it should be the colour of his skin or the place of his birth. It's how we deal with those lapses in judgement that makes us who we are.

Australians accept this as the greatest gauge of success: to fail once, to pick yourself up and have another go. Perhaps it's our convict heritage, but we are a nation of losers made good, descendants of those who settled here in search of a second chance. To fail is not Australian. It is human. But it is distinctly Australian to overcome the failure, to counter bad luck.

The team ethos dictates we take collective responsibility for the errors of the individuals. This in turn implies an understanding that justice in the professional football codes is often unfair.

Punishment is often meted out poorly; players are often blamed for others' deeds. A coach savagely rebukes a player at half-time for throwing a pass that was intercepted for a try, while the real culprit escapes retribution. Coaches can't hear everything said on the field.

The omerta of the clubhouse requires the subject of his abuse sit head down, acknowledging the error, willing the tirade to end while silently knowing another player called for him to pass the ball. The call may have been a priority one, meaning the culprit used the code word that dictates his call must override all others.

Former dual international John Gray, a Great Britain forward in both rugby codes (plus an English county cricketer before playing first grade for North Sydney and Manly), says, 'I have often thought how little of what is said on the field is ever understood on the other side of the boundary fence. The crowd have no idea, although the person with the best chance of knowing what is said is the coach.'

Dual rugby World Cup finalist Nathan Grey elaborates, 'I sometimes sit in analysis sessions and wonder why a certain player doesn't put his hand up, acknowledging the error. Teams try to promote taking responsibility for your own actions, yet some are still quick to make excuses and others don't own up. It doesn't go unnoticed by other players. We do talk about it afterwards.' Shakespeare observed in *Measure for Measure* that, 'Some rise by sin and some by virtual fall,' and many footballers would identify with this.

The hierarchy of authority in football is also unfair. 'What would she know? She never played,' someone who played football only at school might say. 'What would he know? He never played grade,' says someone in third grade, through to 'What would he know? He never captained Australia.' Yet the decent men at the very pinnacle of the pyramid understand such exclusive thinking causes a sport to become a closed system and stagnate. Good men appreciate the role of talent and luck.

Historical TV vision of Ron Barassi, winner of ten AFL premierships as a player and coach, strutting across the field suggests he managed teams much the way Jack London's sadistic captain, Wolf Larsen, skippered the *Sea-Wolf*: an unrelenting taskmaster who tolerated neither mental nor physical errors.

Or you could imagine him as the 10-year-old Margaret Thatcher, who objected to a school presenter complimenting her on her good luck upon receiving a book prize. 'Luck had nothing to do with it,' the future UK Prime Minister said. 'I deserved this.'

However, when Barassi speaks of Stan Alves, now a commentator in Melbourne, his words are soft and sombre, faintly tinged with sadness. 'I often think of him,' he says. 'He played at Melbourne for 12 years and never played in a final. That's the same length of time I played there. If I'd been born the same time as him, I wouldn't have either.

'Stan did win a premiership at North Melbourne with me when I was the coach,' Barassi adds, hinting he is pleased to have helped Stan finally prevail. 'He lost a 14-year-old son, killed in a level-crossing accident. He was sacked by St Kilda as coach. He has had sad times.'

While Barassi's point is the unfairness of history, Gerard Healy, another former Melbourne player, Brownlow medallist and AFL commentator, makes the same point about geography. 'Where you lived was important in the 1970s and 1980s,' he says of a system, pre-salary cap and draft, where Melbourne clubs were assigned zones of recruitment throughout Victoria. 'If you lived in Melbourne's zone, you didn't play finals footy. Great players played at clubs where they slavishly performed their duties, such as Robert Flower, a highly decorated player at Melbourne who played in only one final – the last of his 15 seasons with the Demons. The same with Bob Skilton at South Melbourne.

'The tribunal can also be unfair, rubbing out players from a grand final. This is a life sentence for some blokes. The stewards recognise this in racing, allowing jockeys to ride in the Melbourne Cup and then do three months. It was also unfair in the 1960s and 1970s, pre-State of Origin, when state teams were picked on a formula of three players from the top clubs and one from the bottom club. If Bob Skilton took up the one spot and you played for South, you didn't get a look in.'

Any rugby league player not at St George during the Dragons' run of eleven successive premierships would argue it was unfair to be born at this time as well. And the current generation of Dragons would curse the retributive cosmic forces that have seen the club lose every grand final they've played in in the 1980s, 1990s and the new century.

North Sydney, perpetually cursed by bad luck, bought Wests' Barry 'Barney' Glasgow, a prolific field goal kicker, because they believed he would turn narrow losses into wins. The moment he arrived, the league dropped the value of the field goal from two points to one.

Barassi made 17 grand finals as a player and coach, yet the 1958 loss still sits underneath his eyelids at night. Melbourne were headed for their fourth successive premiership that year, set to equal Collingwood's cherished record, when both teams met in the grand final.

'I've always thought about that match,' Barassi said one day while we sat sipping coffee at his 'office', the Street Cafe in St Kilda. While waiting for him to arrive in my car outside the cafe, I'd watched him stride down the street, dressed in T-shirt and shorts, still gazing at the world with an upturned chin, as if daring someone to take a poke at it.

He was five minutes early, took a seat in the corner and laid his mobile phone on the table. He looked alert, fit and prepared, just as he approached football games. The logo on his shirt celebrated AFL in Papua New Guinea. He explained he was in serious training, preparing to walk the Kokoda Track in July 2006 to celebrate his 70th birthday.

As he ordered two coffees, I mentioned the track's treacherous surface, saying it was slippery with many roots. 'That's good,' he chuckled, his eyes narrowing wickedly. 'Do they fly them in?'

But we were there to talk football. 'We were the best team on the year. They were the best team on the day,' he said of the 1958 Grand Final. 'That can be unfair. There used to be a challenge thing in the VFA where if the top-of-the-ladder team was beaten, it had the right of challenge. But I don't like that idea. I don't like the challenge. Sometimes football is unfair, but it's one of the beauties of competitive sport. There is a lot of luck – both good and bad – in football. You experience it as a kid and then as a teenager. In 1958 they threw the tough stuff at us, and half of us took them on and the other half didn't take them on. I've often thought if we were united we could have won. Good on Collingwood for protecting their record of four in a row.'

There are many who see Barassi as godlike, someone who walks on water. In fact, he did just that when he carried the Queen's Baton on the final approach to the MCG for the Opening Ceremony of the Melbourne 2006 Commonwealth Games, walking across the Yarra along a submerged pontoon. But he's also suffered personal injustice, accepting blame silently.

He was once savaged by his old club, Melbourne, when, as Carlton coach, he made a comeback in order to record 50 games with the club, making his sons eligible to play with the Blues under the father and son rule. The Melbourne coach, an old team-mate, was highly critical Barassi would choose the Demons, then in the doldrums, to register his milestone.

Barassi explained, 'I intended to play only the one game so my two sons could play with either Melbourne or Carlton. I just had to pick one game where I reckoned we could win with me on the field. It just turned out to be Melbourne.'

Barassi had basically popularised the handball game – moving the ball via hand passes rather than kicks – and he was frustrated none of the Blues could initiate it. 'I also wanted to get back on the field to get the handball game going again. Anyway, the opposition coach said I was diminishing them by choosing to play against Melbourne.'

Then, to demonstrate he wasn't all-powerful at Carlton, he volunteered another story. 'My match committee dropped me one week before the finals in 1968 when I was captain-coach,' he said, a major gamble considering there was not a single premiership player in the '68 team. 'They were right. It made me so glad I chose people on the match committee who weren't yes-men. We did win the premiership without me as a player, although I was coach. A few of the selectors had a meeting beforehand and decided Barassi was finished as a player.'

I turned the conversation back to his comeback match and his public humiliation over the noble motivation of helping his sons into history. 'Did your sons play with Carlton?' I asked, aware his own father had played for Melbourne before losing his life in World War II at Tobruk.

'They didn't become players,' he replied, looking away. A curtain had come down briefly between us, providing a rare glimpse of the burden of playing your father's game with your father's name.

Accepting blame on behalf of others is a long-standing tradition in Australian sport. Swimming great Dawn Fraser was suspended for ten years, partly for stealing the Emperor's flag at the 1964 Tokyo

Olympics, taking the rap for a male hockey player who took 30 years to own up.

In a grand final an assistant coach, monitoring fatigue levels, makes the call to substitute a player whose replacement commits a horrendous error that changes the course of the game. The head coach shields his assistant, accepting responsibility.

In the rugby codes, a scrum erupts and a referee blows his whistle, penalising a player for throwing a punch, while suspecting it is retaliation for a more heinous, unseen act. Yet the whistle man knows he is forced to act because the violence is visible to the crowd and, more importantly, to the men who appoint him. This was brought home to three billion people around the world when Frenchman Zinedine Zidane was sent off in the 2006 World Cup final for a head-butt to the chest of an Italian player. Zidane's reaction was so swift that everyone knew the Italian had said something cruel and personal, but Italy went on to win the biggest prize in world sport, playing against a ten-man French team.

Representative selectors are also guilty of abandoning players with blood on their hands. They may incite a player to be aggressive to stir up meek team-mates whose selection was their responsibility. The player is sent off, suspended and vilified, but he stays silent, refusing to 'give them up', while the selectors are reappointed for another season of all-expenses-paid trips around the country. Shakespeare's words in *Richard III* are fitting: 'Our bruised arms hung up for monuments.'

Les Boyd insists NSW selectors entered the Lang Park dressing room on the eve of the Origin match where he was suspended, admitting they had chosen a weak pack and basically telling him the Blues' hopes rested with him creating mayhem.

'One of the selectors came up to me about a week after I was suspended. He said thanks and I asked, "What for?"' Boyd recalls. 'He said, "I really thought you were going to shaft us for what we said before the game." It never really entered my head to do that.'

The inherent unfairness of football is not confined to the field. A player cuts corners at training and everyone has to run an extra lap of the oval. Someone damages property on an end-of-season trip; no-one outs him and everyone shares the fine, often well in excess of the cost of the damage.

It can be argued that in all of life, not just team sports, justice errs on the side of what is intrinsically legal, rather than what is inherently right. The gap between the court of law and the court of public opinion was evident in the OJ Simpson murder trial. The former NFL player followed the advice of his lawyer and stayed out of jail – but for what result? The reputation of the Juice's lawyer became ten-times greater, and his became ten-times worse.

Unfairness in team sports is replicated in the military. The 1962 movie *Billy Budd*, based on an unfinished Herman Melville novella published after his death, captures this collision between what is deemed fair and what is deemed lawful.

Budd is a likeable, softly-spoken seaman with a shocking speech impediment. The cruel master-at-arms, John Claggart, played by Robert Ryan, sadistically uses flogging to suppress the crew. The master targets Budd mercilessly, who, when confronted in a hostile situation, can't defend himself because of his uncontrollable stammer. The captain and the senior officers, including one played by Peter Ustinov, are a humane group who cannot abide the master's tactics. When Claggart hauls Budd before a hearing, he goads him to the point of collapse. Budd lashes out and hits the master, who falls awkwardly and dies. The officers, who witnessed it all, hold a court martial and compassionately find Budd not guilty.

But the captain argues that they have reached a verdict in accordance with conscience rather than law. Recalled to a second hearing, they are torn by a choice between their hearts and their duty under the law – and they vote for Budd to be hanged. The movie has a telling exchange between two officers.

Lieutenant Seymour: 'Wyatt, we do not deal with justice here, but with the law.'

Lieutenant Wyatt: 'Was not the one conceived to serve the other?'

Substitute the word 'law' for the need to have a victim and you have justice in professional team sport.

Only a diversion, such as a common enemy, alleviates the unrest of the crew in Melville's story. As Budd hangs on the yardarm, a French ship appears on the horizon and the team ethos dictates they ignore their own wrong and divert their energies to destroying the French.

Two parallel trends exacerbate the growing conflict between players and their club administration – coaches are keen to empower players in order for them to impose their own discipline, while boards are increasingly sensitive to the expectations of sponsors and fans.

A year after the tempest of sexual assault allegations in rugby league, Newcastle players visited Bathurst on a pre-season trip, producing a tale reminiscent of *Billy Budd*. A young forward, Dane Tilse, entered a dormitory in the university town and sat, inebriated, on the bed of a female student who was spending her first night away from home.

The NRL, savaged by the loss of corporate sponsors from the bad publicity of past pre-seasons, demanded justice be swift and lethal. The player had his contract cancelled and did not play again that year, the punishment being disproportionate to the crime but not out of step with society's expectations at that time.

The Knights played listlessly for months until a distraction arrived in the form of long-time captain Andrew Johns and his inspirational performance for NSW in the Origin series. Forgetting the incident in Bathurst, they made a late but ultimately unsuccessful charge to avoid the wooden spoon.

Players complain that the game's punishment for their off-field behaviour is disproportionate to society's penalties.

When international second-rower Michael Crocker had a squabble with his best mate outside a Bondi hotel, police needlessly intervened and he was arrested and subsequently fined $700 by the courts. The Roosters hit him with a $10,000 penalty and released him to negotiate with other clubs. He is now playing in Melbourne.

The bad boys are not amoral. They know right from wrong. The problem is that all too often they simply choose the latter.

When former North Melbourne champion Wayne Carey was exposed for having a sexual relationship with Kelli Stevens, the wife of his vice-captain and best friend, Anthony Stevens, it generated debate in every club and code. The relationship was discovered when the pair were caught together in the bathroom of a teammate's house during a party.

Carey had broken male sport's biggest cultural taboo, yet adultery is not a crime.

Allan Langer, the former Brisbane Bronco and Australian halfback, volunteered that the same thing would not happen in rugby league. 'Alf' dismissed the prospect immediately, saying, 'We would have had someone on the door.' Langer was wickedly – and jocularly – suggesting the Broncos were so united that if guards were necessary, it was only to exclude outsiders.

A short time later, 2,000 kilometres away at an annual sportsmen's lunch in Melbourne, former Carlton player Jim 'The

Terminator' Buckley was asked the same question. Would the Carey–Stevens incident have happened in his day? The response was the same: 'We would have had someone on the door.'

Buckley was at the function held at the Melbourne Savage Club at the invitation of former Carlton president John Elliott, who was subsequently banned from the club because of his bankruptcy.

All great athletes carry the seed of cruelty, and I recognised it in Buckley. Being one of the league's best players requires a meanness cultivated like a prized bloom. It's their job and their passion to beat the other player, undress his weakness.

I asked Buckley's former coach, David Parkin, about him one day as we sat at the kitchen table in Parkin's Hawthorn duplex. When old coaches meet, niceties are discarded.

'Do you want a cup of tea?' teetotaller Parkin asked, the prospect of beer not even considered.

'No,' I answered.

'Good,' he said and sat down quickly so the discussion could begin.

There was none of the carotid-artery-throbbing intensity AFL viewers saw of Parkin in quarter-time talks, just two old coaches exchanging views without needing to varnish words, cutting straight to the chase.

'He was a nasty little bloke,' he said of Buckley's wiry malevolence. 'A terrific player. When expectations were very high, he delivered.

'Jim Buckley had all the cheek in the world. He came from a lovely family. I don't know where he got his toughness from. Perhaps he got his hard edge because he got tipped over early in his career and knew it was the only way to survive. He had a good chest and wiry physique, so he could deliver the power hit. He could get under them and give them a good whack. He was known as "Whistling Death", because he came in under them like a stealth bomber. He'd hit you from beneath. He hurt blokes when they least expected it.

'He was a jockey from Kyneton and was mates with all the Melbourne jockeys. He occasionally rode track work. He'd get together with the jockeys on Sunday morning, and they'd all be punching up if someone hadn't told them about a sure thing the previous day.

'One night after a game, he king-hit me and two others. He'd just learnt he'd been dropped to the seconds and got nasty. He hung one on all of us.'

Asked if he punished Buckley, Parkin, showing a fine understanding of football justice, said, 'No. He was terribly sorry later, remorseful. He was like that. He won the best and fairest award at the club in 1982, a premiership year, which tells you something about his ability.'

Maybe history will judge Buckley more generously than 'King' Carey, who twice tarnished his crown after his infidelity was exposed.

Three years after the bathroom incident, fuelled by a few pre-speech drinks at the bar, Carey stunned a crowd of about 200 guests at the Surfers Paradise Demons Football Club when he opened with a joke about his affair with his vice-captain's wife. Maybe he was trying to alleviate the embarrassment by getting it out in the open early, but it didn't work.

'He broke the ice by making fun of the situation of being in the toilet with Kelli, saying he would not have been in trouble if she hadn't followed him in,' one guest was reported as saying.

Another called out to him, 'Stop talking about crap . . . We want to hear about football.'

Another asked the two-time premiership skipper, rated by many as the best AFL player of his era, 'Did you play any football, or did you spend your whole time shagging?'

Carey's marriage ended in February 2006 when his friendship with a Melbourne model was revealed, leading his father-in-law, Terry McMahon, to say Carey would be 'going out in a box' if he ever fronted the McMahon family home in Wagga.

Most bad boys become settled citizens and you wonder whether their badness helped turn them good. Shakespeare expressed it best in Measure for Measure: 'They say, best men are moulded out of faults, and, for the most, become much more the better for being a little bad.'

Blocker Roach, whose three sons are all destined to be good athletes, has subsequently solved the mystery of the comment coach Gibson made to him at Balmain Leagues Club all those years ago. 'I didn't know what he was talking about at the time,' Blocker says. 'He was saying we have to use the fear we all have. My eyes used to roll like poker machines, and I suppose he thought I was scared.'

To be a good footballer, particularly a prop like Blocker, the player must force his body to perform actions his mind is deadset against. For a player to accept that deal on a consistent basis, he must have a sense of something greater than money and individual awards, be it faith in a deity or a coach, an unbreakable bond with his team-mates, or a profound fear of failure.

'If you want to be any good at something, especially boxing or football or wrestling, you have to have that bit of madness in you,' Blocker believes, his eyes growing to the size of pocket watches. 'Look at "The Undertaker" in the wrestling. He's about seven foot and 500 pounds, and his eyes roll. He's a loony, like me and Gorden Tallis and Les Boyd. But we all came from nothing. We were like the black fighters. We had to be a little mad.'

Blocker once lacerated me in the Balmain dressing room for something I had said on TV about his work rate, the psychological violence of his outburst terrifying an audience which grew larger but more distant as his voice went higher. Telling Blocker to calm down was like ordering a lion to go easy on the red meat. Looming over me, his chest seemed broader than any barrel or bass drum in common use.

Still dressed in his Tigers' jumper, he was like a giant orange fridge gone berserk; its magnets suddenly come to life.

Only my right hand, clutching a pen, separated us.

'I'd shove both ends of the pen up your arse if I could,' he claims he told me. But we survived the encounter to appear on TV together, collectively denouncing the work rate of others.

Broncos and former Australian coach Wayne Bennett, a Queensland Father of the Year, also understands fear. When he resigned as coach of the Kangaroos – the Australian national rugby league team – after a drama-filled tour late in 2005, he said, 'The biggest fear I had when I agreed to coach Australia again was that we would lose a game or a series, but if I let fear get the better of me, I would never get out of bed.'

Six weeks earlier, I had caught up with him at the Swiss-Grand in Bondi, just before the Test match against New Zealand and, as it transpired, the first loss in Sydney by the Kangaroos to the Kiwis in 46 years. The loss, coming on top of the Broncos' fifth successive failure in post-season matches, forced many pundits to declare it the late winter of his coaching career. And what a cold time it had become!

After the Sydney loss he attended a press conference, warning media that Australia, who had already lost the cricket Ashes mid-year, could not expect to stay at the top of sport forever. Editors turned on him when he offered the warning, demanding he do something to correct it, but Bennett knows football is a war game: you can't recruit and build armies overnight.

His warning proved prescient. The Wallabies endured embarrassing defeats over the following weeks in Europe, and the Kangaroos lost to New Zealand in the Tri Nations final in Leeds, the first failure by Australia in an international series since 1978.

On the Kangaroos' return, Bennett did something out of character. In order to avoid the media at Brisbane airport, he accepted the invitation from a Qantas employee to slip out a side door. He was widely lampooned and shortly after resigned as Australian coach.

In an interview he gave me with the *Herald*, he admitted to hating himself for his rock-star run to his car at the airport. He also conceded he was intensely troubled by the question of his identity, meaning he couldn't reconfigure the borders between man and myth, the margins between public and private.

'I regret taking the backdoor way out of the airport,' he said, his voice thick, as if something had lodged in his throat. 'If I had my time over again, I wouldn't do it. I can't bring it back. It's done and I have to live with it.'

His decision not to talk to the media on arrival in Brisbane was made on the flight. Back at the terminal in Hong Kong, he had stolen a sideways glance at a copy of the *Herald* that assistant coach Craig Bellamy was reading. 'It was a photo of [Anthony] Minichiello with his shirt off and Willie Mason,' he said of a scene at The Church in London, an Australian-themed, barn-like bar favoured by backpackers.

Feelings of betrayal cascaded over him. He had expressly forbidden the Kangaroos to visit the party venue following their 24–0 loss to New Zealand in the Tri Nations final. Scenes of the players celebrating the end of the long-standing win streak didn't sit comfortably with him, and he believed the players had agreed some penance was to be paid.

'We didn't go to The Church,' he stuttered to Bellamy. 'What's this? How did this happen?' Then the answer cut through his fury and everything became clear.

It was last year's photo.

'They were waiting for us to go to The Church and stuff up,' he said, yet more evidence of what he perceives to be a media of jackals. 'When we didn't, they got a photo from last year. How do you win here?'

Although aware the job of Kangaroo coach comes with built-in criticism, he said he could not reconcile the attacks on his predecessor, Chris Anderson, for leading the team on a beer-fuelled trip through Europe two years earlier – famously dubbed a Contiki Tour by Mason – with attacks on him (Bennett) for being an authoritarian figure who never lets players relax.

Like Parkin, Bennett is a teetotaller, and it's no coincidence that both their fathers were heavy drinkers and the coaches are close friends. Bennett believes his abstinence is based on defusing genetic dynamite. He lived a childhood played out in the haunting Toni Childs song: 'I've got to go now . . . The time bomb's ticking.'

He lovingly sat beside his father on dad's long bus trips to play football, but the alcoholic rages were something else. 'My experience is if you get drunk, you're dealing with a wholly different person,' he said. 'The game has never been in more turmoil, and it's mostly drink related.

'I had some rules in England for the drink, and when I got home I found I'd been criticised for that. We had fun; we had some great nights, but someone said I ruined their parties. If I'd gone the other way and imposed no controls, it would have been a disaster. I would have been crucified.'

The Kangaroo tour coincided with the impending death of Northern Ireland international and Manchester United star George Best. NRL chief executive David Gallop, who spent a day with

Bennett in Leeds, says, 'He was particularly troubled that a nation could begin mourning someone who had allowed alcohol to ruin his life.'

Three days after Bennett resigned as Australian coach, the ARL appointed Ricky Stuart, the Roosters coach, as his successor. There was a suggestion Stuart's campaign to rid the Roosters of their party-boy image assisted his appointment, particularly when a report by Kangaroo tour manager John 'Chow' Hayes was tabled at the same meeting. Hayes observed cases of binge drinking on the tour.

In the *Herald* interview, Bennett had repeatedly said, 'You are damned if you do and damned if you don't,' and the subsequent furore confirmed this. When Stuart was appointed and it was implied Bennett had been soft on the binge drinkers, Bennett was understandably furious, breaking another one of his rules to ring a Brisbane radio station to protest.

The coaching king had become the drama queen.

All of this came on top of Bennett sacking his three Brisbane assistants, all past favourites of his as players. It offered his critics the opportunity to say Bennett wore the scowl of a prison guard way too long on the job and should hand in his keys. 'The skinny coach', or 'Longneck' as Langer dubbed him, was as silent as an oyster on the subject, but after resigning as Australian coach, he re-signed with the Broncos for five years, intent on resurrecting the club where he has been its only coach.

His longevity in the job derives from his interaction with players. He is genuinely concerned for their futures and they recognise this, a paradox considering they are members of an instant gratification generation. They want heaven without dying – fast food and overnight weight loss. They abhor dead air; they must always have something to amuse them. They have the attention span of a gnat. To them, history is now.

On the Kangaroos' tour, Bennett took them to France and the Western Front. One player, staring at a monument in Amiens, said, '1914–18, fucking hell. The war went for four years . . . That's unbelievable.' No surprise, therefore, that when the team voted where to go for lunch, they opted for McDonald's. (Bennett disappeared, holding up the bus, returning with a giant baguette.)

Perpetually wired to the present, the Kangaroos shocked old-timers like Chow on their knowledge of England's Premier League soccer players. Because they have so much free time, they rarely miss a top soccer match on Foxtel. They linked up with Manchester United's then injured captain, Roy Keane, who attended one of their matches, and Bennett met with Coach Sir Alex Ferguson.

At the time, Keane sounded off publicly about some of his teammates not having a go, accusing them of wearing Rolex watches but not putting time into their preparation. His outburst mocked the very meaning of Man United, but Bennett actually said he wished more senior footballers would be as honest as Keane.

However, a few days later Keane was gone from the club, a victim of simple economics. It's cheaper to sack an ageing captain than a half dozen rebellious up-and-comers, angry at what their skipper said.

Back in Sydney, when Bennett and I had sat around a table in the bar of the Swiss-Grand, it was noticeable how Kangaroos such as prop Mark O'Meley joined us, taking a quick taste of the conversation before departing.

With the oldies talking, they never take time for a long dinner.

It wasn't long before Bennett, Chow and myself were the only three left at the table. The topic turned to bad boys and Bennett sat on my right side, watching every word I wrote as he dictated his thoughts slowly, allowing for my inadequate shorthand.

'I have a great love of the rogue,' he began. 'I love them because

I'd like to be them sometimes, but I can't. They are always fun to be around. They are always the first to put their hand up and have a go. Invariably, they can laugh at themselves.' Like most of us, he relishes the Australian capacity to self-deprecate.

'But they've also got lots of initiative,' he continued. 'Because of their out-there personality, they get knocked down a lot. I love their irrepressible spirit. They get back up there and have a go again. They get knocked by society, and less and less is there a place for them in society. It is something which worries me. They have a freedom of spirit which endears them to me. My dad, my brother were one of them. They've been close to my heart. But I couldn't put myself through all that emotional turmoil every day. I've got to be in control of my emotions every day.

'For them it's a roller coaster. I've always sought their company, always stood up for them. I've fought more of their battles for them than they'd ever know. There's another group of society that doesn't like their spirit. They'd like people to be like me – boring and no fun to be with. The term I use for them is larrikin, but it's not politically correct. Mateship and larrikinism are the signatures of Australia.

'You hear a woman say, "His wife doesn't like him," yet he's the bloke you want to be your mate. Chris Johns, Allan Langer, Stephen Walters, Gorden Tallis, my uncles, my own footy mates, some of the coppers I worked with ... They are the blokes you look forward to going to work with. I could never understand, whether it be as a coach or a policeman or a team-mate, how you had to justify them, explain them. It's what I love about [legendary adman] John Singleton and [the late former Broncos' part-owner] Porky Morgan. They are going to do something. You never tire of being with them.'

After he'd finished and I put away the notebook, he said farewell and I headed to the toilet, the pace of Chow's beers having an effect. As I exited the gents, Bennett was waiting outside.

'Put Tom Raudonikis down in your notebook as one of them I like being with,' he said. Then he shuffled uncomfortably and looked down at the tiled floor before saying quickly, 'And yourself too.' With that he was gone.

That's about as emotional as Longneck allows himself to be. All the perpendicular adjectives ostensibly apply to Bennett – upstanding, upright, upfront, straightforward. His only weakness is supposedly Mars bars, and it's hard to pin any vice on him, although he once confessed to me that he was looking forward to Madonna's Brisbane performance.

Because Bennett can't be demonstrative, he compensates by being a master puppeteer, a clever manipulator. When Langer returned from English club football to inspire Queensland to an unexpected triumph in a State of Origin match in Brisbane, Bennett, the Maroons' coach, crept behind the last row of seats in ANZ Stadium towards the end of the match. There, stooped so no-one could see him, he initiated an Alf chant that carried, like a verbal Mexican Wave, around the ground.

For Bennett, it was personal redemption for virtually forcing Langer to retire from the NRL and head to England, yet he couldn't allow himself to be seen showing so much emotion.

He actually likes the references to him as being joyful as a toll collector, as excited as an undertaker. When he gives speeches, he often quotes his favourite description of himself – written by me: 'I have seen men mid-vomit looking happier.'

It's convenient to conclude the larrikins have disappeared from football. After all, full-time training means playing football has become a job.

Professional athletes became software the moment media companies began buying teams, turning grounds into theme parks and the games into 'programming' for pay TV networks. Players acquired the flatness of cartoon characters and became nothing more than the bits and bytes of entertainment empires.

Coaches aid the process by teaching players a form of 'footy-speak' where nothing is said that could end up as ammunition on an opposition team's bulletin board.

The media, aided by a vigilant public reporting everything via increasingly ubiquitous electronic means of communication, chronicles every misdemeanour, forcing players to go underground. It is the height of hypocrisy for the media to lament the loss of larrikins, while simultaneously magnifying every misdeed. 'Atrocities' are as keenly tabulated as point-scoring records, yet the media bemoans the disappearance of colour from the game.

Bennett's trainer on the Kangaroo tour, Billy Johnstone, counter-argues that players have *not* changed in the 30 years he has been a player and fitness advisor.

'The average player hasn't changed,' he says. 'Ninety-five per cent are from working-class families and a lot are from small, bush communities. It's still all about mateship and not being big-headed. There's still a lot of clever banter in the dressing room, and they play practical jokes and put shit on each other. But because of the salary cap, there's a lot more movement between clubs compared to my time when there were a lot of one-club men.

'You'll always get your sooks, whingers, larrikins and tough guys. If I've noticed one thing across the board, it's with representative teams and the way they are mollycoddled. Perhaps it's because they are elite players. But they will get off their arse and help you carry an esky or unload ice off a truck.'

Every coach and trainer has his favourites. Johnstone, also a former No. 1 contender for the Australian middleweight boxing title, says, 'Jacob Lillyman is my favourite at the Cowboys. He's a bushie and his old man owns a cattle property. He rides bulls, but with his first pay cheque he bought a computer. His old man came home one night from mustering and saw the computer open on the kitchen table. He wanted to know what the TV was doing sitting on top of a typewriter. He went down to Brisbane and walked into one of those Subway franchises for a sandwich. When they asked him if he wanted any stamps [redeemable coupons], he said, "If I want to post a letter, I'll go to a post office."

'My man at Canterbury was [hooker] Jason Hetherington. He once went on *The Footy Show*, and they made some comment about how well Daryl Halligan was kicking. "Yeah, you wouldn't like to be his dog," was his reply. He knew how to lighten up a tense moment. He bought a cattle station west of Rockhampton when he retired, and I left my dog there when I went down to see my family at the Gold Coast. He certainly educated my dog. When I came back, it had skin and shit off it everywhere from falling off the back of his ute.'

If the traditions of outback Australia are reflected in Lillyman and Hetherington, Manly and Wests Tigers' John Hopoate gave the code a bad-boy reputation. Hopoate, like heavyweight boxer Mike Tyson, became a symbol of pre-packaged calamity.

When Cowboy players complained about Hopoate inserting his finger up their backsides, it found its way into media outlets everywhere. The venerable American magazine *Sports Illustrated* mentioned it in its weekly 'Sign of the Apocalypse' column. Comedians quipped Hopoate would go down in the 'anals of history' and that he would be recruited as a telecaster on the late news, providing a 'short news up-date'.

Hopoate was suspended for 12 matches for the rectal attacks, but was he exclusively to blame? Weren't there reports of his coach and team-mates at Wests Tigers laughing at team meetings when vision of Hopoate 'dating' opposition players was shown? And which coach encouraged him to do it in the first place? After all, it's an effective way of drawing a reaction from a player, forcing him to retaliate and lose possession of the ball. Plus, like anything that happens at the bottom, so to speak, of a scrum or ruck or maul, it's difficult to detect.

But bad boy Hopoate, a practising Mormon and father of eight, copped all the blame, telling the media, 'I will emerge from this a better person. I can't believe what I have done. Everyone deserves a second chance – I know I've had some chances, but nothing like this.' In a later chapter, you will see it's obvious Hoppa was given multiple chances and was eventually banned from the game for a year for threatening a touch judge during a match involving one of his sons.

During this latest drama, Wests Tigers won their first premiership. The players, during a Mad Monday celebration, visited Campbelltown – part of the territory of the joint-venture club – to celebrate with fans. Hoppa's mother, Mele, who lives in the area, carried two giant buckets of chilled watermelon juice to the local stadium, striding straight into the dressing room, oblivious to the possible nakedness of players. The watermelon juice, she explained, would be a good antidote to the hangovers.

She also missed the contact with players. Another son, Albert, also a talented player, was away doing two years of Mormon missionary work.

There's a strong argument that bad boys like Hopoate aren't bad for rugby league. They deliver reverse cachet. The code burns brightest when the fireflies of controversy dance around it. Drama is the code's oxygen and inertia its enemy. NRL research actually confirms this.

Chief executive David Gallop told a meeting of club chief executives one November that research revealed fans actually enjoy what he calls the 'soap opera' of the game. Okay, there's 'good' soap and 'bad' soap, and Hopoate certainly harmed opponents when he hit them high, causing one to be hospitalised with a severe concussion.

But it's unlikely his actions caused one fewer fan to come through the gate, or TV ratings to fall. Sure, his anal exploration, abuse of officials and striking opponents harm the game in the corporate boardrooms where the decisions on sponsorship are made. But rugby league has never done well out of the top end of town.

The working-class code would have to undergo a generational makeover if it was ever to attract dollars from squeaky clean insurance companies and banks. The Commonwealth Bank abandoned its sponsorship of an elite schoolboy competition following a series of ugly brawls and switched to chess. Most of the city's marketing men went to private schools, and their preference has always been rugby union and Aussie Rules. The Hopoate incidents gave them an opportunity to joke derisively about rugby league's goon image and caveman level of intelligence.

Hopoate was the code's Oil Can Harry for four years, the man in the black hat, cape and moustache who invited everyone to throw rotten fruit at him. But it can be argued that it's better to have a visible target than the subterranean ones that really damage the game. Anything that undermines the integrity of the game is worse than a high tackle, providing it does not end a player's career. Hoppa diverted the blame from where it should have been directed; salary cap rorts and sexual assault allegations attack the game's heart, along with cheating referees.

Leaguies argue it is unfair that the code receives all the bad publicity, with Ricky Stuart, a former Wallaby, saying after his appointment as Kangaroo coach, 'A lot of other codes go out and socialise much more than rugby league, but rugby league is the most scrutinised.'

He was referring more specifically to rugby union. Nathan Grey, now playing with the Kyuden club in Fukuoka, Japan, agrees, adding, 'League players are under the spotlight more but should know the media is always after something.'

The only time Super 12/14 football dominated every pub conversation in the way Hopoate did was following a racist sledge by Waratah second-rower Justin Harrison against a South African player. Harrison used the soap opera to wash his mouth out, making an apology that generated another back page lead. Some will see his apology as an act of redemption, but it's usually just designed to bring the soap opera to an end.

John Wayne, in the movie *She Wore a Yellow Ribbon*, said, 'Never apologise, Mister. It's a sign of weakness.' But John Wayne, remember, was just acting. And his real name was Marion.

There is an endearing simplicity, an unvarnished directness about the way rugby league owns up, one that makes it so appealing to its followers. When Craig Young left Wollongong to sign with St George for the '77 season, the Dragons invited a few players and their wives over for dinner at the club bistro to meet the new signing. Craig's wife, Sharon, accompanied him and conversation soon focused on the future.

'The great thing is Craig is leaving a club where everyone called him Fat Albert,' Sharon said of the Wollongong club where the big prop was lampooned for his size.

Within seconds Robert Stone, Craig's future partner in the Dragons' pack, guaranteed the nickname made the transition to Kogarah. 'Pass the salt, Fat Albert,' he said while Sharon looked on, horrified, aware that the one person who hated the name the most had unwittingly passed it on.

The story was told at the funeral of Stone, who died from brain cancer at 49. Among Stoney's many nicknames was 'Stretcher', because he was once carried off by ambulance men on a stretcher but was sufficiently recovered to be seen dancing with his wife, Ann, at the club's disco later that night. Stoney and I had a tense relationship during my six years coaching the Dragons, mainly because I dropped him to reserve grade a couple of times. Of all the duties required of a coach, dropping players is the worst. Stoney made the task horrendous. A school teacher, he insisted on detailed explanations for his relegation and always had logical alternatives. I nicknamed our debates 'Yaltas', because they lasted as long as the World War II conference at the Black Sea resort.

One night, to avoid the discussion, I instructed the club doctor to find something wrong with Stoney's knee, rather than drop him. When the doctor ruled him out, Stoney shook his head in amazement, insisting he had been playing with the same unstable knee for years. When I confessed a decade later, Stoney revealed he had extracted an admission from the doctor years earlier.

Maybe it's the inherent unfairness of football, but men at odds feel the need to resolve things. Only the bitterest feuds endure.

When it was apparent Stoney's illness meant the St George 2005 reunion could be his last, he phoned me to determine whether I would be there. He loved reunions. He scored the opening try in the 1977 Grand Final replay with Parramatta, romping 20 metres, but as the years rolled by he teased team-mates that he had received the ball in goal and run the entire length of the field for the try. His phone call came while I was driving to the airport to catch a plane to Turkey for a walking trip. I was scheduled to return the day following the reunion, meaning I would miss it.

On the night of his funeral, where the attendance was larger than some crowds you would see at football games, we gathered in a special function room at the St George Leagues Club. Ann had been with Stoney when he made the phone call to me, and she expressed sadness that her husband and I had not sat down together before he died. But we had. When I returned from Turkey, I went to a St George game, knowing he would be sitting in his wheelchair on 'Stoney's slab', a concrete section of Kogarah Oval where ex-players meet. The entire stadium could have been named after him given the efforts he made to have it renovated and ensure the Saints stayed at Kogarah.

His beanie-covered head was resting on his left shoulder and a blanket protected him from the winter chill. He looked up, recognised me and I kissed him on the cheek.

'You'll be all right, mate,' I said, clearly lying. But it seemed to be what he wanted to hear.

When I told Ann of the meeting, the grief consuming her momentarily lifted. Football wives understand resolution. The game dictates we sort it all out. Perhaps Stoney had tried to tell her of our meeting, but his speech had become tortured.

Of all the messages read at his funeral, one that resonated most was a letter from Graham 'Shovels' Olling, Stoney's old opponent at Parramatta. The letter, resolving the ancient conflict between these old front-row forwards by setting out Olling's respect for Stone, had been written when it was apparent the disease was serious.

Resolution for misdirected blame and praise take time in football. In 1979 the prize for Western Suburbs Player of the Year was a car, and it went to hooker Ray Brown. Brown had joined the club from Griffith, and within a few months he was chosen to play for Australia, a swift but warranted rise. Only on a one-year contract, he began negotiations with Manly during the semifinal period. Brown was young, immensely skillful and versatile and a future captain of the club. We took his loss badly.

About a decade later, one of Wests' selectors, Ray Hill, told me Brown was not the genuine winner of the car, a black Sigma. He said the team captain, Tom Raudonikis, had polled the most votes, but club president Bill 'The King' Carson ordered the car be given to Brown in a desperate attempt to retain him.

Somehow over the next decade, I stuffed the story up and believed winger Warren Boland, who captained Wests the following year, had won the car. The years rolled by and one night, fuelled by beer, I told Raudonikis that Boland was the real winner in '79, not Brown.

He chuckled with a wicked mix of glee and malice, delighting in the Magpies' bumbled efforts to retain Brown, while simultaneously enjoying the prospect of teasing Boland, who, like Tommy, also lives in Brisbane. They meet at NRL games in their roles as radio commentators.

A short time later my phone rang and it was Boland, saying, 'Why didn't you tell me about the car?' I explained that I learned of the deceit well after I had left Wests and, had I been aware of it, would have blocked it.

Boland good-naturedly volunteered that he was surprised that a winger had polled the most votes, given the top form of so many other players that year. But something gnawed at me, and I resolved to question Hill at Wests' forthcoming reunion in order to get it right.

Hill, who later died from throat cancer as a result of a life of cigarette smoking, struggled to speak, each word emerging as a whisper. However, his memory was clear. Carson had approached him and the other selector, Jim McMillan, and asked who had polled most votes. Both produced their personal statistics, showing Raudonikis the winner, but the King overruled them, saying, 'We've got to keep Brown.' As it transpired, all three men in the saga left Wests: Brown to Manly and Raudonikis to Newtown, both at the end of '79, and the King to the beyond when he died of bowel cancer in early 1985.

Shortly after the reunion, I called Raudonikis and told him I had some good and bad news.

'Give me the bad news,' he rasped, but I knew how to draw a reaction from him and told him the good news first.

'You were Western Suburbs Player of the Year in 1979,' I said. The years have all rolled into one for Tommy – separate honours, distinctions and selections merged with the hazy recall of disappointments.

'That's good,' he said of the 1979 honour, not making the link with Brown and uncertain of what was coming next.

'The bad news is you won the car,' I told him.

The reaction! The dawning took an instant. The phone exploded. In place of the scorn he showed at Boland missing out was fury the club had cost him a car.

'Dirty bastards,' he spat out, before unspooling the years in his mind. 'Dumb. If I'd have won the car, I would have stayed.' And the truth is, Raudonikis's sense of obligation is such that he would have.

A month after my revelation – in the week leading up to the 2005 Grand Final – I travelled back from Suttons Forest in the NSW Southern Highlands with Brown. As a senior executive in Aristocrat, manufacturers of poker machines, Brown had asked me to address his clients on the forthcoming big game. I had never discussed the black Sigma with Brown, nor ever told him how much I regretted his leaving Wests.

As we chatted, the countryside flashing by, my mobile rang. It was Tommy. He wanted to meet for a beer. During the conversation I twice mentioned Ray was sitting beside me and each time Tommy said, 'Tell him I want my car back.'

Caught between the emotions of avoiding the ancient issue and wanting to resolve it, I finally blurted out, 'Tommy wants his car back.'

Brown's response produced instant relief. 'I know all about the car,' he said, nodding sagely.

It transpired that he had heard of the rigged vote from another source and long since rationalised it, although unaware of the identity of the genuine winner and the confusion surrounding Boland.

'If they'd been up-front and told me they were giving me a car to keep me, I would have stayed,' he said. 'It just shows you how incompetent and stumbling and slow they were with negotiations.' So the real winner would have stayed out of a sense of obligation, and the false winner would have stayed out of a sense of being wanted.

That's football.

BAD BOYS AND BAD BLOOD

We relish rivalries because they force coaches, those creatures of regimentation and ritual who rarely look past this week's opponent, to admit the truth: some games are more important than others.

Ray Wilson, a premiership player at Hawthorn under the venerable coach John Kennedy, was invariably shocked by Kennedy's approach to games against Melbourne. Kennedy (later to become AFL chairman) was an austere, conservative school teacher. He was the voice of calm, calling for the return of Latin to the Sunday mass, for the preservation of the corner store, for the past against the troublesome future.

'We were a group of young men in awe of John,' Wilson says. 'He was smart, didn't swear and he'd go home to his wife. But as we approached games against Melbourne, he'd become irrational. Emotion would overtake logic. In the language of today, you'd say he'd lose it. But he was driven by a pain from the past, which we didn't understand because we couldn't appreciate the dominance of Melbourne over Hawthorn in the 1950s when John was a player. Melbourne were the dominant overlord of that decade, winning five out of six grand finals. He was crying out against their power and influence in the league. It really got to him.'

Perceived privilege is at the heart of many sports rivalries – a view that one team has an inherited, undeserved and unjust advantage over another via superior wealth, or the conniving of officials. It's a hatred that persists because one side has gained too much power, as in a bad marriage. The rivalry can endure well after the original reason for the perceived injustice has disappeared.

In Scottish soccer, Celtic–Rangers is an ancient enmity based on sectarian strife, although nowadays there are probably as many Protestants as Catholics playing for Celtic and vice versa. In terms of a purity of hatred that involves politics, social class and, above all, religion, there is no greater bitterness, yet it probably persists more in the minds of the fans than the players.

When Pope John Paul II died, all sport in Italy was suspended the following Sunday. Precisely one week later, in a Scottish Cup semifinal between Hearts and Celtic, Hearts fans jeered during a moment of silence for the Pope. While sport and religion have a unique ability to unify people, they can have the opposite effect when bad blood between the fans boils over.

When AFL fans talk club rivalry, they usually point to Carlton–Collingwood, but both clubs have been traditionally successful, save for brief periods of penury and proximity to the bottom of the ladder in recent decades.

In terms of a historical, sociological rivalry, Melbourne–Collingwood is an old school enmity – the silvertails versus the other side of the tracks; Melbourne Grammar against the parish schools; the old-money toffs versus the new-money John Wrens.

The annual Anzac Day fixture between Collingwood and Essendon generates passion, but it's not long term, despite attempts to resurrect memories of the 1990 Grand Final between these two clubs when a wild brawl, involving officials, broke out during the quarter-time break. In fact, everyone's second favourite team seems to be the one playing Collingwood. This was particularly so when Collingwood's ubiquitous, irrepressible president, Eddie McGuire, called the football for Channel Nine. The perception grew that Collingwood's seemingly regular 'match of the round' status was unearned. But Nine has lost the AFL rights and McGuire has moved to Sydney as network chief executive, obligating him to promote rugby league.

McGuire is the 21st century equivalent of Joe the Gadget Man or the Fuller Brush Man. Nicknamed 'Eddie Everywhere', his link with Collingwood will inevitably diminish. A future joke awaits: What is the difference between Eddie and God? Eddie is everywhere, except at Collingwood.

With the emergence of a national competition and shared stadiums, the old enmities between players and officials at neighbouring suburban clubs, such as Richmond and Collingwood, have largely dissipated.

In place of the old rivalries have come the local derbies in the provinces. The Fremantle–West Coast battle has generated more fights over the past 15 years than between any other two clubs. Equally, there is intense feeling in Adelaide and Port Adelaide games, and their players carried the punch-up from the pitch to a pub one Sunday following a match.

If any club had a reason to pick a fight with the money clubs it would be Footscray, or the Western Bulldogs as they are now called. They lost six future Brownlow medallists over 15 years, yet don't have entrenched enmity with anyone.

The AFL introduced a salary cap before rugby league did and also have a player draft, meaning attempts to even up the talent pool are well-entrenched.

In rugby union, former Wallaby coach Bob Dwyer agrees local derby match-ups have real venom. 'Manly versus Warringah is intense; Easts versus Randwick is another and Sydney University against Randwick was always competitive when Dave Brockhoff and Bob Outterside coached.'

Outterside (Randwick) and Brockhoff (University) would stand at opposite ends of the field, hurling abuse at each other. As one former player observed, 'Each would spend the week trying to steal an advantage from the other. It was certainly 16-men-a-side rugby.'

The annual fixture between NSW and Queensland is a bad blood game, with current Wallaby coach John 'Knuckles' Connolly admitting that during his decade-long stint as Reds coach he once gathered the Queensland players together shortly after he had experienced a heart attack. Speaking in hushed tones at a celebratory dinner to mark his return to health, he said, 'I tell you, having a heart attack was nowhere near as painful as the time we lost to NSW.'

Nathan Grey, educated in Southport but imported to the Sydney-based Waratahs, says, 'Queensland versus NSW has been a massive rivalry. The two teams play for the Templeton Cup [named after esteemed Queensland coach, the late Bob Templeton] and it's held in massive regard. We hadn't beaten Queensland since Super 12 started, and when we beat them in 2005 for the first time, we put a bottle of Grange in the cup and everyone had a sip.'

In rugby league, Souths and Balmain had some nasty exchanges when Mario Fenech and Benny Elias were opposing hookers. However, the officials of the two clubs get on, unlike the Rabbitohs and the Roosters where the players shared breakfast at Aussie Stadium, but their respective hard-nosed leaders, millionaires George Piggins and Nick Politis, refused any attempts to broker a merger.

Some country towns have a rivalry that endures, certainly in the minds of those who lived through them. Parkes and Forbes in western NSW are fierce opponents, and Ted Goodwin is enshrined in the record books as a man who committed a sin usually punishable by hanging – coaching both towns. He led Parkes to premierships in 1983–84 and Forbes in 1987.

However, another former St George premiership player, Ian Walsh, who was raised in the region, has sadder memories of the rivalry. On a trip to Wagga by Men of League (a past players' association), he told us Forbes people will 'never forgive me' for playing in a grand final where he was not residentially qualified. 'I should never have played,' he said over half a century later. 'They would have won without me.'

In terms of a bitter rivalry at all human levels – player, official and fan – nothing in my ten-year first grade coaching career and two decades in the media thereafter surpassed the Wests–Manly rivalry.

In football terms, they were the bitterest confrontations since Athens and Sparta. For years I chose not to write about it, despite frequent appeals by rugby league fans, principally of Wests where I coached from 1978 to 1981, to do so. Maybe I wanted the distilled enmity to settle in order to take a clear look back at the events.

Eventually I put 6,000 words together and told the story in 2005 at the annual Tom Brock Lecture. The night is normally attended by academics, trade union officials, administrators, journalists and the occasional playwright, such as Alex Buzo, or author, such as Tom Keneally – both former speakers at the function dedicated to a former South Sydney stalwart interested in the history of the code.

Kevin Ryan, a former St George and Canterbury player, ex-member of Parliament and barrister, also attended. Nicknamed 'Kandos' because he was as hard as cement, Ryan is a New Age thinker from a Stone Age period of the game, always interested in social issues.

Ron Massey, Jack Gibson's long-time coaching colleague, also attended, warning those who should have listened that the Dragons and Eels were not playing well and were no guarantee to make the grand final. Jack Mundey, the former Builders' Labourers boss who led the green bans that saved much of Sydney from developers, surprised all by making a rare social appearance. A former Parramatta and Wentworthville player, Jack was clearly interested in the origin of the bitter struggles between the Fibros and Silvertails that had Marxist class warfare as its core.

The night was strange in the way it invoked history. Geoff Prenter, a leading rugby league journalist through the 1960s, 1970s and 1980s, arrived with a copy of the final edition of the defunct *Sun* newspaper. He brought it along to show me an article I had written, and, as he opened it up in front of Mundey, there was an article on the same page about the old conservationist. If that's not a coincidence, what about the date of the lecture itself? It was World Peace Day, hardly the most appropriate date to reveal, after more than a quarter of a century, the story of a war.

The so-called Fibro–Silvertail war persists in loyal Magpie pockets on the northern beaches when old footballers meet, but from 1978 into the 1980s, the meeting of Wests and Manly created huge TV audiences, big crowds, a multitude of cut eyes and bloodied noses, but no broken jaws or serious long-term injuries.

It began on 18 March 1978 in Melbourne at a playoff between Wests and Manly for third place in the official Wills Cup pre-season competition. The game was played at the Junction Oval, St Kilda, along with an Aussie Rules match and a soccer game – all packaged as a Festival of Football, a unique and never-to-be-repeated event.

It was a toe dipper by St Kilda, who were interested in forging links with rugby league in the event of relocating to Sydney – a move the Swans took five years later.

The rugby league game was played last of the three, meaning there was a mass exodus of European Australians after the soccer, and the crowd thinned to a few curious sentinels to history. Manly won, but it was a pyrrhic victory with five Sea Eagles taken to hospital by ambulance.

A game, which was supposed to be an exhibition of skill, turned into a bloodbath. It may well have set rugby league's cause in the Victorian capital back twenty years, because it wasn't until 1998 that the Storm were established in Melbourne.

I now live in Melbourne, regularly attending Storm matches, a small act of redemption for my role as Wests coach in 1978. Perhaps guilt motivated me to be the only first grade rugby league coach to welcome the Swans to Sydney when they came to stay in 1983. Coach Ricky Quade introduced every one of the 50 players in his squad on the stage of the Opera House. Ernest Hemingway could have been talking about me when he wrote in *African Journal*, 'He carried remorse with him as a man might carry a baboon on his shoulder. Remorse is a splendid name for a racehorse but a poor lifetime companion for a man.'

Guilt plays a small role in my visits to John Gray, the Manly hooker who was one of the five taken to hospital after the match at St Kilda. Gray was also at the Brock Lecture, along with his partner, Karen. I see a lot of them at their Lavender Bay unit, just around from Luna Park with splendid views of the glittering harbour.

Gray had a fall from a balcony, which makes it difficult for him to walk. People say rugby league, because it toughens the body, saved him from a life of quadriplegia, but the reverse is the case. Doctors told him the attrition in his neck from packing into 6,000 scrums and enduring tens of thousands of front-on tackles weakened the protective bones in his neck.

When he split with his wife, I actually played cupid for him and Karen. I met her for the first time when I was having a drink with friends. She mentioned John, indicated she hadn't seen him for a long time and would like to meet him again. One of the advantages of mobile phones is immediate follow-up, and I had his number within seconds.

Later, John confessed to me that all his scrapbooks had been destroyed in the emotional conflagration that followed his separation from his first wife. One day, with the aid of a copy boy, we retired to a discrete corner of the Fairfax library and resurrected his complete history, including photographs and stories from other publications. He tipped the copy boy $100 and sent the librarian a huge bunch of flowers, but he knew he didn't have to reward me, considering the punishment I directed his way in Melbourne in 1978.

I've raised that battle in my conversations with Gray, and he says, 'It was a bloodbath. They hit me like a missile. I said to Jack Danzey, the referee, "Hey, Jack." We used to go to the same church. I said, "This is supposed to be a model demonstration game." It was a bloodfest. I remember coming away with stitches in my eye and chin. Bob Higham, our club doctor, sewed my chin up with loose stitches. He was a gynaecologist. When I got to Sydney I had 26 micro-stitches put in my chin. But amazingly we all got on a bus together after the match and drank beer together all the way back to Sydney.'

On the forward journey the atmosphere had been chilly, particularly when the plane was diverted by fog to Essendon airport. The two teams grouped separately at the small secondary airport, waiting for a bus that was obviously still at Tullamarine. Eventually one turned up and the Manly players filed aboard first, consistent with the born-to-rule syndrome that I ascribed to them. We assumed another bus was to carry us to our hotel, and we continued to stand on the concrete until I said to Les Boyd, the fort on feet I'd recruited from Cootamundra, that I sensed both teams were to travel on the same bus.

Les and I entered, sat down and Manly second-rower Ray Higgs, who had clearly not seen us board, began making snide remarks about the Wests players standing outside, as if we were residents of what would now be called 'Boganville'. Perhaps it was John 'Dallas' Donnelly's ugh boots, or Bruce 'Sloth' Gibbs's Canadian jacket, or Graeme 'Snake' O'Grady's polyester flares, but he derided us, possibly to curry favour with his new Manly teammates, having left Parramatta at the end of the previous year following a pre-grand final dispute with coach Terry Fearnley.

Boyd began to puff up like an angry toad and, with eyes bulging and knuckles whitening, he hissed to me he was getting off the bus.

It's worth interrupting the story of the Fibro–Silvertail war to recount a similar experience a teenage Ron Barassi had with a bus outside the MCG.

'We played an Under-19 curtain-raiser before the seniors at the MCG, and rain caused the match to be transferred to another ground,' he recalls. 'The other team was Richmond. They organised for these two buses to pull up outside the MCG. We filed onto ours and they filed onto theirs. I heard them say, "Look at those Melbourne poofters in their gaberdine overcoats."'

Barassi laughs in his crinkle-eyed way at the memory. 'We were regarded as ponces,' he says.

Asked to elaborate, he indicates the vitriol was one-way. 'I'm well above class warfare,' he asserts, demonstrating his philosophical objection to the term 'working class' with his next sentence. 'A good rich man works. I come from a working-class family. Melbourne were associated with the Melbourne Cricket Club and, in the days before zoning, they drew players from the private schools. But our coach, Norm Smith, was a grassroots, working-class person. The Melbourne footy club under Norm Smith would have joked about anything that was a stopper to teamwork. The Catholics got up and sang Irish songs and the Protestants got up and sang Scottish songs, and we all laughed about it.'

If Barassi's silvertail club had no enmity towards Richmond, it wasn't replicated at Essendon airport in 1978, especially when a St Kilda official arrived and informed us both teams were travelling on the same bus. Furthermore, he explained, we were staying at the same hotel.

Manly chief executive Ken Arthurson immediately objected to the accommodation arrangements and insisted Wests be dropped at the designated hotel and he would find the Sea Eagles another. The mood was crackling with anticipation, and it was tailor-made for my bad blood view of rugby league.

Confrontation lies at the essence of sport, even cricket. Batsman against bowler, or in baseball, batter versus pitcher. For some, rugby league is still ARL versus Super League. I sat with a woman at a Wests Tigers lunch before the 2003 Roosters versus Penrith grand final. She was a lifelong Balmain supporter and indicated she would be cheering for the Roosters.

Insofar as this match was being promoted as the battlers from the west, Penrith, against 'the new Manly', the Nick Politis led Bondi Junction Roosters with plenty of money and even more influence, I expressed the view that a supporter of a team who had its origins around the wharves would support the Panthers.

'They're a Super League team,' she said with disgust for the rebel league started in 1995 by Rupert Murdoch as a battering ram to achieve product for pay TV.

I pondered whether her view undermined my philosophy that sociological warfare is the basis of sport, but I eventually concluded that Rupert Murdoch's billions can change the demographics of entire nations.

The St Kilda dressing room became a great psychiatrist's couch for my core belief that confrontation is central to rugby league: attack versus defence, ball carrier versus tackler, Wests wives in denim versus Manly wives in fur, corporate box versus standing on the hill, hot pies versus cucumber sandwiches.

I knew I didn't have to deconstruct any of the raging psyches inside that seething dressing room: Tom 'The Kraut' Raudonikis, who lived for a time in a migrant camp at Cowra; Dallas from the abattoir town of Gunnedah; Sloth from the timber town of Oberon; Snake from Liverpool; Ron Gitteau from Blacktown; John 'Joe Cool' Dorahy from a Lidcombe butchery and others from the inappropriately named western suburb of Regents Park.

There was something universal about that Wests team that I didn't ever see again, a psychological unity born from the fact they all came from similar money, which is to say not much. They sang from the same hymn sheet. They relished the dressing room universe of biting sarcasm and evil tricks, tormenting each other with fervour and affection. Nothing was sacred. No-one ever had to offer a penny for someone else's thoughts. The Wests players had the advantage of desire, and, as history teaches us, hardly anything is more dangerous than that.

I once showed them the George C. Scott movie *Patton*, and they instinctively identified with it. I didn't compare sport and war. Seeing the grim realities of war first-hand taught Hemingway that 'abstract words such as glory, honour, courage ... were obscene'. Similarly, it devalues the deeds of the fallen by comparing them with men who play football on a grass field for 80 minutes.

But the Wests players loved the line in *Patton* where the gruff old general says, 'A soldier's job is not to die for his country; it's to make the other poor bastard die for his country.' They intuitively understood this. The simple dichotomy appealed and the choice was clear. Hit or be hit. Consciousness or darkness. Night or day. Victory or humiliation.

The approach to war in the maxim painted on the chapel wall at Sandhurst, the college that trained officers in the British army, including poet Wilfred Owen, didn't appeal. '*Dulce et decorum est pro patria mori*.' 'It is sweet and fitting to die for your country.'

There was universal, instinctive hatred of the image I painted of Manly's beach culture – handsome half John Gibbs with sunglasses parked in his blond hair, climbing out of a Mazda RX7 on the boulevard at Manly. The decision of Arko, Manly's chief executive, to relocate the Sea Eagles to a superior Melbourne hotel, playing right into my hands.

When Manly played an aggressive first half and the Wests players entered the St Kilda sheds complaining, I released the hounds. Unfortunately, my half-time talk was taped by the earnest president of the St Kilda club, who had been invited into the room to learn about rugby league.

I had noticed in the first half that the two touch judges had little idea a linesman has two main responsibilities: to act on incidents in back play and adjudicate where the ball goes into touch. Because they were Melbournians, the two touchies concentrated only on the flight of the ball, as though they were boundary umpires in AFL. I therefore gave the order that every time a Manly kicker dispatched the ball downfield, the second marker had to fly at him like a missile and put him on his back.

There is something surreal about a coach ordering violence. It's not an out-of-body experience but quite the opposite: a saturation of the senses. It's akin to having dynamite strapped to your person. A feeling of power, yes, but with a constant undercurrent of danger.

The tactic of hitting the kickers in back play certainly worked. It was also basically responsible for John Gray, John Gibbs and others leaving the ground courtesy of St John's ambulance.

*

Jack Danzey proceeded to referee quite a few Manly–Wests games, and I remember speaking to him years later. With a semi-excited stutter he said, 'I'd wake up on Sunday morning when I had a Manly–Wests game and I'd start to tingle.'

When Jack had a heart attack in the mid-1980s, I knew what was responsible. The man in charge of the next Wests–Manly game, Dennis Braybrook, also had a heart attack about the same time as Jack and later died.

The media had already anticipated, indeed, partly precipitated, the fury of the next game with headlines such as 'Battle of Lidcombe Shaping Like a Lulu'. Getting violence and sex into one headline was uncommon then, but a Wests fan, noting the hypocrisy of the media salivating at the prospect of an all-in brawl and then condemning it when it happened, wrote a poem and sent it to me: 'The media declares it's violence we dread; you can savour the scenes in our full-colour spread.'

On the day of the match, the fans sensed a brutal battle and Lidcombe banged and rattled like a 1963 Valiant. I intimidated prop Dallas Donnelly in the dressing room, questioning his preparation, because someone had reported him drinking eight schooners at the Railway Hotel the evening before. The limit I imposed in those days was three – enough to get you to sleep. It was probably not enough for someone who weighed 130 kg but far more than today's players, who are so fit that their body fat percentage is as low as the interest rate on a current account.

The dressing room before a big game is like a reactor core. Intensity, emotion and ambition feed off each other until they've grown into a hellish contagion. It's an electric feeling, like when a boxer bounces on the balls of his feet before the opening bell or a soldier flicks the safety catch of his rifle.

When a coach takes on one of his behemoth players in this environment, you can almost see the steam curling up around them, like smoke from a vent in the earth. If you could actually peer inside the players' heads, you'd see complicated circuitry that operates without a kill switch. Because they are forever processing information about the alignment around the ruck, calculating how to attack and defend them, they are amongst the smartest players on the field. However, the rest of the world doesn't see these giants that way. Who would expect subtlety from a sledgehammer? Fans treat front-rowers like fast bowlers: dumb and big.

But Dallas half knew I was role playing when I went on a finger-stabbing tirade, invading his personal space in front of the whole team, predicting Manly's Terry Randall would dominate him. The other half of him wondered whether I was fair dinkum, and it made the atmosphere incredibly tense, like going to war, without the prospect of death.

My tirade ended with him looking at me through refrigerated eyes and saying, 'You'll know how I'm going to go after one minute.'

I did. He tucked the ball under his arm and ran at Randall with a cocked elbow, igniting a brawl where Les Boyd raked the head of another Manly player lying on the ground. The ramifications of the May '78 match were enormous, with Donnelly and Boyd cited on TV evidence.

Milton, in *Paradise Lost*, minted two phrases so relevant that they remain – even today – as four-centuries-old clichés. 'Heaven on Earth' describes the post-match euphoria in the dressing room and 'all Hell broke loose' at league headquarters afterwards.

Manly's Stephen Knight, a former Wests player, had been sent off, but no Wests player had been punished with more than a penalty. It seemed to us that Arko, whose name always had the mandatory adjective 'astute' preceding it in every newspaper article about him, had lobbied for action from Phillip Street.

Boyd and Donnelly were both suspended, and it was about this time when Phillip Street called in St George and Parramatta players and their coaches, together with those from Manly and Wests, to protest the darkening nimbus of aggression gathering above the game.

Ron Casey, then prominent in TV and newspapers, rang and warned me the NSWRL had a copy of the tape given them by the shocked St Kilda president. As I recall, Ron and I concocted a story about taping without permission and the injustice of ambush material presented at disciplinary hearings, and the matter wasn't raised. Ron got his story and I got off, an early example of how the media and clubs cooperated then, as they occasionally do today.

The Fibro and Silvertail tags were in widespread use by then, two terms that easily rolled off the tongue. I got the Fibro from the houses I saw as I drove to training with Tom Raudonikis from Blacktown, and the Silvertail came from a term I saw in a Frank Hardy novel.

Wests supporters began to dress down for games and became curiously quiet about their address if they lived in bluestone houses in Strathfield. I knew a pharmacist from Ashfield who left his chemist shop at noon on Saturdays, drove home, took off his coat and tie, wore a boilersuit to Lidcombe and carried two narrow slats of fibro, nailed together at one end. He stood on the hill, holding the fibro pieces in front of him, opening them into a V when we scored a try.

Warren Boland, Wests captain in 1980–81, told me recently, 'For a long time I had a piece of fibro, about six inches by two inches. A fan gave it to me. I don't know why I kept it, but it seemed to have symbolised something.'

Manly retaliated by trying to expose us for being, as Manly coach Bob Fulton once accused me, 'closet silvertails'. Ken Arthurson was quoted in the papers in 1980, noting our club doctor, Bob McInerney, drove a Rolls Royce; our president, King Billy Carson, owned a Mercedes and the third grade coach, Ken Gentle – a property valuer – had a Saab. Arko also resurrected Wests' era in the late 1950s when the club was known as 'the Millionaires' because the licensed club at Ashfield had bought big-name players.

I have often thought Manly played it wrong, trying to dress down to us. With the glittering array of talent at the club, they should have proclaimed their riches, daring people to beat them, confident of their superior skill. Interestingly, after a quarter of a century Manly have finally woken up to this. A group of local businessmen who raise money for the club have a box at Brookvale named 'Silvertails' and an unofficial Manly web site is headed 'The Silvertails'. (A confession: I have actually helped them raise money by debating Tom Keneally, Manly's No. 1 ticket holder, at their request.)

Manly officials now admit, after their rejection by the NSW Central Coast when they were known as the Northern Eagles, they prefer to be loathed than loved.

I'll also confess that the siege mentality – the 'league-is-out-to-get-us' view of the universe which I preached – is, in the long run, essentially self-defeating. It encourages you to look inwards, play negatively, feel inferior to the opposition and not take risks. We did not perform well when we moved into the city to play at the SCG, almost as if we did not deserve to be there.

In retrospect, I wish I had read the words of the great Negro League baseball pitcher Leroy 'Satchel' Paige, the Cornbelt Confucius from Missouri, whose words would free up any athlete: 'Work like you don't need the money. Love like you've never been hurt. Dance like nobody's watching.'

The only coach I have seen successfully combine a siege mentality with expansive, deserve-to-be-here football on a long-term basis is Brisbane's Wayne Bennett. His Queensland players forever moan about southern injustice at the judiciary and with referees, and Bennett fuels it, but in the 1990s they discarded the chip on their shoulders when they took the field, playing a loosey-goosey style.

Yet there was curious comfort at Lidcombe about being Phillip Street's despised club.

When I was attempting to find a very inspirational pre-match speech for the team before the next encounter against the Silvertails in 1978, I unashamedly mined the speeches of Winston Churchill to find an appropriate one. 'Hitler has said he will wring the neck of England like the neck of a chicken. Some chicken. Some neck', seemed relevant. So, with the Wests players listening intently before the match, I recounted the recent history of discrimination by the NSWRL against Wests: the suspensions on video evidence; the first players in premiership history to be cited, not on what the ref saw, but what he didn't see; and other perceived and imagined injustices.

Finally I said in reference to Kevin Humphreys, the president of the NSWRL at the time, 'Humphreys has said he will wring the neck of the Magpie. Some magpie. Some neck.'

Bob McInerney, who never missed a diatribe, pulled me aside and asked, 'Did Humphreys really say that?'

'No,' I whispered. 'It's bullshit.'

Dr McInerney replied, 'It doesn't matter. It's the type of thing he would have said anyway.'

Les Boyd, a lifelong capitalist who now owns half of Cootamundra and has only ever voted Liberal, was never comfortable with the 'oppression of the working class' view I expressed. 'I don't believe that bullshit you tell us,' he volunteered after a tempestuous game, an hour after his eyes had retracted into his head. 'But I make myself believe it.'

In fact, many of the Wests players voted Liberal. I reminded Raudonikis of this when he spoke at rallies in Brisbane, protesting

John Howard's workplace regulations. Rather than sing Catholic versus Protestant songs, as Barassi's Melbourne team did, we'd argue about politics, this being only three years after 'the Dismissal'. It intrigued me that while players like Boyd and Raudonikis were so fiercely right wing in their politics, when Shane Day, our hooker, brought along 'Fanfare for the Common Man' to play before games, they all embraced its music and meaning.

But Wests' identification with fibro didn't help us when we went in search of a corporate sponsor. One of our well-meaning committee men, John Cochrane, once walked into the offices of James Hardie and explained how we were known as the Fibros, a material they produced. The manager abused him, pointing out fibro was excellent building material, and there were fibro homes in salubrious suburbs – how dare he associate it with a working-class team. Cochrane scurried away and, not so long afterwards, James Hardie announced a sponsorship with Parramatta. Given the company's later association with respiratory illness, I'm relieved we never carried its name on our chests.

Victa Motor Mowers sponsored us, and we had their name on our jerseys when the Brookvale game was played in 1978. Afterwards, I remarked to a representative of the sponsor, a serious-minded chap, that he should sell plenty of lawnmowers based on the exposure in the high-profile game.

'Yes, but none over here,' he muttered.

A story circulated, which is confirmed by former Manly international prop Ian Thomson and winger Tom Mooney, that Manly coach Frank Stanton recruited a Vietnam War hero to address his team in an attempt to match the crazy motivational tactics of the Lidcombe Svengali. Manly thought we were simply mad, whereas we knew we were a *good* team that was mad.

The army major arrived by helicopter at Brookvale Oval, flouting air regulations according to our spies. He spoke of teamwork, sacrifice, physical and mental courage, survival and even ripped open his battle garb to reveal bullet holes. He jutted out his square, militaristic jaw and said, 'Any questions?'

In the audience was Ian Martin, Manly's much-underrated utility player, nicknamed 'Ima' from the popular TV series *My Favourite Martian*. The previous year (1977) Ima went bush to play football and shoot pigs, the interregnum year between two premierships, a pointer to Ima's value to his club.

Ima put up his hand at the major's invitation and, because he was considered the least of the Manly players to be impressed by rhetoric, his interest was interpreted as a huge victory for the strategy of importing the soldier.

'Yes,' said the major, inviting Ima to speak.

'Can I have a ride in your helicopter?' Ima asked.

Wests prime tactic in matches was to ignite a brawl early and then revert to football while the opposition spent 80 minutes seeking to get square. We always believed, in the hysteria of the publicity, that our football talents were grossly undervalued and actually hoped the opposition would think of us only as brawlers.

Manly won the only really important match against us that year – the final at the SCG refereed by Greg Hartley, who was promoted from reserve grade for the final premiership round. We found our match in his intimidating demeanour, threatening us with, 'I'll get you black bastards under the posts.'

If only referees were wired then.

Most coaches who didn't have a team in the finals, including those like Jack Gibson, predicted a rort, and Hartley disallowed two Wests tries (a story related in a later chapter). Hartley and Arko understood each other and, let's face it, if you have the richest team, you've got to win. It's like Chelsea, owned by the Russian oil baron

Roman Abramovich, and Real Madrid's deep pockets under the stewardship of Florentino Pérez. You don't go to watch them play as much as you go to see them pay off.

I turned Hartley's refereeing into the start of a brand-new bray. It was more ammunition for our psyches, more bullets to fire at injustice.

The following year, 1979, Manly had a poor season and missed the playoffs. To us, that was like Bill Gates walking down the road with a can after his car has run out of petrol, or Paris Hilton staying at the People's Palace.

The infamous *60 Minutes* footage showing Wests players slapping each other's faces was shot in the Lidcombe dressing room before a match against Manly that year. Ray Martin was the reporter on the story and, in his initial approach to the club, raised the suggestion that the energy Wests players expended was fuelled by pharmaceuticals. We were incensed and offered him entrée to everything at the club for a six-week period.

All he found was face slapping and a fiery exchange between Boyd and Brown, which was replayed four times in the quarter-hour segment that ultimately went to air. The reaction in Phillip Street to the show was fury.

With all the solemnity of a papal election, and almost as much smoke blowing, delegate after delegate, including Manly's, stood and howled how they were appalled. But when Wests and Manly met at a Brookvale match in 1980, the Sea Eagles ran onto the field with blood pouring from their noses, victims of a fierce dressing room slap-up. A quarter of a century later, a national TV audience witnessed St George Illawarra coach Nathan Brown slap three players on the sideline at WIN Stadium during a game against Manly in 2004. After being so reviled for the tactic, every time a coach slaps, I reckon I should get a royalty.

The truth is the face slapping was an invention of our in-your-face trainer, Dave Dickman, but, consistent with rugby league's blame ethic, I took the rap.

One night at training during the 1979 semis as the Wests players ran their lap of Lidcombe, I noticed three hang back at the rear of the peloton – John Dorahy, Ray Brown and Les Boyd. I asked Raudonikis, the captain, what was up, and he told me they were discussing a big offer from Manly.

Arko's plan was to ruin our future semifinal prospects and fortify Manly's. Players destabilised by big midseason offers is still a challenge, but in the late 1970s it tended to happen at season's end. This 40-year-old problem can only effectively be countered with a draft system.

There was a mass exodus of Wests players in 1979 – Dorahy, Brown and Boyd left for Manly, and Raudonikis and O'Grady went to Newtown for John Singleton's riches. Of course our enemies blamed the face slapping. To them, the once stable club was a bizarre, reverse-theme *Survivor* cast, as if getting off the island was the only goal.

But we knew money was our problem. Rich clubs think the most important thing in football is spirit. Poor clubs know it is money. This was illustrated in the inaugural A-League grand final between Sydney FC and the Central Coast Mariners, where Sydney captain Dwight Yorke was paid more than the entire Gosford-based team. And Dwight Yorke set up the goal to Steve Corica to win.

Wests picked up Terry Lamb in the Canterbury junior league, Jim Leis in Tamworth, John Ribot and Ted Goodwin from Newtown, Paul Merlo from Penrith and Ross Conlon from teachers college to fill the gap. All quickly identified with the Wests' ethos, Goodwin reporting for training at Lidcombe in a torn black

T-shirt and ragged shorts. (He later confessed he thought old clothes would impress me.) Leis played for Australia, as did Ribot in his new position of wing. Merlo played for NSW and, of course, Lamb became an icon of the game. Conlon later represented Australia.

But we had to change our tactics. Only Dallas was really interested in a punch-up. We became movers of the ball, spreading it quickly, tiring the bigger teams – the same approach as the 2005 premiership-winning Wests Tigers. Interestingly, the opposition sought to match us, just as our opponents in the late 1970s wanted to brawl. So the big teams tried to play our style of touch football and weren't suited for it.

The history and heartache of the two year Fibros versus Silvertails battle came to an unusual head-to-head denouement early in the 1980 season. In a brilliant piece of scheduling, the NSWRL, allegedly anxious to avoid another Manly–Wests bloodbath, drew the two teams to clash at Lidcombe on April 20, aware that three former Magpies had switched clubs. The fallout would guarantee this much: one team would come away with a new reason to dislike the other.

The Wests players were so pumped up they needed drool buckets. A tremendous wall of sound erupted when Wests ran out, the kind of roar that comes not just from the throat but from the soul. The muscular chorus of boos seemed fuelled more by bile than beer. Dallas stood on the sideline and reviled the Silvertails with incendiary words, basically saying what a Wests team with two internationals (Goodwin and himself) would do to the Manly team with ten.

It worked.

The game was played in a gathering rage, and when former Magpie Ray Brown walked over in a conciliatory, concerned way, sticking his head into a posse of Wests players examining our prone halfback, Alan Neil, Dallas told Brown to piss off. Wests won 19–4 and the Wests faithful belched and farted and leered at Manly as they left the field. Arko had the hide to call us ungracious.

But the season was played with a patented formula of individual opportunism, selflessness, innovative game planning and emotion, all fuelled by perceived disrespect, rather than a feeling of socio-economic disadvantage.

Bozo Fulton, a former Manly player and Manly coach, was then in charge of the Roosters. He was convinced our almost invincible record at Lidcombe was the result of listening bugs I had placed in the visitors' dressing room. So he arranged for all his players to dress at the home of halfback Kevin Hastings who, in a bizarre twist, happened to live at Lidcombe. The players arrived at the ground by furniture truck. They ran onto the field, as if they were horses galloping down the ramp of a float, and went on to beat us, thus reinforcing the myth of a bugged dressing room.

In 1982 I moved to St George and Terry Fearnley tried to change Wests' culture, ostensibly consistent with the 'turn the other cheek' ethos he had established at Parramatta. Warren Boland says of the difference between Fearnley and myself, 'If a heavy squall of rain came, Terry would quietly open an umbrella. Roy would stand out in the rain, defying lightning to strike him.'

Boland also recalls us travelling to a trial game at Young, and again there was no bus to meet us. 'There was a copper on the plane and the paddy wagon met him at the airport,' Boland says. 'We all piled in the back and were driven to the cop shop in the main street. We all climbed out, a Saturday morning, and I remember thinking, how appropriate ... The Wests boys have arrived by paddy wagon.'

Fearnley stayed at Wests one year and took seven players with him to Cronulla, committing the same sin as Ray Brown. The Magpies never mind anyone leaving the club, but you can't just use the joint.

Fearnley cost King Billy Carson the presidency, because the rest of the committee wanted Laurie Freier, who had coached Wests to a reserve grade premiership. Freier did eventually get the job, but by then he had been coach at Easts and tarted up his attire. He made the infamous error of coming to games at Campbelltown dressed in a light-tan leather suit with a zipper at the rear, although Laurie's sexual preferences were certainly not directed that way. Laurie also occasionally supervised training, riding around on a horse because his bad knees prevented him from jogging.

Warren Ryan, who coached Wests in the mid-1990s, was criticised for arriving at Campbelltown by helicopter after his appearances on Channel Seven. Wests fans don't like their coaches dressing up or travelling in style.

Tom Raudonikis, who understood this, bought a home in Campbelltown when he succeeded Ryan and travelled around the shopping centre in the back of a utility, exhorting the crowd via a loudspeaker to 'come to the game'.

John Bailey, my former assistant coach at the Dragons for six years, also understood the fibro philosophy when he succeeded Freier, who was sacked midseason. On 7 August 1988, when the new coach assembled his team at Orana Park, Campbelltown, the *Herald* reported Bailey's pre-match address. It concentrated on what he called 'the Claymore Kids'. 'These are the kids who live in the Housing Commission area at the back of Campbelltown. Nobody drives slow through Claymore, because they'll rip your hubcaps off. I told the Wests players every Claymore kid aged 3 to 16 was at Orana to see us beat the moneyed men from Manly. As soon as I finished my talk, the club came in and promised every player $500 if we won.'

Now, rewarding players with money while simultaneously motivating them to beat those with money may sound hypocritical, but double-standards have never worried rugby league.

Bailey certainly demonstrated he was the new bearer of the flame in life's long war against the unspeakable Silvertails, telling the *Herald*, 'The Wests officials had tears in their eyes and the players had the love of the club in their hearts.' Wests players derived comfort from being thought of as hard hats. Maybe it was knowing that their fathers were working on assembly lines or farms that made the Wests team play hard and relentlessly, as if trying to score on the first tackle was taking a moral short cut.

Penrith played as if similarly motivated when they won the 2003 premiership: rugged, home-grown men in the tradition of outsiders and strivers, ex-students of local schools who grew the sport from its roots. They seemed to have earned their stature through dogged determination, guile and sacrifice. To many of the people who lived between Blacktown and the foot of the Blue Mountains, these were men in whom the fans saw a brighter, better reflection of themselves.

Most teams try and establish themselves as underdogs, drawing comfort from the fact they have nothing to lose and everything to gain. I'm told by a former Eastern Suburbs player that coach Bob Fulton turned this psychology upside down on the eve of the 1980 final against Wests, a humiliation for the Magpies.

In a moment of raw honesty, Fulton impressed the Roosters when he said, 'Roy Masters harps on about fibro houses. Would any of you really want to live in a fibro house? I'm happy with my home at Fairy Bower.' Yet when Bozo was coach of Manly in the mid-1990s, he encouraged me to write a story in the *Herald* describing the fabulously talented Sea Eagles as a team of lunch pail men, players who go to work with cut sandwiches, men who roll their sleeves up and get their hands dirty.

Most teams welcome underdog status, and it's the first thought expressed after a win over a star-studded team. When Parramatta, one of the league's megarich clubs, beat Manly 22–20 in March 1989, coach John Monie said, 'We haven't the brilliant individuals of Manly. We have to graft for everything we do.'

The crowd was highly energised by the game, as they were in the first weekend of the semifinals when they played Manly, and I wrote in the *Herald*, 'Even before the confrontation, the differences between the supporters was apparent. Parramatta fans arrived in twos, because that is all they can fit on a motorbike. Manly fans just arrived late. Parramatta fans have nice tattoos. So do their husbands. The Silvertails from the north like to sneak in a nice bottle of red. The Fibros from the west just like to sneak in. Supporters of both clubs like their wine, but Parramatta fans spell it with an "h".'

The reaction from Parramatta supporters was hostile, one fan asking whether he should pour all his red wine down a sink and buy a Harley. They pointed to their wealthy homes around Castle Hill. They wanted to be thought of as underdogs, but not as far down the social ladder as the Magpies.

There were some contradictory aspects about Lidcombe worth recalling. Wests were the first club to allocate a 'dry area' for families, inconsistent with the view that we kept a keg in the dressing room. Wests were also the first club to feed journalists, offering tea and scones with cream and strawberry jam – a practice I tolerated because I hoped it would deliver sympathetic copy. We also sent plastic buckets into the crowd, seeking funds when an international rugby union player from Drummoyne was dying with leukaemia.

It's interesting to reflect on the influence the Fibro–Silvertail war had on those Magpie players who represented Wests in the years before 1978, such as Noel Kelly, Chow Hayes, Pat Thomas and Co. They are part of a group of 28 former Wests first graders now living on the northern Sydney peninsula who call themselves Fibros. At a Wests reunion much was made of the fact that they couldn't get down to their local watering hole quickly enough the Sunday night after Cronulla thrashed Manly by a record score.

In preparing the Brock speech, I asked Boland what he recalled of the Fibro years, and he reaffirmed my suspicion that I approached all football games as life's best chance to exact revenge. Confrontation was the essence of my view of the universe, but sociological differences gave the Fibro–Silvertail feud a more violent meeting point.

'When we played Manly, you were on about their Porsches,' he said. 'If it was Canterbury, it was the hypocrisy of the family club. Penrith blokes walked around with a cigarette packet rolled up in the sleeve of their T-shirt, tight shorts to impress the sheilas and sunglasses hooked into their hair. You had a line for everyone. It was more about motivation than class warfare. That said, it was more pointed when we played Manly.'

Some will call it Roy Masters's puppet theatre of dunderheads, but Boland registered one of the highest scores in the HSC in his year. If a successful coach is one who can 'get into your head', I suppose I was living in a three bedroom fibro built on the fault line between the two hemispheres of Wests' brain.

For Boland to recall all this a quarter century later, it's probably worth reflecting on the effect those Fibro–Silvertail days had in all our lives.

I met up recently with Mark Muloch, the son of a NSW deputy Premier, and he enthused about those games, offering a window into his family life. His mother would have toasted sandwiches and cups of cocoa ready on trays at 6.30 pm so the entire family could watch Rex Mossop hosting the Fibros against the Silvertails.

*

When you are at a game with fellow tribesmen, it's like sneaking a blanket over your head when you're a kid – suddenly the bad world goes away and nothing outside that little warm space matters. The old palaces where games were then played had a lot to do with it. Lidcombe, Cumberland, Henson Park, North Sydney Oval and Belmore, in their quirky ways, added so much to the experience of going to a game. When those relics were abandoned, the emotional attachment they engendered with their teams died.

To be a football follower back then was an act of faith, and sport was ironically far more interactive than anything Bill Gates conjures up for us now.

In the old days there was this curious contradiction: the more someone was celebrated as a Kangaroo, the less he belonged to Australia. He was Wests' Kangaroo or one of five Kangaroos at St George. His club was so proud of him; he belonged to them.

Today, a club doesn't possess its good players. They belong to the rights holder, the TV network. They're generic stars. The salary cap forces them to behave like leaves in the wind, switching clubs for higher offers. Clubs also value national cachet over their suburban identity, calling themselves Sharks rather than Cronulla and Western Bulldogs rather than Footscray. Super 14 teams are known only as Bulls or Cats or Highlanders, seeking some globally marketable uber-team status like Man U, even though many Australians don't know whether these teams are from South Africa or New Zealand.

NRL players now tend to live at either Cronulla or Coogee and travel across 20 suburbs to attend training. This much is certain: by 2010, too many footballers, teams, entire clubs will have long forgotten the concept of home, and too many children will have never known it. To many, home is a provisional notion – a unit or flat on the highway of personal advancement. But it can also be a place where you kick a football with your kids or sit with former team-mates at a reunion.

Because I live some of the week in Melbourne and read about American sports, I get the feeling that Herculean efforts, such as Plugger's goal tally a few years back, or American baseballer Barry Bonds's home run record, or Joey Johns's points tally become quickly shopworn, a clip we've seen once too often, diminished by TV's endless repetitions.

As we gaze into this century, never minus the remote, eyes glazed and numb, our greatest act of imagination might be to remember the time, only two decades ago, when we sat *together* at sporting events, sharing personal thoughts and glorious moments. Ground records being broken each week indicate more people are going to games, but are they sharing the experience?

There is isolation, even in the crowd, as modern stadiums resemble home entertainment centres. People sit watching cricket, packed together like freckled mangoes in the sun. Each has a headphone and they follow the commentary silently. Football fans can often be seen transfixed by the big screen, as if a game only acquires legitimacy through the cathode rays of TV. Paradoxically, the personal isolation we experience has something to do with stadia managements' desire to pack us in. People are getting larger, but seats are getting smaller. The only time I've been grateful for the steeply tiered Telstra Dome, with its narrow rows, was when red-headed, long-legged dancer Rhonda Burchmore sat behind me at a particularly dull Essendon game, her knees resting sensuously on my shoulderblades.

With Wests and Balmain merged, supporters of the joint venture live in Leichhardt terraces, Strathfield mansions, Lidcombe fibro, Auburn weatherboard and Campbelltown brick veneer. A Manly supporter actually faxed me a map, published in the *Herald*, showing more fibro houses on the northern beaches than in the rest of Sydney, with the bilious, triumphant scribble, 'Exposed by your own newspaper.'

As I told the audience at the Brock Lecture, if I were still coaching Wests and Arko came up with that, I'd say all those fibro homes were relics of the 1960s, holiday homes built by wealthy doctors and lawyers who thought they were too good for the decent folk of the western suburbs.

At a personal level, the Magpie–Manly feud flared briefly via the bad blood between Bryce Gibbs of Wests Tigers and Kane Cleal when he played for the Sea Eagles. Gibbs is no relation to the Sloth, while Kane is the son of Noel 'Crusher' Cleal, who played for Manly when Bailey's team beat them at Campbelltown. The pair loathe each other, Gibbs having been suspended for striking Cleal in the SG Ball final in 2002, breaking his jaw. Cleal received a five match suspension in 2005 when he balanced the ledger with a reckless high tackle.

I talked with Crusher at Tom Keneally's 70th birthday party, a month or so after Wests Tigers won the premiership, and he told me the venom was such that his son could not watch the grand final. 'It's not over,' Crusher said softly of the feud.

However, West Tigers coach Tim Sheens revealed he had been approached from player manager Wayne Beavis, who represents Cleal Jnr, gauging his interest before Kane switched to Souths. Sheens said he raised it with Gibbs, who dismissed Cleal, saying, 'He's not taking my spot.'

No-one can quite explain the origin of the feud, with most ex-players simply shrugging their shoulders and erroneously guessing, 'It must be over a sheila.'

Coaches and players go lockstep through life, inextricably bound up by coincidence and fate, not unlike parents and children, cops and robbers, priests and sinners.

It has long been assumed there is bad blood between Barassi and one of his former players, Brent 'Tiger' Crosswell, a player who allegedly didn't yield to Barassi's discipline. Opposing players accused the highly educated Crosswell of being 'a great agitator but not a great gladiator', a stirrer who exited a brawl when it became serious. Newspaper photographs of Barassi striding to a quarter-time break, his jaw thrust out, rain coating his hair and collar, as if he was a modern-day Ahab steering his ship to a vengeful destiny, are sometimes assumed to be the coach preparing to savage Crosswell.

Yet Barassi is proud of their relationship: 'I won four premierships as a coach and he was in every team. He didn't win a premiership with any other coach, and I didn't win one without him as a player. We are joined at the hip. I gave him the sack at North, and I turned up again at Melbourne where he was playing and he said, "Not again."

'Like Sam Kekovich, he could have been one of the greatest players ever. When he was at Carlton, we were playing Hawthorn and I put him on the wing as a stopper against one of their star players. At three-quarter time we were on our way to a record score. I think we won by 30 goals at the end. He said, "Can I do my own thing in the final quarter?" I said okay. He kicked six goals from the wing.'

Crosswell has had a long battle with Ménière's disease, a neurological condition affecting the inner ear. The concerned former coach said, 'I stayed with him for four days in Hobart one Christmas recently. His health is the best it's been. He's on a new medication.' The relationship between coach and player is a tangled web that only goes straight at the end. Quite often, the need for one to be loved intersects with the need for the other to be right.

Because AFL has no effective competitor as a winter sport in Melbourne, clubs are less defined by social class. There is no analogy in the rest of Australia for the almost chromosomal role AFL plays in Victoria. It is like ice hockey in Canada. Aussie Rules is symbolised by Collingwood president Eddie McGuire – omnipresent. Everywhere and in everyone. Even Melbournians who loathe the game understand its nuances.

Victorians actually believe it is the manufacturer of good character. It is both myth and mathematics. Aussie Rules is to Melbourne what rorts are to Sydney – a functioning ideology.

Sydney is effectively divided into rugby union followers in the eastern and northern suburbs and rugby league fans everywhere else, including the vast western suburbs.

Alan Schwab, the former AFL executive who died in tragic circumstances in a Sydney hotel, often told me in the early 1990s how intrigued he was by Collingwood's classlessness, although the club's occasional boorishness would suggest the word applies via a different meaning.

'Fair dinkum,' Schwab would say, his voice like a whispered shout. 'A brain surgeon I know can't wait to get into a pair of jeans and get down to Victoria Park with the mob on the hill.'

The economic Darwinism of ground rationalisation, with Collingwood now playing at the MCG and its offices and facilities located in the nearby modernistic Lexus Centre, has undermined its working-class image. Now, all Melbourne clubs play either at the MCG or the roofed Telstra Dome, further minimising suburban rivalries. The old grounds where teams played, such as Essendon's Windy Hill, are now training complexes.

The globe seems goitered with these domed stadiums that create stratification within a club's fan base. Corporate boxes have turned stadiums from shared communities to stratified societies. The clue to this came long ago when the mob at the MCG booed the members for not doing the Mexican Wave, as if they were afraid to spill plates of antipasto on their laps. I witnessed this at the

SCG in the mid-1980s when corporate boxes were built in the first tier of a new stand, just above the concourse where fans stood watching the match.

A brawl once broke out in a corporate box hired by an advertising agency. A husband had objected to the lecherous attacks on his wife by another adman in the box. The two men began fighting, pouring chardonnay over each other and stabbing away with asparagus spears. The mob standing on the concourse turned to watch, their backs to the action on the field, delighting in the police attempting to separate the brawlers.

The plethora of glass boxes today effectively divide a stadium into people who want to see the game and people who want to be seen at the game. Changing demographics and ground rationalisation have created such a sameness with football clubs, Tom Keneally jokes that it is better to think of them in terms of religious orders or faiths.

If you are a Collingwood supporter, absorbing all the abuse and ridicule probably involves a lot of Calvinism, in the sense that it helps to believe everything is predestined. Certainly the way fans live with supporting Collingwood is Calvinistic, although, curiously, the club has a Catholic heritage, which may explain why they all have a cross to bear.

To be a Collingwood fan is to enter a world of floods, parting seas and woes of Biblical proportions. Fathers have passed Collingwood to their sons, who have passed it to *their* sons, as mothers have to their daughters – as though it is by the will of God. The doctrine of predestination certainly explains the way they rationalise some defeats. Only by the grace of God, and not by a failure of their full-forward, do they lose grand finals. The Calvinists' God also marks certain souls for damnation, and the MCG can resemble a giant church in the final quarter when the Magpies are well behind. The Collingwood faithful becomes a vast, sullen congregation. Victory may be sweet, but epic collapse is unifying.

But they always turn up the following weekend, knowing all they can do is wait for God to do his work, even if it includes more damning misery.

The other Magpies, Sydney's Western Suburbs, were friar-like in the sense we dressed roughly, were poor and enjoyed sitting around yarning and having a drink. Keneally admits, 'Manly were the Jesuits, mainly via the influence of Arko, plotters behind the scenes. South Sydney in their heyday demonstrated many traits of a muscular parish clergy – they drank and they liked sheilas. St George are interesting sociologically in the sense that the area has many battlers, but it also has some pretentious suburbs of the old, established order. Their hard forwards, like Kevin Ryan, remind you of the Christian Brothers, while their swift backs belong to a more glamorous order.

'Newcastle, like Wests, are friar-minded,' Keneally continues, 'while the Broncos are above them all – the College of Cardinals. The Bulldogs are the Knights Templar – good at desecrating sanctuaries.'

While the Bulldogs' salary cap abuse and problems with the police over sexual assault allegations stamp them as the epitome of a bad-boy club, the various cultures of the club reflect the changing demographics of society, particularly with their recent strong Lebanese following.

'When Bullfrog Moore was in charge, everyone had to be a practising Catholic to get a start,' Keneally says, although the truth was the three Mortimers were all Protestant. 'Then they employed Hazem el Masri [a prodigious goal-kicking winger and Muslim] and were able to say, "At least he's not Protestant." So now they are the crescent and cross team. They certainly behave with all the brio of crescent and cross. They are as troubled as the Holy Land.'

This is not to say all Lebanese follow the Bulldogs. St George Illawarra and Parramatta also have a strong Lebanese following. I met a successful young Lebanese businessman shortly after the

Wests Tigers premiership, and he told me how he came to follow Balmain.

'I was like the girl in the *Jerry Maguire* movie where he came into a room full of women and expressed his love for her, beginning with "hello",' he told me. 'She told Jerry, "You had me at hello," and that's the way Balmain had me.'

Significantly, the one club for which no-one had bad blood no longer exists in the top grade. North Sydney was a Franciscan club. For core virtues they embraced humility, poverty and a love of nature. Visiting teams were welcome to North Sydney Oval, and the car park attendant always managed to find a space, no matter how late your arrival. Their doorman was the most obliging and cheerful in the league. Their poverty derived from their lack of success – their last premiership was in 1922. The old fig tree at the ground, a convenient meeting point, symbolised their love of nature.

But, like baseball's Chicago Cubs, they were cursed.

While a disgruntled fan damned the Cubs for not allowing his goat into the ground, thereby damning the team to seasons of endless futility, the Bears were said to be cursed because their field was built on sacred Aboriginal ground.

The Bears may not have invented the concept of lovable losers, but they certainly perfected it. They signalled a move to Gosford, hoping a new stadium would impress NRL administrators who, in 1998, were intent on reducing the number of teams in the league. Heavy rain on the Central Coast delayed the construction of the stadium, forcing the Bears to be itinerants, reducing their home crowds and generating the excuse the hard-hearted rationalists needed to evict them from the league.

Instead, Penrith was chosen to stay in the NRL, a club whose only recent boast had been winning the 1991 Grand Final. Yet if

Norths' usually reliable goal kicker, Daryl Halligan, had been on target in the preliminary final, the Panthers wouldn't have made the grand final. Norths lost 14–16, with Halligan kicking one goal, compared to six in each of the two preceding games.

We needed Norths so we could be reminded that the light at the end of the tunnel is sometimes an oncoming train, that redemption isn't automatic and there might not be a next year. It's a dismal lesson, but it stops us from taking comfort in our calamity like Collingwood, from presuming success is the natural order of life, from counting on a cosmic corrective. The Bears were a reminder that as you meander through sport, it really can get worse than this.

Had the Bears survived, they could have been the equivalents of the Boston Red Sox, or, even more recently, the Chicago White Sox. Both were similarly cursed. The Red Sox finally exorcised the ghost of Babe Ruth to win the World Series after an 86-year drought, and the following year the White Sox, whose players were guilty of throwing a World Series in 1919, finally won it again after 87 years. Now their place in the sporting pantheon is assured; they are the St Jude of sports, the patron saint of lost hopes, a spirit to be summoned at the bleakest of moments. A Red Sox fan celebrated the Boston win with a personalised number plate, which could also be a neat summary of the Fibro–Silvertail war: 'ITZOVA'.

BAD BOYS
AND BIRDS

A taped-up laundry bag with the distinctive markings of the Holiday Inn, Leeds, did a few solitary laps on the baggage carousel at Charles de Gaulle airport in Paris on 22 November 1994 before Kangaroo tour manager Geoff Carr finally claimed it.

The team, embarking on the French leg of the tour after a successful Ashes campaign in the north of England, had used the hotel as their base. Carr could only assume a player had forgotten the parcel in the haste of climbing onto the team bus headed for their Paris hotel. After all, the Kangaroos had spent the previous evening drinking beer and bourbon after winning the deciding third Test 23–4 at Elland Road and most had not slept.

'We went back to the Rugby Football League headquarters for a reception and Bozo [coach Bob Fulton] ordered champagne,' Carr recalls. 'I remember having an argument with my English equivalent, David Howes, over who was paying. I said "not me" and he said the same. But Bozo kept ordering. The players were not used to champagne, and they were pissed by the time we got back to the hotel.

'We had to be on a bus at 7 am to catch the flight from Manchester to Paris, so I decided not to sleep. I gave an instruction to all players to have their gear outside their room at the Holiday Inn so it could be loaded onto trolleys and onto the bus. I then made an arrangement with the head porter – who had a master key – to enter any room, pull the player out of bed or pack up anything he had left in the room.

'Some of the players had their wives over there, but they were staying at a different hotel. Bradley Clyde slept at his wife's hotel, and she rang the club doctor to say he was too crook to travel. He was so crook the doctor had to wheel him from the hotel on a trolley, wearing only his swimming trunks. He took him by private car to the airport where he was again wheeled in and left semi-naked on a luggage trolley until we could get him in a tracksuit. Some of the players back at the Holiday Inn had to be dragged out and their luggage packed, but they all made the bus.'

It seems the staff were zealous following the orders, opening each room, advancing in the early morning darkness to the wardrobes and loading everything onto trolleys in the corridors.

'When we landed at Paris, I saw this plastic bag do a few circuits of the carousel, so I took it off and took it to my room,' Carr continues. 'I planned to meet Bozo for a drink on the Champs Élysées, but as I was about to leave, curiosity got the better of me and I opened the bag. In it were lady's boots, slacks, vest, shirt, teddy and jewellery. What could I do except think of some poor young woman back in a hotel room in Leeds waking up at 11 am and wondering how she is going to get home with nothing but a sheet?'

Either that or a Kangaroo had decided to leave his expensive cross-dressing habit in England!

It's not unusual for some English women to develop relationships with single players on tour. After all, the players are young, fit, healthy, often handsome and, if a woman is interested in a physical, short-term relationship with a male who won't go down to the local Leeds boozer and boast of his sexual conquests, why not? Some of the English groupies admit this and, when the national team returns to the same hotel years later, reignite relationships.

During the October–November 1995 World Cup, the Kangaroos returned to the same hotel. A young woman, nicknamed 'Barry Beath' – not for any resemblance to the former St George forward, but because it was rhyming slang for her teeth, which were badly decayed – was a regular at the hotel. Acknowledging that her smile was not her most attractive quality, she willingly identified herself as Barry Beath and admitted she craved physical connection with athletic young men, even following some into the gents' toilet to determine their interest.

I once spent a half hour in the lounge bar of the Leeds hotel, observing Barry while drinking a couple of pots. There was nothing false about her, including her teeth. Dressed in a tight-fitting black dress, Barry moved around the tables of players and was treated courteously. They put her beers on the team tab and those not remotely interested in her sexually talked football.

Wives of sporting heroes tend to accommodate the reality of their husband's adventures overseas in many ways, denial being one of them. But sometimes wives accompanying their men on tour get caught up in the locker-room larrikinism.

The former chief executive of the Canberra Raiders, Kevin Neil, was staying with his team at the Holiday Inn, Leeds, in 1997, along with the Australian cricket team. The footballers were participating in the ill-fated World Club Challenge, an expensive and one-sided competition between Rupert Murdoch's Australian Super League teams and the English clubs.

The North Queensland Cowboys were also in town and one of their long-term players was, well, long in more terms than one.

Neil recalls, 'The cricketers' wives were with their husbands in the lounge bar and the well-endowed one did a helicopter in front of them.' A 'helicopter' is a manoeuvre where the rotating action of the hips sends the penis into a spin. 'All the wives cheered. Their husbands were happy because their wives were happy.'

However, two years later, when Penrith's Craig Gower performed the same penis pirouette at a Bondi hotel while the Australian team was in camp, a female Irish backpacker took exception to his antics. Gower, then 21, had been egged on by his team-mates to perform the circus act during a pre-Test match bonding session but, following the complaint by the backpacker, he was banished from the team and replaced.

Maybe wives on tour apply a double-standard, but they are universally attuned to groupies at home.

Cathy Roach, wife of former Balmain international Blocker Roach, addressed a forum for women at the Intercontinental Hotel, Sydney, hosted by the NRL. It was not long after the NRL announced a $1 million education and welfare package following two years of accusations of sexual assault by the Bulldogs in Coffs Harbour.

Roach, a lovely, caring, generous woman with innate Irish decency, told the forum, 'The groupies of today appear to be more aggressive than ever before. Maybe it is a society thing, but I notice the girls who ring up my boys are more forward than we ever dreamed of being.' Cathy is protective of her three lads – the first trio ever to be selected in a top school's water polo team – and made it clear that girls can be as predatory as boys.

Wendy Brentnall, wife of former Canterbury international fullback Greg, said, 'The biggest issue discussed on the night was the young girls hanging around after games and the question of whether the boys are educated to handle it.'

Their views were validated two years later with the release of the film *Footy Chicks* at the Sydney Film Festival in June 2006. The film, where the NRL offered access to players but no funding, shows raw and confronting images. It focuses on three groupies who admit to their predatory search for footballers from AFL, NRL and Super 14. One scene has them alighting from a taxi and adjusting their provocative parts, saying, 'Breasticles in place.' One groupie is shown putting a footballer on hold, saying, 'I'll fuck you later. I've got to go with two other boys first.' Another, who admits to only wanting to have sex with footballers, holds up a mobile phone screen saver and says, 'That's him. He loves his body, and so do I.'

Polly McCardell, a NRL media manager who once worked for the Bulldogs and now accompanies teams in Australia and overseas, says that within a year of the Coffs Harbour firestorm, players had become wary. 'I don't see as many women in the foyers of hotels, or in the players' rooms anymore.'

Oblivious to the furore, a former international strolled into a representative training camp and said by way of greeting, 'Any buns, boys?' ('Bun' is football language for group sex.) The players were so horrified to even be caught up in the suggestion of a gang bang that they covered the distance to the door more quickly than they'd ever scored a try.

Broncos captain Darren Lockyer observed at a function in Brisbane that the Bulldogs were poised to win a wave of premierships. Referring to John Raper, Lockyer joked, 'St George won 11 premierships with one Raper, imagine how many Canterbury will win with a team of them.' The reaction was universal condemnation and Lockyer was forced to apologise.

Compare this with the action of comedian and broadcaster Wendy Harmer at the same Intercontinental Hotel dinner attended by Cathy Roach and Wendy Brentnall. Harmer, a member of a

Manly female support group called the Eagles Angels, threw a bun at the waiter. It was a neat piece of symbolism, considering the debate over group sex was the reason the women attended the forum.

'Wendy threw a bread roll at the waiter and chased all the men from the room,' Cathy Roach says.

Few males crack jokes about sex in rugby league now.

At the Dally M Awards at the Sydney Town Hall, held 18 months after Coffs Harbour, an attractive female journalist sitting next to me, bored perhaps by the endless presentation of trophies for the prop of the year, halfback of the year, coach of the year, etc. made probably the only sexist remark on the night. 'Who do you reckon will be Bun of the Year?' she quipped.

And at the NRL directors' table there was horrified silence when the code's only female director, Katie Page, part owner of giant retail chain Harvey Norman, said, 'She's got nice legs' in reference to Telstra executive Holly Kramer, who was on stage to present an award.

Men reached for their beers, others checked their watches. Finally, ARL chief executive Geoff Carr told Page, 'You can say that. We can't possibly say that.'

It reflected some cosmic comeuppance to the code because Kramer, probably the only woman in Town Hall to receive a compliment about her femininity that night, is married to Malcolm Noad, a former News Ltd senior executive hired as chief executive of the Bulldogs in the wake of the Coffs Harbour disaster.

So what was this Coffs Harbour bombshell that had such a Pearl Harbor-like effect on the code? It was a sorry saga that linked two of the nation's major interests – sport and sex – yet the more it dragged on, the more difficult it was to separate the victims from the villains.

Allegations of sexual assault against six Bulldogs players during a pre-season training camp at the NSW mid-North Coast holiday resort sent seismic waves through rugby league, infuriating women's groups, angering former players and providing ammunition for other codes.

It followed a complaint the previous year, at the same hotel, when a 43-year-old single mother of five alleged that two Bulldogs had non-consensual sex with her. No charges were laid in either incident, although the policeman in charge of the second case, Detective Chief Inspector Jason Breton, made it very clear in an emotional press conference that he was frustrated having to make a recommendation to the DPP not to proceed.

Detective Senior Sergeant Gary McEvoy disagreed. McEvoy was in charge of the investigation, called Strike Force McGuigon, until replaced by Breton. McEvoy left the police force in February 2006 due to stress related to the enquiry that took 11 police officers two months to investigate. 'I would go so far as to say that on Sunday 22 February, 2004, there was no woman raped in the pool area of the Pacific Bay Resort,' McEvoy told Graeme Hughes on 2SM's *Talkin' Sport* in May 2006. Hughes and his brother Garry – the Bulldogs football manager who was sacked in the wake of the enquiry – were both members of the club's 1980 premiership team.

'A very vicious sexual assault' was Breton's description of the case. It was a story that caused a forest of trees to be felled and the great squid fleets on the Indian Ocean to be put to sea to provide the paper and ink to cover it. The young woman, a 20-year-old mother of an infant son, refused to speak to the media and the Bulldogs have never publicly told their side of the story, except to criticise reports they deem to be inaccurate.

The Charlesworth Pool at the Novotel Pacific Bay resort in Coffs Harbour is little more than a standard hotel pool, but it seemed to occupy the entire world of rugby league for two months.

It was in a car park near the pool that the young woman was found sobbing, wet and distraught. She told hotel staff she had been gang raped by up to eight Bulldogs by the pool.

She admitted to police she had visited the resort three nights earlier and had had consensual sex with four players on that occasion. She had booked a room in the backpacker's hostel that forms part of the Plantation Hotel where the Bulldogs adjourned after a pre-season match against the Raiders. There, she had sex with one of the four Bulldogs she had been with earlier at the resort.

He accompanied her back to the resort at about 5.30 am in a cab, and a pool technician told police he observed them having oral sex on the pool deck in broad daylight. By 7.15 am, when the pool technician returned, the pool was deserted. At 8.30 am an ambulance was called to the resort to take her to hospital.

So what's the best guess why she was found alone and hysterical?

The Bulldogs probably made it very clear she had been used and they wouldn't be seeing her again. At the Plantation Hotel, she had already been rejected by Bulldog Willie Mason, who had nothing to do with her at any time and refused even to travel in a cab with her.

What could have aggravated her distress was that the same men who had indulged her, even buying her drinks and playing poker machines with her, were later rude, dismissive and callous, and the one who had apparently cared for her the most was going back to Sydney by plane.

So why would a woman expose herself to such ignorance and ignominy? A barman at the Plantation Hotel in town explains it succinctly. 'It's two-to-one here,' he says. 'There's two girls to every guy in Coffs.'

City footballers with their rippled abs, tanned bodies, sharp wit and big wallets temporarily redress the imbalance, and they don't tell the whole town about you. Plus unemployment in Coffs Harbour is double the national average. It's as hard to find a bloke as it is to land a job.

But why did the police defend her so publicly? Perhaps because of medical evidence of aggravated sex, even though that does not rule out it being consensual.

Although it was clear many of the Bulldogs had breached the club's code that women not be brought back to the team hotel, the club went into bunker mode. The Bulldogs are the most ruthless of the NRL's clubs, enjoying a reputation for insularity and siege mentality. They have a contagious contempt for the media that mitigates any sense of responsibility on the part of their players. The club almost courts danger, consistent with the advice of W.C. Fields: 'Always carry a flagon of whiskey in case of snakebite. And furthermore, always carry a small snake.'

Although the Bulldogs fined six players for breaching the club's own rules, it refused to name them, thereby impugning all players and their partners by association. Some of the wives were understandably seething, wanting the innocent husbands to be publicly cleared.

Bulldog Corey Hughes, nearly two years after Coffs Harbour where he was not involved in the allegations, faced rapist taunts from a group on a bucks' day outing as he left Kembla Grange racecourse. A furious, if intoxicated, Hughes chased the name caller onto the group's minibus, belted him and was fined $10,000 by his club.

The shame, not name attitude is not confined to the Bulldogs. 'One in, all in' or 'What goes on tour, stays on tour' is the football way. In any case, officials at the club did not want to pre-empt, through publicly announcing their own fines, the outcome of the police investigation.

There is a hitherto unwritten, sad postscript to this story.

In February 2006, when Newcastle and Cronulla players visited Coffs Harbour for a pre-season match, the same young woman met both buses. Officials of both clubs, aware of her identity, gently asked her to leave. It appears the woman had 'certain issues', as the DPP put it, which prevented charges being laid and the possibility of her telling her story on TV.

So who is wrong? The defenders of Canterbury who point out the woman enjoyed the experience so much she backed up two years later to two teams, or the Bulldogs themselves for exploiting this woman?

About the same time as the Coffs Harbour firestorm, Melbourne executive director John Ribot was interviewed by Victorian police when a woman accused two Storm players of sexually assaulting her. Police showed Ribot security tape of the woman leaving a night spot with a jockey-sized male.

Asked whether the male was a Storm player, Ribot unhesitatingly said no-one in the entire organisation resembled him. The diminutive male did not appear tall enough even to push a pen in the club's clerical division, let alone a scrum. However, Ribot called a team meeting, asked whether any players had sex with the woman from the club on the night in question and two immediately volunteered, insisting it was consensual.

As it transpired, the Victorian police did not rewind the security tape far enough. A further study of the tape showed the woman leaving the club with the two Storm players and the trio later returning, the two players chatting amiably with each other, the girl a few paces ahead. Another tape at a nearby 7-Eleven store showed the woman entering and buying condoms.

One of the players admitted having sex with the girl, while the other desperately tried to gain an erection. Afterwards, she had a shower.

When the woman returned to the club, she then chose the jockey as her next partner, and it was vision of him that the police first acted on when they interviewed Ribot.

It took her a week to file the complaint, indicating she expected some follow-up response from the players.

News Ltd, owners of the Storm, were furious with Ribot for not informing them. However, Ribot, a former international winger, believed the stories told by the players and insisted on keeping their names confidential. After all, Ribot had experience with women demanding hush money.

While boss of the Broncos, he dealt with a case where a big forward was accused of sexually assaulting a girl when he pushed her away by placing his hand on her breast. At one point during the Melbourne saga, the woman indicated money would solve the problem. She demanded $400,000 and when Ribot told her the player didn't even have $40,000, he then received a solicitor's letter accusing him of intimidation.

Ribot, who acted honourably, suffered. His refusal to inform the NRL of the investigation was part of the ammunition News Ltd used when they sacked him.

It might be assumed the Storm players were not punished in any way. The name of the flaccid player has never been revealed. Although he enjoys a reputation for being extremely well-endowed, he must also endure 'soft cock' jibes.

Furthermore, public opinion had become hostile to footballers in Melbourne, particularly the rugby league variety, and the pair endured a month fearing a future jail sentence. Some of the more elitist, up-themselves Melbourne-based Aussie Rules commentators, desperate to please the AFL, kicked rugby league hard. They speculated why the no-neck code produced rapists while the pencil-neck code did not. Melbourne's ABC radio station, 3LO, asked me that very question, and I recall warning morning host

Jon Faine not to become too moralistic about AFL because a few cases lurked in the nether world of the code.

Within days, allegations of sexual assault surfaced against two St Kilda players, who were immediately named by then chief executive Brian Waldron, now, ironically, boss of the Storm. However, this may have been necessary because a TV reporter incorrectly named a Saint not involved.

In a sewer-like environment such as this, who can control what floats to the surface?

Further allegations were levelled against three AFL players in Adelaide. Swan Michael O'Loughlin and Port Adelaide's Peter Burgoyne and Adam Heuskes paid around $200,000 to a woman at the centre of rape allegations in Adelaide in 2000, leading to the AFL threatening to rip up the contracts of players who paid hush money, and discipline clubs and agents involved.

While the Bulldogs were in Coffs Harbour, I was with NRL chief executive David Gallop in Dubbo, part of the pre-season promotion of the code with 60 footballers visiting 25 country centres in NSW and Queensland. We were staying at the same motel as some senior Roosters.

Around breakfast I observed a father, clearly annoyed, remonstrating with his daughter, who had emerged from the room of one of the single players. The couple had met at a function the previous evening and, when the girl had not arrived home, the father tracked her down after questioning her friends. If there had been an official, formal protest lodged by the father, or the daughter, Gallop would have been sitting on top of a conflagration.

Neither of us had witnessed a criminal offence, but it was a precursor to the moral debates that followed. Only one thing united past players during the whole sorry Coffs Harbour–Melbourne Storm sagas: the possible physical mistreatment of women.

The first Coffs Harbour incident – men hiding in the bathroom, playing tag, deceiving the woman into thinking the same footballer was having sex with her – was not new, no matter how offensive it was to many. In Shakespeare's *Measure for Measure*, one woman is substituted clandestinely for another in what was called 'the bed trick', deceiving a ruthless Italian count. But any suggestion of harming women physically, or reviling them afterwards, horrified past players.

Privately, no-one denied 'buns' or group sex occurred in the football environment, although the new term 'chop up', which superseded bun in the language of the code, hinted of the mistreatment and diminishment of women.

Men who see nothing wrong with violence on the field were repulsed at the thought of a woman being abused, even verbally, after group sex. The abuse of a woman, rather than using a woman for sex, is deemed to be the greater problem.

During this time I met up in Melbourne with a former international sportsman whom I occasionally see. He confessed to being haunted by an incident that occurred during an overseas tour.

Two players were having sex with a woman when the team captain walked into the room and dropped his pants. The woman took an instant dislike to him and refused to let him join in. Furious, the rejected captain struck the woman on the jaw. I recall some of the former star's confession: 'I was as weak as piss ... I should have done something ... I was scared he had broken her jaw ... I was gutless.'

The sexual assault outbreak led to some serious philosophical re-evaluation of the views of all football men, some prompted by the vigorous questioning of wives, whose cross-examination skills would be the envy of Tom Hughes QC. Because there were so many incidents in such a short time, it was assumed sexual assault had reached epidemic proportions in Australia.

I remember looking at contemporary overseas incidents and found that over one seven-day period heavyweight champion Mike Tyson was sentenced in Indianapolis for raping a beauty queen in his hotel room, and a 31-year-old New York City woman accused three members of the New York Mets of raping her at Port St. Lucie, Florida, the site of the Mets' spring training base. The same week three Hampton University basketball players were charged with sexually assaulting a female student in Virginia. In yet another incident, a woman withdrew a complaint that she had been raped by a former NFL defensive back out of fear, the prosecutor said, that she would be 'victimised once more' at a trial.

Some of the bow-tied sociologists had a field day, pointing out that sporting teams emphasise the exclusion of outsiders and, in exclusively male sports, the ultimate outsiders are women. It follows, they argued, that women may thus be seen as less than human, objects to be exploited without a second thought.

Others pointed to the exalted status of the modern athlete, the special privileges accorded them and the army of club officials and managers who protect them. It reinforced the view that sexual assault was on the rise because players believed money and fame would always rescue them.

But it's also possible that victims of sexual assault are now more willing to come forward than in the past. Nor should it be ignored that allegations are just that – allegations. Perhaps the media was less aggressive in the past.

In *A Hack's Progress*, London-based Australian writer Phillip Knightley notes he was hired to cover the French leg of a Kangaroo tour in the 1950s. The team visited a brothel in Paris and one player refused to pay, sparking a violent altercation with a bouncer. When Knightley enthused about the story to his Australian colleagues, they told him they didn't write about such matters.

The 2003 Kobe Bryant case demonstrated the problem of separating fact from fiction with superstar athletes.

A young woman accused the US basketball star of sexually assaulting her in a Colorado hotel. After generating mountains of publicity, the case was dropped by prosecutors during jury selection when the accuser refused to testify. The US's highest paid basketballer came dangerously close to a full-blown trial and a possible long-term prison sentence. In the eventual settlement, it's generally believed the young woman received a handsome payment, and Bryant's wife was seen wearing a ring that challenged the Hope Diamond for size.

The case highlighted the conflict between the perception of the athlete as a star and the reality of him as an individual. The exploits of footballers and basketballers between the lines make them heroic; their carefully constructed corporate images make them iconic. But when the star athlete steps outside the lines, it's an encounter between heroes and hero worshippers with potential for exploitation on either side.

The fury over Coffs Harbour forced many league men to defend themselves against accusations that they perceive women as nothing more than notches on a gun. It is a view many find offensive in a football code that was the first to appoint a female club doctor (St George), the first to have a female club chief executive (Cronulla) and the first to have a female director (Balmain). The longest serving State of Origin official is the NSW team physiotherapist, Liz Street (since 1992), and women greatly outnumber men as ARL development officers. But the animosity did lead to a serious re-evaluation of the increasing professionalism of the code.

Money has brought full-time training and with it the isolation of players from the mores of the rest of society. They are cocooned from the community, immune from its leavening influence.

When yesterday's part-time footballers went to the local pub after training, they were rebuked for any manner of sins, including losing by 40 points and looking sideways at someone else's girlfriend. The modern player now lives twenty suburbs from his team's home ground and drinks only once a week, often in an inner city disco, sometimes on his own.

As salaries have risen, so have expectations. When the modern player acts boorishly, people send emails to media organisations reporting the behaviour of 'the overpaid bighead'.

The full-time professional training environment of the modern player certainly attracted criticism at the forum for women run by the NRL. Cathy Roach and Wendy Brentnall pointed out how it isolates young men from their wives, girlfriends, grandmothers, sisters, daughters and aunts, who once identified a football club as a Sunday night home away from home.

'If you see generations of women around a club, it will rub off and promote respectful attitudes to women,' Cathy said. 'Young men need to see women in those roles and not just the *Sex and the City* attitude of life today.'

Wendy, who once worked in the office of the Melbourne Storm, was gobsmacked at the evidence from wives of players of Sydney-based clubs who attended the meeting. Wendy, accustomed to the culture of the Bulldogs in the 1970s and now part of an inclusive club where members are forced together by their relative isolation in Melbourne, said, 'There were wives from the same club at the Sydney meeting that didn't know each other. I found that a bit sad. Compared to the Canterbury days [when it was referred to as the "family club"], I've got to say I was shocked.'

For a time, it appeared the Bulldogs were so removed from their fans, sponsors, the media, even other clubs, that they may well have been in a witness protection program. Malcolm Noad, brought in to resurrect the Bulldogs from this threatened disconnect, admitted he had not considered the role women could play in the way Cathy Roach and Wendy Brentnall identified.

'I think they're right,' he said. 'What I have identified here is that a lot of young players are not exposed to many people outside of rugby league – not just women. They come in so young. They only have their mates from school and football.'

For a time, the saga emotionally distanced fans from the game these men play. Was the golden triangle of youth, money and celebrity out of control? Maybe the fans worry about results and the players care about their lifestyles. It tended to reinforce the view that professional footballers, including English Premier League players, are like high priests who serve a god in whom they do not believe.

Only five months earlier, a similar crisis had destabilised the rock solid Premier League in England when a group of players were accused of forcing a 17-year-old girl to have group sex in a £400-per-night London hotel room.

Within weeks of the Coffs Harbour revelations, a Brisbane woman spoke on Channel Nine's *60 Minutes* about being assaulted by up to 20 rugby union players in the mid-1980s.

Around this time I wrote a column in the *Herald* based on a conversation between a former rugby union international, Jeff Sayle, and a leading player manager, Wayne Beavis, the previous day.

'Come on, mate,' Beavis told Sayle. 'Surely you blokes get up to gang bangs, too.'

'Yeah,' replied the long-term Randwick player, coach and manager, 'but the difference with us is we kiss them afterwards.'

Sally Loane, then an ABC broadcaster on Sydney morning radio whose first husband was Dr Mark Loane, a former Wallaby captain, was apoplectic. She was horrified at what I had written, abusing me for suggesting rugby union players practise illicit sex or break their marriage vows. She invited an Australian Rugby Union (ARU) acolyte to speak on her program of the social development programs run by the code for which she has long been a standard bearer.

Sayle wasn't making light of the Coffs Harbour situation. He was making a wider point: group sex did occur in rugby union, but the women involved were treated royally.

Former dual World Cup centre Nathan Grey, happily married with a young child, says, 'The stories are the same in rugby league and rugby union, but the media focus is greater in league with the spotlight on them. But I've got to say I think the rugby league guys are dumb about it. You've got to be nice to people. Overstep the mark and you are in trouble.'

Still, the player handbook for the football program at an American university for presumably intelligent young men suggests that ethics might be far from commonsense. It has deemed it necessary to include a section entitled 'Date Rape/Social Policy'. It advises, among other things, 'Never initiate sexual intercourse if the woman is intoxicated or passed out.' Imposing new rules is different from changing an ingrained culture.

Nor is it accurate to say all rugby men are sensitive to women's wishes. A Wallaby coach told me of a player who, after having sex with a girl in his hotel room, put on his pyjamas. (Who else but rugby players wear pyjamas on tour?) The girl asked the player what he was doing and he told her he was going to bed. 'But how am I getting home?' she asked, and he suggested she take herself home. 'But you took me home last night,' the young lady said.

Whereupon the tourist said, 'So? You know the way.'

The woman immediately went downstairs and made an official complaint to the manager of the team.

In another incident, Wallaby Wendell Sailor was exposed publicly for commissioning a prostitute while playing for rugby union club Leeds Tykes. Sailor offered her only half the fee, pleading he was an impoverished South African university student. Both were arrested and Wendell, with his huge contract, had no problem paying the fine.

A mother-daughter combination, accused of stalking members of the Hurricanes team in South African hotels, also ended up in court. The pair, barred from Durban's Elangni Hotel, took legal action against the hotel and management of the Wellington-based Super 14 team. They admit meeting the team at Durban Airport and accompanying them to the hotel for coffee but were 'humiliated and traumatised' when contacted two days later and told they were not welcome in the hotel bedrooms. A booking for the pair at a hotel in Bloemfontein, where the Hurricanes were to play the following weekend (February 2006), had been cancelled by the chain.

The mother had bedded Wallabies in her younger days, with her daughter asking members of the current team to pass on mum's regards to a past champion, whom she says she taught the Kama Sutra.

At the same time Loane was sanitising her code, I had lunch with Ross Turnbull, the former ARU deputy chairman and ex-Wallaby prop nicknamed 'Sir Lunch-alot'. Maybe it's his Newcastle working-class upbringing, but he doesn't varnish the truth. When asked whether rugby union players misbehaved on tour, he related a story that had former St George players Mark Coyne and Brian Johnston and the Dragon's No. 1 ticket holder, Doug McClelland (a former ALP president of the Senate), and me hanging on every tantalising word.

In fact, he had an entire table of eight women sitting adjacent to us at the City Tatts Club in Sydney following the tale with equal interest.

'I was honorary manager of the Sixth Wallabies,' he said, noting that rugby union originally reserved the name Wallabies only for the team that toured Great Britain and Ireland every four years, before surrendering to the commercial opportunity of using the name for every Australian rugby union team selected. But, for the benefit of the leaguies at the table, filling our glasses in anticipation of a long story, he explained it was an October 1975 to January 1976 tour involving 26 matches.

Dave Brockhoff was the coach, John Hipwell the captain and Mark Loane a member of the team. They had played three of the Home Unions, losing each match, and Ireland was the last of the four Home Unions to play.

'We were staying at the Shelbourne Hotel in Dublin,' he said, referring to the ornate, old world, up-market hotel in the centre of town, near St Stephens Green. With velvet curtains and antique furniture, it is a favourite home of visiting teams.

'A first-class hotel,' Roscoe said with a hint of pomposity. 'We were there for days leading up to the Test, along with the chairman of the organising committee of the tour. The committee consisted of one person from each of the unions plus a chairman, who I had become very friendly with. He was an English stockbroker by the name of John Tallent, and he moved in the rarefied circles of the British aristocracy. He was the sort of guy who, if he visited Australia, he'd stay with the Govenor General, in the days we had British Governors General.

'He was staying as a guest of the 7th Marquess and Marchioness of Conyngham. Her name was Elizabeth. Her husband's name, the marquess, was Mount Charles. They lived in Slane Castle, on a 1500-acre estate in the heart of Boyne Valley on the River Boyne.'

Aware I was including the incident in a book, Ross later provided detail of the history of the noble family. 'The Conynghams were originally a noble Scottish family who first settled in Ireland in 1611,' he dicated over the phone one night, insisting the spelling and dates were correct. 'It was where the Battle of Boyne was fought in 1690. We went for a drive after lunch in their Land Rover and went to the field where the battle was fought. It was a decisive battle which confirmed a Protestant monarch. One of the mistresses of George III was the original marchioness. George III had a direct road built from Dublin to Slane Castle so he could root her.'

The leaguies interrupted Ross's history lesson to observe George III was also mad, as in the movie, *The Madness of King George*. Perhaps, it was pointed out, he rooted himself silly.

'The manager of the Shelbourne had given the Wallabies a suite to entertain in,' Turnbull continued. 'Midafternoon Friday, the day before the Test match, there was a knock on the door. John Tallent had this beautiful young blonde woman with him. She was about 35 and I invited them in for drinks. It was the normal thing a manager would do. I had a great relationship with John.

'I was only 32, the youngest Australian manager ever. They were duchessing me like you couldn't believe. John referred to me as "my son". He said, "My son, I'd like to introduce you to my daughter," who was Elizabeth, the marchioness.

'I remember saying, "I suppose I can kiss my sister," and did so, inviting them to sit down. We had a convivial cocktail and she asked if I'd like to come to lunch on Sunday. "I will have Mount Charles pick you up at 10 am," she said.

'It was a beautiful drive out there.' (The Wallabies won their only Home Unions Test against Ireland the day before, suggesting the coming activity did not distract the Australian manager from any of his duties.) 'It was a sunny day and took us an hour to drive there along the straight road,' he recalled. 'Mount Charles's son, Henry, by a previous marriage, was there. The son actually changed the castle to a venue for rock concerts some time later, but that's another story. Anyway, we sat down for lunch – the marquess and marchioness, Henry, John Tallent and me.

'I remember thinking to myself, "Wouldn't my dad be happy to see me now!" It was a very English atmosphere, even though the marchioness was Welsh and we were an hour out of Dublin.

'After lunch we went for a drive and walked the fields where the Battle of Boyne was fought between the Catholic King James II and William III of Orange. During the walk, she spent a lot of time talking to me about interesting times.'

The leaguies again interrupted the prelude to ask if James II was routed – did Roscoe get rooted?

'We went back for afternoon tea, more drinks, a log fire and supper,' he intoned, disregarding the interruption. 'It had been a lovely day. We talked world issues, but it came time for me to go home. "I will take Ross home, darling," she told Mount Charles.

'I remember him saying, "Shall I warm some Horlicks for you, darling?" She said no, and on the drive home she indicated by way of conversation she had spent time in gambling clubs in London with Middle Eastern oil princes.

'It became obvious I should invite her to my room. I spent hours with her. I remember thinking, "If only my dad could see me now." Mum and dad were clerks in the gas company in Newcastle and lived in a miner's cottage in Adamstown. Newcastle to Slane Castle.'

That was all Ross would say, despite the demands for lurid detail from the St George connection.

'Because we were playing the Barbarians at Cardiff Arms Park, I invited her, but she said to leave it as it is,' he said. 'We both moved on. The next day we travelled on the team bus to the airport, and there was an announcement calling me to the phone. It was her thanking me for a wonderful evening.

'The following year, the Australian cricket team went to England for the Ashes series. It was Ian Chappell's tour and my legal firm, Turnbull and Hill, were acting for the cricketers who had signed with Kerry Packer for World Series Cricket. I got talking with Ian Chappell, who told me he had met the marchionesss and she sent her regards.'

The St George group's patient, yet pained, willingness to listen to Turnbull's story, hoping it would end with graphic detail of his romp, were disappointed because it ended at the bedroom door.

Voyeuristic, vicarious sex is not confined to rugby league. Grey says, 'When I came into the Waratahs as a 21-year-old, I was often summoned to the back of the bus where a quartet of big, older players cross-examined me. All over 110 kg, six foot two and me all of 90 kg being summoned and questioned. I had to tell them the story of what happened the night before so these guys with wives and girlfriends could get their sex via this young bloke. Every detail was expected to be revealed.'

In fact, a rare occasion when no detail was requested concerned a rugby league star who also had a story of seduction – by one of the world's great musical icons, Maria Callas, long-time partner of Aristotle Onassis, the Greek billionaire shipping owner who later married Jackie Kennedy.

It transpired the Kangaroos were staying briefly at a London hotel during a 1960s tour and the star player and the opera singer had congress. Years later, while having lunch with the star, along with the Federal Minister for Sport and the Arts, Senator Rod Kemp, I mischievously put the story to the star and he didn't deny it.

'She picked me out in the hotel,' he said. 'She heard I was a young, up-and-coming player and took me up to her room and basically raped me.'

The reaction of Minister Kemp will endure: seeking neither to approve of the story nor diminish the narrator, Kemp commented dryly, 'Well, that is a story which marries both sides of my portfolio.'

But the marchioness and opera singer stories are sideshows to rugby league's main act. One of the world's great supermodels was invited to a soirée at the Newtown home of Alan Jones, Sydney's top-rating breakfast broadcaster and a former coach of the Wallabies and Balmain Tigers.

Alan also spent a couple of years as football manager at South Sydney and periodically invited players to meet celebrities, part of their socialisation process. The supermodel was immediately attracted to one of the rugby league players, a guy with an unusually handsome, cosmopolitan face and very sculptured body. They adjourned from the Jones party to the eastern suburbs nightclub of the late stockbroker Rene Rivkin before retiring to the supermodel's hotel.

Legend has it she gave only one instruction: don't mess with her hair.

The following morning, after a night of rampant lovemaking, she farewelled the player at the hotel door. He paused, suggesting a contact number and a future meeting. 'Piss off' is a summary of her reply, making it clear she had used him, rather than the other way around. Some women reading this may actually cheer the supermodel: 'one back for the sisterhood'.

A more humorous story of women using their wiles to achieve a desired result in sport concerns a Moreland Challenge Cup soccer match between Norton Hill Rangers and Wookey FC in Cheltenham, England, which ended 0–0.

The teams went to a best-of-five penalty shoot-out. Each time a Rangers player stepped up to take a shot, he was flashed by a 25-year-old Wookey fan standing behind goal. Three kicks sailed over the bar, including one that landed in the parking lot. Wookey won 3-2. The captain of Rangers, Lee Baverstock, admitted, 'It definitely got to the lads.'

Nor should it be assumed the wives of footballers blindly believe all their husband's stories, particularly of tours. Former ARL chief executive John Quayle, who played for Australia, has a favourite story of sex and bonding, a tale his wife, Diane, has heard many times.

'It was my first game for Australia and we were in Auckland and I was on my best behaviour,' Quayle says. 'During the day, Tommy [Raudonikis] kept coming up to me and saying, "We're going out tonight, Canon. You're with me."' (Quayle's nickname derived from his father's occupation as an Anglican minister.)

'I'd keep saying, "No, we can't. We've got an official function after the game."

'Tommy said, "No, we can give that a miss," but I eventually convinced him we should make an appearance. We weren't there long and he came up and whispered, "We'll be going in five minutes. Meet me in the foyer."

'I thought I was going to this lovely party at this lovely place overlooking the harbour. We were met in the foyer by this Maori lady a little on the large side, and I noticed a couple of tattoos. It was quite rare in those days for women to have tattoos. But she was quite good-looking and well-spoken.

'In the car, Tommy was doing his usual business [titillating the lady]. But it took us an hour to get there and I was already getting a bit worried. We came to this house on stilts, and there were about 50 motorbikes out the front. All the guys were dressed in leather, and they had tattoos on their foreheads and faces and looked frightening.

'When I later saw the movie *Once Were Warriors*, I said to myself, "I've been there." All I could see were these white eyes. I was really shaken and kept saying to Tommy, "Where are we?" I felt a bit of panic because we were miles from Auckland, but Tommy kept assuring me that we'd be sweet.

'As we walked through the gate, the blokes were patting us on the back. We were in our Australian blazers, and they had been to the game and were saying gracious things like, "You were too good."

'They had a hangi going and everyone was off their face, having a drink, and things were getting wild. I was talking to the blokes but I realised Tommy wasn't there. I went around the house calling out "Tommy", knocking on doors. There were things going on in the bedrooms, but I couldn't find Tommy. I was worried how we would get home because we were at least an hour from Auckland.

'I walked under the house and I could feel this water dripping down, so I went back upstairs and knocked on the bathroom door, saying, "Tommy?" The next thing I hear is, "Canon, come in."

'I opened the door to this incredible sight. There was this big, giant enamel bath, with candles burning around the room, and Tommy and the large lady in the bath. He had a big container of Johnson's baby oil, and he was smearing it over her.

'He's saying, "Canon, get your gear off and get in," but then she would roll on top of him and he'd disappear. When he came up for air, he'd splutter and say again, "Canon, get in."

'Water was splashing over the edge of the bath and dripping through the floor to underneath. Tommy and the large lady were going round and round under the water,' the Canon says of the human rinse cycle. 'There was no chance they could do any business, the way they were rolling and the water, so oily. If I'd got in the bath, it would have fallen through the floor.

'I said, "Let's get home." When we finally left, one of the blokes drove us back.

'The next day, when Graeme Langlands [captain-coach] asked us where we went, Tommy whispered, "That's between me and you, Canon."

Diane Quayle has heard this story many times and her reaction is consistent. 'I bet you got in the bath. That's the only thing you missed out,' she tells him with a mix of suspicion and scorn.

And Tommy's reaction? 'The Canon is wrong when he said she was a large lady. She was a bloody good sort,' making her sound as if she had a body that would cause a monk to chew a hole in a church pew.

Of all the newspaper stories written during the Coffs Harbour debacle, the one that most damaged the code was written in the *Sun Herald*, including the comment 'Some of the boys love a bun', and under the heading 'Players reveal their side of the story'.

NRL boss Gallop had retreated to his South Coast holiday home one weekend during the saga and was relieved when the *Sun Herald* had a tepid story. But he didn't realise it was a first edition story, the Sunday newspapers never giving their opposition the opportunity to follow up early edition scoops.

When he read the full story, it sent Gallop into a spin, holding inteviews with the author and editor. The words were attributed to an unnamed Bulldog player, and the journalist, while not revealing his source, convinced Gallop this was no made-up story.

'Gang banging is nothing new for our club, or rugby league,' was another quote from the player.

So why do 'the boys love a bun'?

The sociologists say it is part of the bonding process – and they are right. Plus, players don't have to talk to the girl afterwards. Group sex, provided the player and woman are alone during the congress – the others being in an adjoining room – also disguises the sexually inadequate. Even if he is revealed as a 'soft cock' or a premature ejaculator or a 'little dick', much merriment is made and it is subsumed into the team, or club, ethos.

One memorable training night at St George, where I was coach for six years, the players from the three grades were full of laughter. You could actually track the humour like a blaze, a spot fire of giggling erupting on one corner of Kogarah Oval and a player sprinting like a spark to another group to ignite the same explosion of side-splitting mirth.

It transpired that a prominent player, then married, had finally succumbed to a temptress who had been stalking him on Sunday nights back at the leagues club. He arranged to use the one bedroom apartment of a single player, a lower grader, for his illicit union. But there was a mix-up with the address, or the key, and the prominent player arrived at the apartment about the same time as the lower grader.

The temptress, who had long harboured a passion for the player, entered the bedroom with him while the lower grader made himself a cup of tea in the kitchen, a room so small you had to leave to sneeze.

Within minutes, the temptress was back outside the bedroom door, fully dressed, staring blankly. Speaking to no-one but herself, she said, 'That was the worst fuck I have ever had.'

That was the punchline of the story that was told and re-told a hundred times at Kogarah Oval that winter night. The prominent player good naturedly endured the countless jibes, a look of resignation on his face.

Rugby union's Grey has a similar story. 'A young guy with the Waratahs had been seeing this older woman, and he was very keen on her. Both were single. She invited him around for dinner but rang about half an hour before he was expected at the house, saying they would now be going to a restaurant.

'He thought he'd missed the boat, thinking it was only dinner. They had a nice bottle of wine with it and he's thinking he's no chance, but she offers him dessert back at her place. He immediately thinks the tables have turned.

'They go to her place and he walks in feeling a bit uncomfortable, and she leads him into the bedroom. She lights candles above the bedhead and they both get their gear off. He's standing there naked and she says, "Make love to me."

He lasts six strokes.

'She says, "You're the quickest fuck ever. You've halved my past record." He drove home shattered. He obviously confided in one of the guys . . . who then confided in 35 others.'

When I coached Western Suburbs, training night disruptions at Lidcombe Oval were commonplace. Club president Bill 'King' Carson introduced a chiropractor to the club, and within minutes it seemed all three grades were queued up to see him.

Of course they were avoiding training, and I instituted a 'queue of one' system where any player who had finished treatment must return to the field and tag another to report to the chiropractor.

Unfortunately, the tag system went in an unexpected direction. One leading player appeared to be with the chiropractor for nearly half an hour and, since he was pivotal to our rehearsed plays, I stormed to the medical room. When I asked a lower grade player where the first grader had gone, he sensed my fury and his eyes looked skyward, to the radio boxes at the top of the grandstand.

I sprinted up the stairs, only to see the player running down them, just as fast. He did not stop, despite my instruction to him to do so.

Sensing something amiss, I entered a radio box to see a leading official of the club, his pants around his ankles, and a groupie, known as 'Wok Eye' because of one lazy eye, giving him a blow job. I berated the pair but she didn't miss a beat.

Wok Eye's vision problem did not prevent her from being asked to adjudicate a short dick competition. The two finalists included a forward, who said memorably, 'It was the only contest I never wanted to win.'

League fan John Singleton loved the stories about her so much he named a racehorse after her. Unfortunately, he misunderstood the cruel language of the Magpies and called the horse 'Wonk Eye'. Unlike Wok Eye, who didn't miss a start, Wonk Eye never won a race.

Incidents such as these go a long way to explaining how the bonding process at the Magpies produced a rare but robust democracy. Even now at Wests' reunions a quarter century after we've left the club, players of the late 1970s and early 1980s gather and speak wistfully of 'Shaz'.

Shaz was tall and very attractive with blonde hair cascading down her back. She loved all the Magpies, although giant prop Dallas Donnelly was her favourite. Not a reunion passes without some recollection of her, the most recent being how she came to the club.

Prop Peter Young, Dallas's best mate, remembered discovering her at Burwood shopping centre while they were doing a promotion. 'We've got a live one here, Pig,' Young said, using his pet name for the unmarried Dallas. 'The blonde's showing interest in you.'

'We followed her into a butcher's shop and got talking to her. We arranged to meet at a pub later in the afternoon, a different one, because she was so good we didn't want to share. Within a day, Snake and Spider had sniffed her out and undercut us.'

Occassionally, Shaz would accompany a half dozen players to the 'Halfway House', a dwelling owned by two Magpies, and cook 'the meat tray', usually won by a player in the pub raffle.

The electrical fittings at the Halfway House were not lavish. The stove was very small and a one bar radiator provided the only warmth, a problem considering it was the middle of winter and was also required to make toast.

Of further concern to Shaz was the fact Dallas insisted she cook in the nude. She'd complain about the cold and the fat spitting on her bare breasts, but Dallas liked a nude cook. He once installed 'Barrell', a roundish, very amiable Wests supporter with whom Dallas shared lodging, to monitor Shaz's state of dress.

'Has she got her gear off yet?' Dallas would periodically ask of Barrell between hands of a card game.

'Still got her pants on,' said the unmarried Barrell, peeping around the corner into the kitchen, goggle-eyed at the sight of the semi-naked beauty. A few minutes later, with the chops sizzling and Dallas's giant gut rumbling, he wondered aloud if Shaz was still wearing pants.

'She ain't now,' said Barrell, warming to the role of Shaz-watcher, spitting bits of toast everywhere, simultaneously excited about her nakedness and desperate for food.

One night an outsider, who had urged his way into the post-pub exodus to the Halfway House, was caught peeping into the bedroom. Dallas threw him out. It predated Channel Ten's *Big Brother*, perhaps the first time someone was evicted from a house for perving, as opposed to providing a perv show for a nation. Shaz later brought her role of naked chef to an end by refusing to cook until all males in the house undressed. Dallas could not convince her to change her mind, but it significantly thinned the numbers who shared the sausages.

Dallas had a magnetic attraction to women.

When I finally decided to leave Wests and coach St George, I travelled with the Magpies to an end-of-season game in Darwin. Dallas would not hear of my leaving, insisting I break the contract with the Dragons. Nothing would distract him from this mission, not even a thousand beers.

Finally, it came the morning of my flight back to Sydney, but Dallas and some of the others were extending their stay. We drove down to Fanny Bay for a few breakfast stubbies and looked out at the almost still water.

The head of a young woman emerged from the ocean and she began walking towards us, evoking instant memories of the blonde in the James Bond movie appearing from the sea in a white bikini. But the gradient of the bay was so gentle, the woman waded 20 metres before it was clear she was not wearing a top.

Dallas echoed everyone's thoughts when he said, 'It's too much to hope she ain't got pants.' Another 20 metres or so, it became apparent she didn't. She continued to wade towards the car and Dallas was transfixed.

I opened the passenger door, collected my bag from the boot, walked to the road, hailed a cab and half an hour later was in the air to Sydney.

End-of-season trips test the toughest of coaches. Triple AFL premiership coach David Parkin recalls, 'In 1981 Carlton went on a pre-season trip to Hawaii, and I got the players together for an early morning run. I was doing the rollcall and noticed a player was not there.' Parkin has a legendary love of discipline, and the veins on his neck pop at lack of punctuality. '"Who's rooming with him?" I demanded.

'The big Yugoslav [Val Perovic] declared he was the player's room-mate and I told him to go and get him. But he threw me the key and says you get him. I was new to the joint and wasn't sure how things worked, so I raced back into the hotel, up to his room, opened the door and there he was with hands behind his head, watching TV.

'"Get down to training, don't you know you're already facing a $100 fine?" I said.

'He rolled back the blankets and there was a girl giving him a head job. "Mind if I'm a bit late?" he said.

'I stalked out the door saying, "It's now $200."'

A former Geelong captain, Andrew Bews, stunned me at a fundraiser for junior football one summer. It was the year following the Coffs Harbour revelations, and the audience at the North Geelong Cricket Club sausage sizzle wanted to know what happened in Bews's era.

'Rat', as he was nicknamed, a 207-gamer for the Cats, told how on end-of-season trips the players would buy a saw and pinch a motorbike helmet. They'd cut a head-sized hole in the top shelf of a tall cupboard in one of the hotel rooms and place the helmet over it, leaving the door marginally ajar so only the helmet was visible. Phone books were collected and placed in the bottom of the cupboard for height adjustments.

While sex proceeded on the hotel bed, players took turns placing their head in the helmet and peering through the visor at the romp.

It took almost two years before anyone told a joke about Coffs Harbour. The comedian at the Wests Tigers grand final luncheon in 2005 made a quip about sex doggy style, before suggesting it was bulldoggy style. 'Everyone standing around watching,' he explained.

Only a recent recruit to the code's administrative ranks could have committed a gaffe of the magnitude of one club official delegated to recruit a new coach over the Christmas of 2005. The new man on the block asked a senior player to comment on the qualities of a prospective coach for whom he had played.

'He's a mad reader,' the player enthused.

Believing the player had said 'rooter' and anxious to ingratiate himself with the culture, the club official said, 'There's nothing wrong with that. We've all been in buns.'

AFL recovered more quickly. At the Essendon Women's grand final lunch at Crown Casino, during a debate that 'footy has gone soft', one woman speaker said, 'I want my man to be Best On Ground and Best Pants Man Off Ground.'

Commenting on a move by a space-challenged Melbourne council to bar anyone hitting a cricket ball for a six, one woman said, 'That's like having sex without an orgasm. Been there, done that.' Victorian women feel a greater ownership of their game and speak with more confidence. Essendon didn't even have a team in the grand final, yet there were 1,000 women at the lunch, all paying $100.

If women are appalled by violence in football, there was no hint of it from the speakers. 'Every woman here would pay $20 to see you clean up Jason Akermanis,' a debater told former Hawthorn tough man, Dermott Brereton.

If women are appalled by stories of yet another footballer arrested by police, one woman debater said, 'I want my son to be singing, "I'm going home in the back of a divvy van" by the time he is 18 months.'

Of course, it was all good fun and a refreshing departure from the Bulldogs' view of the universe that the world outside Belmore is populated by hypocrites and bearers of double-standards. Yet there is increasing evidence rugby league women are assuming some ownership of the game and, hopefully, greater confidence to co-exist in a male sport.

A Premier League match between the Roosters and Bulldogs in 2005 was refereed by Jason Robinson and his wife, Jenny, was a touch judge. Jenny, a mother and a theatre nurse, has also refereed a Jersey Flegg match with two female touch judges. In a 'Here's to you, Mrs Robinson', NSWRL Referees Coordinator, Dennis Spagarino, said, 'She deserves to be there.'

Spagarino also said, 'If some districts, such as Balmain, didn't have female referees, rugby league wouldn't exist.' His daughter, Joanne, sent bad boy/water boy John Hopoate from the field the same year when he challenged a touch judge to a meeting after the match (related in a later chapter).

Rugby league came in for a trashing at the Essendon lunch. 'It has all the charisma of meat trucks colliding by numbers,' one unfunny woman said. But despite AFL women's liberated view, perhaps some rugby league women have always known what they want. I know of internationals who married women who might be considered 'buns'.

For the most part, the couples remained happily married, although one player, when he got drunk, would argue with his wife, sometimes saying, 'I found you in a bun.' This was occasionally said in front of others, drawing a horrified reaction from those observing the altercation.

But she settled everyone with her response: 'Yes, but I'm still the best fuck you ever had.'

To which he invariably agreed, saying, 'Can't argue with that.'

BAD BOYS AND THE BENCH

In the opening act of *Macbeth*, Malcolm describes the calm with which an enemy went to his death: 'Nothing in his life became him like the leaving it.' Footballers, as a rule, behave with dignity when they are sacked. It's said a footballer dies twice – once like the rest of us and, before that, when his career is over. If retirement is such an emotional death, why do they act so honourably?

Mainly because footballers spend their playing lives exploiting weakness in others and are not about to expose that innermost kernel of frailty when all eyes are upon them as they exit the stage. Most are prepared for the moment, being benched or banned occasionally throughout their careers, dropped to a lower grade, sacked as captain, shunned by the representative selectors, dismissed from the field by a referee, suspended by the disciplinary panel, sent home from a tour by the team manager.

This is not to say there aren't some monumental blow-ups, and David Parkin still flinches at the memory of one.

'I got so good at sacking players at Carlton, I could make them sack themselves,' he says. 'We called a player named Adrian Gleeson into my office at Optus Oval and told him he had to go. I had Col Kinnear, my football manager, with me because you need two if you have to verify a story later, should a player kick up when he'd had a long think about it. I talked to Gleeson and in the end he said, "I've had a terrific innings. It's time for me to move on. I've had a great career and you've helped me and thanks for everything."

'He goes out the door, and I put my feet up on the desk and my hands behind my back and say to Col, "Geez, we're getting good at this sacking caper." Then the door flies open and Gleeson storms in and stands over the top of me – "You're a disgrace. The way you treat players is disgraceful." It was 45 seconds of everything you don't want to hear about yourself. I was trying to get my feet off the desk while he was standing over me, giving it to me, but I was stuck there.

'When he left, Col said, "You're getting good at making them retire, aren't you?" I was shell shocked. He'd obviously gone outside and thought about it and thought, *This is the only chance I'll ever get to tell him what I really think.*' (Gleeson is now on the Carlton board.)

Maybe it was karma or cosmic comeuppance, but Parkin admits he departed coaching with a similarly smashed ego. 'When I finally decided in 2000 that I wanted to finish, Jack [club chairman John Elliott] called me in and said, "We want you to stay." 'I said, "Is this a job offer?" and he said, "Yes. We want you to look after the place." I asked did it have a salary? "Yes." A car? "Yeah." I said I'd written myself out of the script, but he said he wanted me to think about it.

'I went into my office and had a little weep. In comes Col and Shane O'Sullivan [recruitment manager], my two best mates.

They said, "What are you going to do?" I said, "I think it is time to leave." They said, "Yes, it is."

'So next day I rang Jack on his mobile. He must have been on a tractor up on his rice farm, because he kept saying, "Who is it?" and I kept saying, "Parkin." Finally, he understood who it was and I told him I was finishing and he said, "Yeah, once you pass the baton, you can't take it back again."

'So my two best mates told me to go and the president had thought about it overnight and also said it was time to go.'

Apart from a life ban, the biggest ignominy is to be sent home from an overseas tour. Tom Raudonikis admits he was almost dispatched back to Australia on the 1973 Kangaroo tour.

'They were going to send me home after I had a blue with manager Charlie Gibson,' he says. 'I was blamed for trouble up the road at another hotel over something that wasn't my fault. One of the top-liners did something, and I copped the blame.' Raudonikis had earlier captained Australia to a win over Great Britain on an icy ground at Warrington. 'The blue with Charlie cost me the Australian captaincy. I captained NSW but never Australia after that.'

A *Lord of the Flies* mentality often exists on overseas tours where there is an elite group at the top and the rest below. The team management is often guilty of fostering it. It is an environment about power and bonding, and it produces discriminatory justice.

In 1978, in France, four Kangaroos were playing cards in the downstairs bar of a hotel when they saw a team-mate pick up a heavy street sign and smash it into a parked Porsche. Coach Frank Stanton confirms that manager Peter Moore was intent on sending the culprit home, until he learned it was his son-in-law, winger Chris Anderson.

Rugby union has produced two celebrated examples of players being sent home from tour. Not only did they leave the touring party without fuss, they have refused to speak about their banishment.

Ross Turnbull, having managed the Wallabies on their Great Britain tour in 1974–75, blames pressure by officials from the host union for both players being sent home.

He says of Keith Murdoch, the All Black front-rower sent home in 1971 during a tour of the British Isles where he scored New Zealand's only try in their narrow victory over Wales at Cardiff Arms Park, 'He was a big country boy from some small town in New Zealand. After the Test match he went to the team hotel across the road from the ground for the celebratory Test dinner, had a few beers and then went to his room. He left his room about midnight and went down to the kitchen for a snack. There was no room service. Wales was then a third-world place.

'He got himself a feed and then went out through a side door of the hotel to get upstairs. He found himself outside the front door of the hotel. He was decidedly the worse for wear, because by then he'd drunk a bottle of gin. A Welsh security guard stopped him and barred him from entering. One thing led to another and Murdoch flattened him.

'The next day, following complaints by the hotel to the Four Home Unions Tours Committee, whose chair was an Englishman, the New Zealand team management buckled and he was sent home. He left the plane in Perth and has been living ever since in a mining town in Western Australia.'

When the famous New Zealand journalist Sir Terry McLean (knighted for services to rugby journalism!) tracked him down, he said, 'Hello, Keith. It's Terry.' Murdoch, who was holding a can of insect repellent, pointed to the label, making it clear Sir Terry should buzz off.

In August 2002 Australian newspapers reported Murdoch's alleged involvement in the death of a 20-year-old burglar found in an abandoned open-cut mine. Murdoch, then 58 and living in the Northern Territory, was questioned by a coroner and twice interviewed by police over the death of a young Aboriginal man, Kumanjayi Limerick, who was caught thieving in Murdoch's Tennant Creek home on 6 October 2000.

Limerick's body was found 15 kilometres from Tennant Creek, three weeks after the robbery, but Murdoch was not charged following the initial suspicious death investigation where he appeared as a witness. The Northern Territory coroner recommended a new police investigation when he delivered his inquest findings, and the renewed inquiry examined whether the crimes of assault or deprivation of liberty had been committed when Limerick was taken to Noble's Nob goldmine the night of the burglary. Police investigations were completed without charges laid.

Turnbull accuses the All Black captain and players of being weak over Murdoch's banishment from the team, saying, 'They should have stopped the bus when he wasn't on it and refused to go on without him. It's a similar story with Ross Cullen, who was sent home from the 1967 Wallaby tour for biting the ear of an Oxford University prop, Ollie Waldron, during a match. His own props weren't protecting him. The opposition props were boring in on Cullen and he told them to stop it. He was physically being hurt, but they didn't stop, so he latched onto the ear of one of them. He was told by senior players to admit nothing, but manager Bill McLaughlin pulled him aside in what he insisted was a man-to-man confidential discussion.

'The chairman of the Four Home Unions Tours Committee would have suggested McLaughlin investigate the incident. McLaughlin seduced Cullen into telling him exactly what had happened. When Cullen admitted biting the prop, McLaughlin no doubt then passed this on to the Four Home Unions Tours chairman, who would have declared over a glass of port, "Send him home. That's what I would do, my boy."

'It was a lesson I learnt when Australian captain Tony Shaw came to me on a tour of New Zealand and I was the manager,' Turnbull continues. 'It was the night before a Test match and Tony said he'd dropped a bloke in the bar. God knows what had happened in the bar, but I told him to zip his lip and go to his hotel room and not answer the door to anyone. A copper came to his room, but he pretended to be asleep.

'The next day New Zealand management wanted to take court action, and I said *we'd* be the ones taking court action. I told them I wouldn't have one of my players verbally assaulted in a hotel bar. New Zealand buckled. We'd lost eight of our best players, plus coach Daryl Haberecht, who'd had a heart attack. But we had to get on with the tour. The next day we beat the All Blacks and Greg Cornelson scored four tries.'

Turnbull describes the banishments of Murdoch and Cullen as 'management problems', accusing British officials of being hypocrites because they did not apply the same high standards to their own players.

'British officials pulled the wool over their eyes,' he says. 'When the British and Irish Lions toured, they had so much money they could pay for the damage and hush it up. A section of the Lions were known as "the hotel wreckers" in the 1970s. I had to put up with this on the 1975 tour of the British Isles. Mick Burton had been sent off in the Battle of Brisbane [an infamous Test match detailed in a later chapter] and they were looking to get square and punish one of ours. They put a lot of pressure on me.

'Four of our players were involved in a minor incident [drinking too much whisky at an official reception] after the Scottish Test. It was blown out of proportion by the chairman of the Four Home Unions Tours Committee and the president of the Scottish RU, Sir John Law, the chief constable of Scotland.

'On the following Monday we were headed to Buckingham Palace for an evening reception with the Queen and Royal Family. At the preceding dinner at the East India Club in St James Square, we took the wind out of their sails by having the boys apologise individually to the Tours chairmen.'

McLaughlin, the Wallaby manager, despised by many players, threatened to sue me when I wrote an article in the now defunct *Sun* newspaper in which I quoted former Wallaby, horse trainer and doctor, Geoff Chapman. Dr Chapman accused McLaughlin of vindictively omitting him from a Wallaby team to tour South Africa, despite Chapman scoring 18 of his team's 22 winning points in a trial match. Chapman said he argued with McLaughlin, then chairman of Australian selectors, at half-time following an incident where he punched Greg Davis, who was pulling his jumper in the line-outs. During an earlier tour of New Zealand, Chapman said he ordered McLaughlin to leave a post-game party when it was reaching an engaging stage. McLaughlin denied both clashes occurred.

Turnbull also had dealings with McLaughlin when the dictatorial official was chairman of selectors for the ARU. 'I was travelling around the country playing rugby and also practising law when the 1969 tour of South Africa loomed,' Turnbull says. 'I had an opportunity to buy a law practice but was worried whether it would undermine my selection. I had to borrow £10,000 to buy the practice, a lot of money in those days. So I decided to have a private word with McLaughlin and asked him if I did make this step, if there was anything which could block me. He assured me I'd be fine and encouraged me to buy the practice.

'I was never chosen for the tour. He never told the truth.'

Turnbull admits he should have been prepared for the disappointment: 'Earlier, there had been the British Isles tour of

1966–67. At that time, they only came every ten years, so you had to be born at the right time. I was, but I wasn't chosen, despite all the experts picking me in their teams. I decided then that I wouldn't allow anything to ever hurt me like that again. I did go to Ireland and Scotland in 1968 and got my cap. My opponent in the Irish Test was Syd Millar [now the chairman of the IRB, the governing body of the code in the world]. It's not a disappointment being chosen for only one Test. What I was upset with was the manner I was treated by McLaughlin.'

But 'Mad Dog' Turnbull has always proven tenacious. Despite bankruptcy, running up $50,000 in bills on corporate credit cards, having his meagre belongings (including Viagra) photographed and printed in a newspaper when he could not pay his hotel bill, he has always bounced back.

Of one of his earlier resurrections, he says, 'After missing the South African tour, in the next four years I built up [with partner Michael Hill, later chairman of the Newcastle Knights] the biggest legal practice outside Sydney. Then I became a stamp collector until Trudy [first wife] suggested there must be something in rugby union I could do.'

It was then he became manager of the Wallabies, earning the grand trip he had earlier missed.

Football's wheel of fortune occasionally makes amends. Rugby union now appears to treat its highly paid touring players more leniently than in the days when they were not paid at all. Maybe it's a paradox of the modern era, but players appear to act less professionally now that they are professional. Or perhaps the great glare of the game, with vigilant media reporting, exposes more wrongdoings.

Certainly, the end came for Wallaby coach Eddie Jones when he did not heavily punish two Test players – Lote Tuqiri and Wendell

Bad Boys and the Bench

Sailor – who were at a nightclub in South Africa until the early hours of the morning, three days before a Tri Nations match against the Springboks.

The day following Jones's sacking – after a commendably honourable performance at his press conference – I saw former Australian cricket captain Steve Waugh in an airport lounge in Sydney.

He had made himself a cup of tea, and we chatted about his book and Eddie Jones. He was happy to talk because, after all, he never missed a match at Lidcombe Oval when he was a kid cheering for Western Suburbs. When Terry Lamb switched to Canterbury, Waugh followed him, but he insisted he is still a Wests supporter. Maybe the Bulldogs' penchant for serial disaster disappointed him, because he shook his head at the club's mention.

Fortunately Wests Tigers finally have a five-eighth to compare with Lamb. 'My son practises his Benji Marshall sidestep every day,' he said.

The conversation meandered to Jones's sacking, the cup of tea cold and forgotten. Waugh opined that the end came when Jones failed to heavily discipline Tuqiri and Sailor, while sending home Matt Henjak, a bench player, for the crime of throwing ice in the nightclub. Although the two Wallabies were former Kangaroos, I remarked that the rugby league culture does not allow late nights on Test eve.

'It wouldn't happen in cricket either,' Waugh said. 'Ten to 12 years ago, that culture was encouraged. It's all self-regulation now. It's up to them how they behave. When you get one million dollars playing for Australia and one hundred thousand playing for the State, it's a pretty clear incentive.'

Two days earlier I met former Wallaby captain John Eales in Canberra's airport lounge, and he delivered the same message, saying there had been a marked change since the beginning of the World Cup era in 1987, illustrating it with a story about former Wallaby prop Chris 'Buddha' Handy.

'Before Buddha's first Test [1978], he couldn't sleep,' Eales said. 'He walked along the hotel corridor, found a room full of journos and drank a bottle of rum. He got into bed snoring at 5 am and woke up later that day to play his Test.'

Still, despite rugby's assurances the Tuqiri–Sailor incident was an aberration, Sailor became involved in another incident outside a nightclub, also in Cape Town, vomiting and pushing a young South African supporter. He was out of the team at the time with a hamstring injury, and many of his former ex-league team-mates joked he should have been given the same punishment as Sri Lankan cricketer Murali for being 'a chucker'.

But a drunken Sailor is big news, and the ARU suspended him for three matches. Former World Cup centre Nathan Grey, has harsh words for Sailor, claiming his actions eroded a culture that took years to create.

'Team culture is so hard to get right; you can lose it like this,' he said, snapping his thumb and forefinger. 'It's difficult to obtain, hard to maintain and easiest to lose. If you've got guys out before a Test, it's so disrespectful to the others in the team. When I heard about it, knowing the culture we built, reading about it, it was so disheartening.

'You do get angry. As an individual, you contributed to that culture and they turned their nose up at it. You don't have to have a sports scientist tell you three nights before a massive game you shouldn't be on the piss. Wendell's second incident, when he was out with a hamstring, is even more frustrating. The ideal way to get over an injury isn't by getting pissed. If he wants to have an impact on the team, he's got to get himself right for next week.' Grey's words preceded Sailor testing positive for cocaine in May 2006. The serial misbehaviour of Sailor and Hopoate spawned a joke: the two have joined one of the world's top bands – 'Powder Finger'.

Wallaby captain George Gregan was continually spared, despite the losses and behavioural problems of his team-mates in South Africa. The ARU showed him enormous loyalty at a time the captaincy in all codes was undergoing a quiet revolution.

In fact, the 2005 premiers in three codes all had differing approaches to leadership. Wests Tigers replaced their long-term captain, Mark O'Neill, with half Scott Prince, whose appreciation of the honour did not stop him signing with new club Gold Coast Titans for the 2007 season and relinquishing the skipper's role with the premiers. The Swans won the AFL flag with six captains, while Sydney FC won the A-League with three.

I half expected Pete Seeger to sing, 'Where have all the captains gone? Gone to graveyards every one. When will they ever learn?'

What has happened to the old man with the C? The traditional model, the player in the decision making position who had proven over a long period to be the best player in the club. Captaincy once involved individual displays of physical courage, good decisions and channelled emotion – the pillars of leadership since the last Ice Age.

It's a model still preferred by some clubs: Newcastle's brooding but brilliant Andrew Johns, Brisbane Lions' inspirational Michael Voss, A-League grand finalist Central Coast's old-fashioned midfielder Noel Spencer.

Is it a case of the professional era – salary caps forcing high turnover of players – retarding the development of natural leaders? Or does professionalism – demanding high standards on and off the field – require multiple leaders?

Grey's coach, World Cup-winning Wallaby mentor Rod Macqueen, argues for the latter. 'It's like a business,' he says. 'You can only have one captain, like you can have only one boss, but it makes it easier if the boss has a number of very skilled deputies with certain assigned roles. If something happened to John Eales on the field, we minimised his loss by having one player calling the plays at the attacking line-outs, another calling the defensive line-outs and someone taking responsibility for the kick-offs. Because the captain, in our case, had his head stuck in a scrum, we had someone else to call the backline moves. The captain in that area would tell Eales the move, meaning he would take responsibility for it.

'With the broader leadership model, you are developing other leaders, which is very helpful for them when they leave sport.'

It took Macqueen some time and considerable resistence to introduce this model, particularly in a code once hidebound by a captain having more power than the archaically named honorary assistant manager.

Eales told me in our Canberra airport chat, 'It's my understanding Rod wanted to replace me but [then ARU chief executive] John O'Neill intervened. But as time moved on, Rod and I worked really well together and achieved our goal.'

Macqueen had come in as a white knight after the reign of the previous Wallaby coach, Greg Smith, ended in personal illness and team failure in 1997. Under Macqueen, Australia won only one of its two Tests on the tour of Argentina, losing the other badly. The Wallabies then drew with England at Twickenham, beating only Scotland.

I checked with O'Neill and he told me Macqueen approached him and said he wanted to replace Eales. His preferred skipper? Gregan. According to O'Neill, he pointed out to Macqueen the decision was not his but the board's.

This dated from the mid-1990s when the Kerry Packer-financed/ Ross Turnbull-run World Rugby Corporation attempted to sign-up the world's best rugby union players in order to counter Rupert Murdoch's Super League. The ARU believed the Wallabies coach at the time, Bob Dwyer, and captain, Phil Kearns, sold out to the WRC. Lest future coaches have too much influence over the captain, the ARU board took the responsibility away from the coach, voting to give itself the power to appoint the skipper.

So, when O'Neill, as the board's full-time manager, was told by Macqueen that Eales wasn't up to it, he acted like most rugby men in a crisis. He invited Eales for a game of golf. If Sir Francis Drake could manage a few ends of bowls before the Spanish Armada arrived, O'Neill could sort it out over a round.

On the last few holes, O'Neill raised the matter. 'How much do you want the job?' he asked Eales.

It became very clear that Eales was desperate to hold onto the captaincy. According to O'Neill, he then instructed Macqueen to have a heart-to-heart talk with Eales, who subsequently remained as skipper and led Australia to World Cup success in Wales in 1999.

I pointed out all of this in a *Herald* column in 2005, concluding it by saying that if O'Neill had not acted, the Wallabies may have had Gregan as captain four years earlier.

One week after the column appeared, I was at Kirribilli House, having been invited by Prime Minister John Howard for Christmas drinks. Eales, O'Neill and Macqueen were also there, never all three standing together, chatting on the lawn overlooking the harbour as waiters circulated, carrying trays of oysters, prawns and smoked salmon. I was conscious of the fact I had not checked with Macqueen for his side of the story, but in journalism, two out of three ain't bad.

Macqueen pulled me gently aside, and it became obvious I had really only researched the story from one side — most of Eales's version had come from O'Neill. According to Macqueen, he went to O'Neill, not intent on changing the captaincy but the Wallaby culture.

After the disastrous loss to Argentina, prior to leaving for England, Eales approached him on behalf of the team. The players were annoyed they were to be based at sedate Windsor and not in

London with all its pubs and night-life. Macqueen interpreted this as a less-than-serious approach to winning the two Tests in Britain.

Whatever O'Neill's conniving and cunning after Macqueen voiced his concerns, it worked – Eales kept the captaincy, Australia won the World Cup and the culture changed.

But a change to multiple skippers, or 'the leadership group' as some consultants hired by clubs prefer, didn't help coach Wayne Bennett on the 2005 Kangaroo tour. Nine NRL club captains toured and it didn't stop Australia from losing the Tri Nations, or management mentioning binge drinking in a tour report.

Furthermore, there appears to be resistance from some individuals and player groups when a long-term captain is dumped. Penrith's Craig Gower, captain of their 2003 premiership team, seethed for months over losing the position following an off-season drunken rampage. Gower made headlines for days when he went to a Sunshine Coast golf resort prior to his wedding in early 2006.

While there, he groped the 17-year-old daughter of league legend Wayne Pearce, became involved in an altercation with Pearce's son, stripped nude, hijacked a golf buggy, put a butter knife to the throat of a journalist and otherwise offended a few guests.

When Pearce woke him up the following morning, Gower couldn't remember anything.

Penrith sent two executives to the resort to investigate and, under the glare of incredible publicity, fined him $30,000 and stripped him of the captaincy. Gower protested his punishment, telling Penrith's long-term president, Barry Walsh, 'You'd think I'd killed someone.'

Walsh replied, 'You have, mate. You killed yourself.'

However, Gower, aware that alcohol and he don't mix, abstained from the 'binge drinking' on the Kangaroo tour, impressing team management. This piece of intelligence was passed on when the

NSW team was chosen for the May 2006 State of Origin match. When skipper Danny Buderus was in doubt for the game with injury, Gower became the shadow captain. Just when his redemption appeared complete, Gower himself was injured in the final training session. He made it back for the third game in July. Like Shakespeare's Borachio in *Much Ado About Nothing*, Gower seems 'condemned to everlasting redemption'.

Football clubs, sensitive to a fan base attuned to reporting every misdemeanour to the media and sponsors nervous about their synergies with misbehaving players, are simply obliged to act.

Around the same time Gower was disciplined by his club, West Coast Eagles Ben Cousins was also stripped of the captaincy when it was revealed he did a runner to avoid a roadside breath test while returning home from a wedding.

Cousins blatantly parked his leased Mercedes sports car across a road at Applecross and outran eight policemen. His mate, Perth real estate agent Nathan Hewitt, also inexplicably did a runner, both men leaving their partners in the car. Hewitt was caught within 100 metres, but Cousins swam across a river and subsequently stumbled into the Blue Water Grill restaurant, shirtless and soaked.

The surprised staff members were cleaning up. 'You're Ben Cousins!' cried one.

Cousins denied it.

When the staff member insisted, Cousins said, 'No, I'm his twin.'

He was eventually allowed to use the phone to call his stranded partner, Sam.

A Perth court fined him $900 after several magistrates ruled themselves out of hearing the case because they were strong West Coast Eagles supporters. The magistrate who did hear the case, Peter Malone, also admitted he was an Eagles supporter but was confident he could dispense justice objectively.

Cousins had previously antagonised Eagles officials for his known association with convicted criminal John Kitzon, known as Perth's Mr Big and also a pallbearer at one of Melbourne's gangland funerals.

Cousins's flirtation with the underworld wasn't as blatant as that of team-mate Michael Gardiner. Following a televised pre-season match, Gardiner raised his crossed arms above his head in the symbol of handcuffs as a gesture of support for a jailed bikie leader.

The Eagles, who have one of the highest revenue streams of any football club in Australia, tolerated Cousins and Gardiner because they delivered on the field and had the support of team-mates. Cousins's replacement as leader, Brownlow medallist Chris Judd, declared Cousins would still be the 'spiritual leader'. The leniency finally expired for Gardiner in July 2006 when he was suspended indefinitely after an alcohol related crash that caused over $100,000 in property damage.

Although most captains take their relegation nobly in public, they sometimes boil in private.

When Wests Tigers captain Mark O'Neill returned from injury, stand-in skipper Scott Prince had already proven himself as a clever tactical leader. Experienced coach Tim Sheens had a delicate situation to resolve, and the media recognised a good story. Sheens tried to navigate a path between O'Neill's ample ego and the team's premiership chances, perhaps suspecting O'Neill wanted the job more for himself than what he could do for the team.

The number of references to the second-rower's unhappiness in the media indicated he was speaking off the record to journalists. To O'Neill, the captaincy was not merely an official designation of leadership but an honour of almost mythical proportions. So, when it was stripped from him, it wasn't merely a C change, it was a sea change.

While the O'Neill family made their resentment to Sheens clear, the coach's only public mention of it was at a celebratory function at

Wests Leagues Club when he obliquely noted that players' wives can be vehement in their feelings.

It would seem the current state of captaincy in the four codes is best summarised by the words of former Socceroo captain, John Kosmina: 'Captains are either arse kickers or arse lickers.'

When it comes to players being totally tarred and feathered – former Manly and Wests Tigers winger John Hopoate is the prototypal bad boy. Over the course of his 13-year career, his moods changed faster than the sky over the ocean. Early in 2005 the former international flankman was banned, sacked and retired all in the space of ten minutes.

During a match against Cronulla, he launched himself at good friend forward Keith Galloway, striking him in the head with his arm after the Shark had passed the ball. His defence? He was attempting a 'shooter', a rush out of the defensive line to force an error.

'It was clumsy, I misjudged it,' he told the tribunal, who didn't buy his defence, suspending him for 17 matches.

The Manly board had already met and decided to sack him, and the troublemaker announced his retirement as he left the hearing. He stayed out of the newspapers for a while, except for a photograph taken of him breakfasting with Galloway at Anthony Mundine's Sydney restaurant.

He was back in rugby league news by the end of the season, banished from the field by referee Joanne Spagarino, the 20-year-old daughter of NSWRL referees coordinator Dennis Spagarino, in an Under-13s match at Leichhardt Oval involving his son's team, Manly Cove, playing a semifinal of the Coca-Cola Cup against Western City Tigers. Hoppa, playing the role of water boy, was warned twice for abusive language before being ordered off for challenging a 22-year-old touch judge to meet him after the match.

Dennis Spagarino, who had recently returned from Italy after representing the family in a contested deceased estate, good naturedly rejected suggestions from his colleagues that Hoppa would wake one morning with a horse's head at the end of his bed.

After delaying disciplinary hearings for months to allow Hoppa every chance to defend himself, the NSWRL banned him from rugby league for a year and placed him on probation for a further four years.

He escaped a life ban because of his 'services' to rugby league.

In December 2005 newspapers reported the ban, with an offer by the NSWRL to help him become a qualified coach. Hoppa, who coached four junior teams, described the ban as 'a good and bad result'.

'I can still go and watch my kids play football, but I can't act in any official capacity,' he said. 'I'll cop it on the chin like I have with everything else that has happened to me.'

It capped a tumultuous year for Hoppa, who began the season calling a ball boy a 'little shit' during a match against the Warriors in Auckland. His verbal attack almost precipitated a strike by ball boys. The boy's sin was not throwing Hoppa the ball immediately when he requested it. The 14-year-old New Zealander, however, was acting according to NRL rules by placing it on the sideline. Afterwards Hoppa phoned the family to apologise, soothing the mother and congratulating the lad for knowing the rules better than he did.

Just one week later he struck Cronulla's Galloway, ending his playing career.

Even before Hopoate was banished by Wests Tigers for famously poking his finger up the anuses of opposition players, he had set some records at the club. In a match against the Dragons, he was sent off, suspended for two matches and fined $7500 for throwing 11 punches. He was also hit with a massive ten charges in a game against Melbourne.

When Manly, where he began his career, took him back after he had served his 12-match suspension for the rectal attacks, he turned out for Parramatta's fifth grade rugby union team while contracted to the NRL, a serious no-no.

He also launched a verbal attack on a referee, after which Manly rested him for a month to improve his fitness, claiming his lack of condition was the reason for his temper tantrum. But two months later, entrenched lack of respect for authority became the obvious reason for his behaviour when he abused a touch judge and was suspended for nine matches.

The day before his return from the suspension, he called a referee a 'dickhead' in an Under-12s grand final between his son's Manly Cove side and Cromer at Brookvale Oval. Hopoate was on the field as a trainer and also abused a touch judge, telling him to 'Shut up, you fucking dickhead.'

Coincidentally, the coach of the victorious Cromer team was the very same NRL touch judge he abused for his nine-match suspension. Because Hoppa was a current first grade player, he was invited to the microphone for the victory ceremony.

Manly junior league officials froze with fear but were shocked at his grace. 'He spoke beautifully and said that the other side was far too good and congratulated them and the referee,' says Manly Junior Rugby League executive director, Peter O'Dwyer. 'I just thought, *Excuse me, I can't believe this is the same bloke*.'

Shortly after this Manly extended Hopoate's contract for a year, although Sea Eagles executive director Paul Cummings, when asked whether he was confident the Tongan international would behave the following season, said, 'That's like asking, can I control the world?'

Like almost all bad boys, Hoppa has no safety catch, no kill switch. But the more intriguing question: why did the club tolerate the antics of the Mormon father of eight for so long? Mainly because he was a team man at training, assisting younger players with advice and generating enthusiasm amongst the older ones.

And he did cop his punishment, as he said, on the chin.

Hopoate began a boxing career after retiring from rugby league, fighting on the undercard of the Mundine–Green bout in Sydney in May 2006. He knocked out a Wollongong journeyman inside a minute and then challenged another bad boy – former rugby league international turned journalist Mark Geyer – to a fight. Geyer's crime? Writing critically about current players in the media.

Even the most wild-eyed bad boys can behave with dignity when benched. One night while I was coaching St George at Kogarah Oval, a tall, very muscular prop forward from Cronulla, Michael Wicks, walked onto the field. It is most unusual, probably unprecedented, for a player from another club to simply walk onto a foreign field and join training. Wicks, dressed for action, joined in the tackling drills, driving the first grade players who were holding pads and skidding them along the grass.

No-one said a word, but everyone wondered what the hell he was doing at an opposition team's practice.

The club directors, watching training, scurried back to the safety of the leagues club. John 'Beetle' Bailey, the reserve grade coach – named after an American comic strip character – avoided the looming danger by inventing a drill that involved him taking his players over the fence surrounding the oval and performing shuttle runs up a darkened embankment.

Bailey's team, from a distance, became a dark but immense and watchful eye.

Wicks was known to have a serious personality disorder. Cronulla coach Jack Gibson, who contracted the big fellow, had a tolerance and understanding of schizoid behaviour because one of his sons died from the disorder. However, Jack had clearly decided Wicks's aberrant behaviour was too much, even for him, and cut the young behemoth.

Someone had suggested he join the Dragons, the nearest club to the Sharks. So Wicks merely joined our first grade team. The problem, as one player later observed in the sanctuary of the pub, was that Wicks had 'muscles on his muscles' and eyes that burnt like giant headlights in the night. No-one knew what ignited the wick, as it were, making him a human volcano, and none wanted to find out.

Yet I had to confront him. Discipline dictated it.

I beckoned to him as I watched players he had flattened peel themselves off the turf. As he approached me, a mist surrounded him, the condensation from his heaving body mixing with the cold night air. I began talking to him gently, explaining he wasn't a contracted St George player. Had the volcano erupted, I was on my own. The entire first grade squad had migrated even further away.

But Wicks took it well.

He asked could he shower, and I escorted him into the dressing room, telling the trainer to accommodate him. They approached him cautiously. I learned later that he covered his entire body in linament and then had a hot shower of such length it drained the water tanks.

Years later, when Beetle and I met to exchange old memories, he recalled the night I was left alone with Wicks. Beetle, who proceeded to coach first grade at Wests when we both retired from St George, said, 'Wicks ended up in jail and when he got out, went to Wests. Everything went well between us until I dropped him.'

*

Nine's camera coverage of the modern game means the NRL is a nine-headed Hydra, able to see illegal action from almost every angle. This was evident midway through 2006 when a vigilant tape operator at Channel Nine observed an incident missed by the NRL review committee. The Nine staffer detected St George Illawarra captain Trent Barrett hitting a Newcastle player with a raised forearm in a tackle. He passed the new camera angle on to the NRL and Barrett, who pleaded guilty to striking, was suspended for six weeks. The story has echoes of early August 1986, when Ten had the TV rights and blond-haired Penrith winger Ken Wolffe had his head in the vicinity of the boot of St George prop Craig Young during a game at the SCG. The referee missed the incident that forced Wolffe to leave the field with a cut forehead.

Craig and I watched the replay together at St George Leagues Club with Sharon, his usually subdued wife. When the cameras missed Craig's boot grazing Wolffe's head, we voiced relief. Except for Sharon, who berated her husband for stomping and chided me for not censuring him. But his 'escape' was short-lived, and the following morning brought sobering news.

Tim Sheens, Penrith's coach at the time, had a supplementary club video taken of the game, and it captured the stomp. Craig, a gruff detective, was cited, as was proper according to the rules.

However, Wolffe broke the unwritten law that injured players do not make matters manifestly worse for those fronting the tribunal. The winger appeared before the tribunal without any bandages, the gaping cut visible to all. Furthermore, according to Craig, he told the panel the date of his wedding would have to be changed because his new bride didn't want him photographed in a turban.

Sheens told the panel, then headed by Dick Conti, who would later become a Federal Court judge, 'You could have put three fingers in the cut.'

Young was given four weeks, the standard penalty then and enough to derail our semifinal campaign. Wolffe didn't appear grateful for Sheens's advocacy, switching to Parramatta the following season.

Conti later told me the presence of a coach at a tribunal had the potential to halve a suspension. However, there were dangers in this because the coach was often required to sit between the player charged and the one giving evidence against him.

I once sat uncomfortably between St George half Steve Linnane and Penrith player Doug Delaney. Linnane was accused of eye gouging the Panthers' brilliant young half, Greg Alexander, and Delaney was a witness. Delaney, sitting on my left, interrupted Linnane's evidence to challenge his account of the incident, leaning past me as I edged forward to minimise the distance between his cocked right arm and Linnane's chin.

Some time later I was staying with Conti on his cattle property in north-west NSW, and he recalled the case, agreeing he had gone – in the language of his stockmen – 'the colour of calf shit'.

Eventually Delaney, a solid Aboriginal lad with the view that the only real justice was the evidence of his own eyes, settled down. Linnane was suspended but was able to laugh at the taunts of a reworked line in a popular song at the time: 'I can see clearly now Linnane has gone.'

The judiciary was the scene of some light moments as well, particularly when headed by the old Eastern Suburbs centre, Dick Dunne.

A winger with a severe stutter appeared before Dick, charged with striking an opponent. He began his defence, torturing himself as he tried to speak, words like 'running' and 'field' taking an eternity to emerge. Finally, Dick cut him short and asked, 'Did you hit him or didn't you?'

The relieved player was quick to respond: 'Far, far, far, fuckin' oath I did.'

My wife, Elaine Canty, sat on the AFL tribunal for nine years and she reports similar humorous moments. 'There were times when it was actually an advantage being a woman,' she says. 'Whenever we heard a "squirrel grip" case, I was the only one in the room whose eyes weren't watering.'

In the days before national judiciaries, there were serious inequities with punishment.

Gerard Healy played for Victoria in the February 1988 Bicentenary Carnival in Adelaide. 'South Australia and Victoria played in the final,' he says. 'Gary McIntosh was a willing combatant for South Australia, a rare beast in the 1980s, who didn't come to Melbourne to play. He had a punch-on with 'Diesel' Williams. South Australia won the title. Both players were reported. Each went back to their respective tribunals. Diesel got two weeks and McIntosh was given a hero's welcome at the tribunal and knighted. That was the game where six Victorians were reprimanded for going out midweek. I was one of the imbeciles who took it seriously.'

This was the era when innuendo surrounded some tribunal chairmen, including a now retired NSW Supreme Court judge, with whispered accusations of deals behind closed doors for players to plead guilty and receive an agreed penalty. It led to a changed system of set penalties in the NRL.

Cases are heard by a panel of ex-players, rather than lawyers and representatives of referees, or the public. Few proceed to the tribunal because players know in advance the grading of the charge in terms of how many games they will miss and therefore take the benefit of the discount available for pleading guilty.

Of the ex-players who sit on tribunals, few have more first-hand experience of justice than former international prop Royce Ayliffe.

Ayliffe was captain of the first Australian schoolboy team to tour England, a team of 16-year-olds. I was the coach and, early in the second match in a game against a Lancashire team, I was joined on the bench by Ayliffe. I asked him why he had left the field, and he indicated the referee had sent him off for ten minutes. It was the first time a sin bin had been used in international rugby league.

The referee, a school teacher, believed it was apt punishment for Royce, who greeted his young opponent in the scrum with words to the effect that the English did not wash. Royce had played first grade in Wollongong as a schoolboy. His much older team-mates, some of whom had toured England with Kiwi teams, encouraged him to confront his opposites as they had done, with words like, 'You stink, you Pommy bastard.'

I caught up with Royce recently at Junee RSL Club during a Men of League weekend. He recalled how Jack Gibson recruited him to play for the Roosters around the time he enrolled in a physical education course at Teachers College. Because he earned a pittance as a trainee teacher, he aspired to win the Roosters' $200 club Man of the Match award. One day the prize was his, and he was jubilant.

'Unfortunately [team-mate] Arthur Beetson had asked me to go down on the field so he could get a rest while the trainer came on. The trainer asked me what was wrong and I winked at him, saying Arthur needed a rest. Unfortunately the trainer later told Jack and he immediately ordered the award go to Bruce Pickett. It cost me $200.'

Almost a decade after the NRL introduced the system of set penalties, the AFL adopted it. The intention was to create transparency, but the most famous case in the first year of its operation in the AFL suggests we were looking at something through opaque glass.

The Barry Hall case, where the big, bad Swans forward was charged with striking St Kilda's Matt Maguire, reeked of a done deal. If Hall was found guilty, the Swans' best player would miss the grand final.

Most of Melbourne was behind the Swans, who had not won a flag since the 1930s. Everyone, except grand final opponents the West Coast Eagles, wanted Hall to play. But Hall had struck Maguire in the stomach, forcing him to go down, almost in the comic book manner of someone who had run into a tree he hadn't seen.

The AFL match review committee, headed by former Hawthorn coach Peter Schwab, made themselves look good by charging Hall. However, Schwab submitted a charge that he must have known Hall would beat. He deemed Hall's behaviour 'reckless' as opposed to 'intentional', which would have attracted a more serious penalty. Tantalisingly, that left the second part of the charge – whether the incident was behind play or in play – already decided by an earlier case.

Weeks before, Collingwood full-forward Chris Tarrant had escaped punishment when it was deemed his proximity to the ball made him actively 'in play', as opposed to the more cowardly 'behind play'. An AFL video, produced to offer guidelines on the operation of the new set penalty system, also suggested Hall was in play.

The tribunal heard hours of evidence but took four minutes to find Hall not guilty of the charge of striking behind play, deeming the Tarrant case a precedent, and the AFL video put the exchange clearly in the proximity of the ball. After all, Hall was close enough to kick a goal while Maguire lay spread-eagled on the turf.

Everyone came out smelling of roses, even Hall, who was represented by Terry Forrest QC, the barrister who only days earlier successfully defended bouncer Zdravko Micevic, the security guard who was charged with causing the death of popular cricketer and broadcaster David Hookes. Hall was able to put his hand up and say, 'I did it'; the match review committee was seen to be serious by laying a charge, and the tribunal were good blokes for letting him off.

With no Melbourne team in the grand final, the debate in the days leading up to the case was academic, rather than passionate. Nevertheless, the city seemed relieved when Hall escaped a suspension. It appeared that everyone wanted to see him play. I advanced this theory to George Foster, an Australian-born Stanford University professor of business, who always comes to Sydney and Melbourne to attend the grand finals. He asked the logical question: if the AFL was so desperate for Hall to play in the grand final, why didn't the review committee give him the lesser 'in play' charge in the first place? Because they would have been accused of going soft.

As it was, Schwab and company further sandbagged Hall from penalty by grading the punch 'low', at the bottom end of a four-tiered scale. Yet the punch dispatched a fit, young, 96 kg, 190 cm athlete straight to the ground, and some swear they saw him vomit. Maguire was lampooned for taking a dive, but a six-inch punch delivered to the solar plexus can do a lot of damage.

Hall bars only one topic from discussion in his colourful career – his days as a boxer. Leading boxing trainer Johnny Lewis trains Hall and predicts that when Hall's AFL career is over, he could be a serious contender for the Australian heavyweight title.

The day before the grand final, my wife took me to an annual lunch hosted by the former AFL tribunal chairman, Brian Collis QC. It's a traditional affair; judges, barristers and former AFL tribunal members gather in the basement of a bluestone chambers in the heart of Melbourne's legal district.

Also in attendance was former Hawthorn premiership player Richard Loveridge, a lawyer and member of the tribunal that found Hall not guilty of the more serious infraction. Loveridge was initially first emergency to hear the case but was called up when another tribunal member disqualified himself after being heard to say of Hall, 'I think he's in a bit of trouble.'

In a vague, rambling discourse, Schwab, the guest speaker at the lunch, made a tepid reference to the Hall case, yet it was the topic everyone wanted to hear about. Later, I looked Loveridge square in the eye and asked if he had no alternative but to find in favour of Hall, given the nature of the charge as laid.

His answer was reminiscent of the British Chief Whip in a BBC political thriller who told a journalist, 'You might say that. I couldn't possibly comment.'

It seems Shakespeare summed up the problem of former players sitting on tribunals best when he referred in *Romeo and Juliet* to those 'who stand so much on the new form that they cannot sit at ease on the old bench'.

While Hall's appearance before the tribunal meant that he didn't miss the grand final, Ron Barassi was famously suspended on the eve of the 1963 finals, and he believes the video would have saved him. The Melbourne skipper was reported for striking a Richmond player who had a reputation for staging free kicks. The Demons tried to have a Channel Nine videotape admitted in evidence, but the tribunal wouldn't allow it.

Barassi was suspended for four matches. He missed the finals series, and his team lost the preliminary final when the stand-in captain was a late withdrawal and a key player was injured in the opening minute.

'It happened one game back from the finals,' Barassi said of the incident, still clearly angered by the perceived injustice. 'I've got no doubt I was innocent. He [Dean] took the ball from me in the pack, and I came down and belted the ball on his chest. He launched back as if he had been hit by an uppercut, still holding the ball on his chest, mind you.'

I raised the improbability of Barassi using an uppercut when he was above the player, and he said, 'That's right,' almost triumphantly, as though he was pleased someone from another code had recognised an ancient inconsistency ignored by the then VFL judiciary. 'Frank Adams, an injured Melbourne player sitting in the grandstand, watched him [Dean], and he says the player didn't touch his jaw for five minutes afterwards.'

Barassi said he still laments the case was not heard in an official court where strict rules of evidence apply before a person is convicted.

'The ball went out of bounds and the crowd was booing me. There was a throw-in and [Melbourne coach] Norm Smith sent the trainer out with an instruction. He yelled out to me, "Go off the ball," but I thought he said, "Go *for* the ball." The noise was so . . .,' and he shook his head at the memory of the high-decibel level of the game, bringing his hands to his ears. For an instant, he was Mel Gibson in the Thunderdome. 'So I stay on the ball and the roar continues. The trainer comes out again, and again I think he is saying, "Go for the ball," when he's saying, "Go off the ball." I say to the trainer, "What does he fucking think I'm trying to do?" And it happens a third time.'

I interrupted to ask how this related to the earlier incident, and he seemed annoyed I didn't see it was further evidence of the injustice he suffered that day.

'It shows my state of mind,' he said, as if the present tense applied. 'I was annoyed my coach didn't think I was doing what he asked. There weren't any videos allowed in those days. They wouldn't let us show film or a photo which showed him still holding the ball on the ground. How could he have copped that big a whack and still have the ball?'

It occurred to me that Barassi related the story without once mentioning the player who had taken a dive. So I asked the name of his opponent, and he said, 'Roger Dean, Richmond. He was the captain.'

This is not to say Barassi, the most legendary name in AFL, was always innocent. He once scuffled with Essendon captain-coach Des Tuddenham on the sideline.

'They had to do something,' he said of the action by officials. 'We were hauled up before the beaks. You can't have playing coaches fighting with non-playing coaches. I was worried about what he was doing to one of our players at the centre bounce. The player came to me [at quarter-time] and complained, and I said I'd seen it. I went to the umpire and spoke to him, which you are not allowed to do, but he did nothing. So I positioned myself where Des had to go past me [to resume playing]. As he approached, I opened up verbally. We tangled.' Barassi chuckled at the memory. 'He took a button off my blazer. He's a fiery bloke, and it's not as if I'm placid. We laugh about it now.'

Racial sledging has been 'ousted' in recent years as minority players take a stand and microphones pick up evidence. The offending remarks in the past usually derived from the shorthand language used by footballers. Attacking players are defined by their most obvious physical characteristic. 'Watch the black bloke' is a warning in the same league as 'Get the fat bloke'. But there are racists on either side of the boundary fence.

One landmark day at Victoria Park, Melbourne, St Kilda player Nicky Winmar walked over to a section of the Collingwood crowd that had been hurling racial taunts at him and deliberately and proudly peeled up his jumper to point at his exposed dark skin. The publicity that gesture generated guaranteed the AFL would get serious about racial sledging.

Yet, at an earlier time, Carlton's Syd Jackson, another Aboriginal player, used racial taunts as a ploy to escape a judiciary charge, even though it seems that he invented the abuse.

I challenged Barassi on this, saying it appeared to contradict his inherent sense of fairness. 'I didn't know anything about it,' he said. 'I didn't know it was being used as a defence,' adding that Jackson's defence was organised by the club president, George Harris.

Race and Barassi collided one day at Footscray's home ground when he arrived to see the 'welcoming' banner proclaim: 'We like Our Asians. Up Yours Barassi.' In the pre-match publicity, Barassi had made a remark about Footscray being 'full of Asians'. It appears his concern about drugs ended with him being accused of inflaming another serious social issue – racism.

'I remember the Footscray mayor gave me a serve,' he said. 'I've lived in St Kilda for 27 years, and so have a lot of drug addicts. I think I said a lot of them have gone to Footscray because St Kilda is too expensive to live. Everyone knows I hate racism, so it didn't get far. I certainly got a shock when I saw the banner.'

When the story was first relayed to me at a Savage Club sportsman's lunch, it was done in whispered tones. I sat opposite Barassi and, coincidentally, Professor Geoffrey Blainey was beside him, also accused of inflaming racism when he spoke out against rising immigration levels of Asians in a speech on a slow news day.

While coaches have been castigated by the media, fans and their boards, it's rare for a coach, sitting on the bench, to receive a message from an opposition player.

'I got the arse from Carlton,' David Parkin once told me, 'and was replaced by Robert Walls who was at Fitzroy. We changed jobs. Fitzroy played them early at Princes Park, and I wound-up a bloke named Ross Lyon to sit on Wayne Johnston, who I'd coached at Carlton. Lyon wasn't the quickest bloke about, but he had a mean streak. In AFL, when you bounce the ball, you can line a player up and get a hit from behind. They were called 'centre bounce take-outs'. If you did one now, you'd get a 20-week suspension. A bloke comes in off the square and thumps the bloke going for the ball because he's just got his eyes on the ball.

'Ross Lyon was the best in the comp at it. I told him to get Wayne Johnston early. At the first centre bounce, [Ross] flew in and nicked him. The second bounce, he just winged him. The third time, he missed him altogether. I was sitting there in the coach's box and I got a message from the Fitzroy runner. He told me he had a message from Wayne Johnston. It must have been the first time in AFL history where a runner delivered a message to a coach of an opposition player. The message was, "Tell Parkin he'll have to do better than that if he's going to get me."'

Johnston was nicknamed 'The Dominator' and later 'The Fibulator' because he was frequently caught out massaging the truth. 'At Carlton we had a Blow Flies 11, a team chosen from those who were caught telling lies,' Parkin explained. 'No-one wanted to get in the team, but Wayne Johnston was captain-coach 11 years in a row.'

Johnston was only one of three legendary bad boys Parkin coached, the other two being Jim Buckley and David Rhys Jones. 'Buckley and Johnston were admired because they weren't just snipers. They could play. If they had no skill, they'd have no respect, but they could play. Johnston definitely had white line fever, but I needed to give it to him at the end of each quarter for him to play at his best. He had this inner belief, but he had to be kept wound-up.

'Another bad boy I had was David Rhys Jones. He was rubbed out more than anyone. He could not run past an opposition player without treading on him, giving him a punch, spitting on him, abusing him, or all of the above. I sat there mesmerised one game just watching him do it.'

While players have been sent off and sent home, suspended, fined, sin binned and dropped to a lower grade and captains demoted, it's rare for a player to get rid of a referee.

According to John Gray, who played for Great Britain's rugby league team against Australia in the third Test at the SCG in 1974, football justice has strange ways of making amends.

'We had a good lead at half-time, but then I saw Kevin Humphreys [ARL chairman] go into the referee's room at half-time,' Gray recalled. '[Australia's] Keith Page was the referee, and we were robbed by a flood of penalties against us in the second half. It was such a rort that it led to neutral referees. The next year at Headingly, Great Britain was playing France. Keith Page was the referee and I was about to take a kick at goal. Page said something to me which I thought was designed to distract me, and I said, "You robbed us in the last Test. Are you trying to do it again?"

'He had a heart attack on the spot. I've never told this before, but that's what happened.'

Australia's oldest-serving official in charge of referees, Eric 'The Bosun' Cox, a former World War II navy man, confirms Page had a heart attack at Headingly, retired and later died in the United States.

Humphreys rejects outright any discussion with the referee, saying of Australia's second-half rally, 'The suggestion is an affront to the great performance of [Australian captain] Graeme Langlands. In any case, I was the one who initiated the move to neutral referees at international fixtures.'

During the same conversation with Gray, he went on to tell of his own tangle with football justice, vividly recalling a match at Redfern Oval. 'Charlie Frith was Jack Gibson's No. 1 young and very obedient henchman. When we came to play Souths at Redfern Oval, it was apparent Charlie was following me wherever I went. As soon as I had the ball in hand, Charlie was there like a shadow. As you can imagine, this became tedious . . . Did he fancy me?

Although he was obviously trying to put a big hit on me, Charlie was at a tender age of football, so there was no chance of me not being conscious of his whereabouts.

'As Charlie was also playing in the front row, I had a couple of conversations down the line of, "Charlie, leave me alone. Disappear on the other side of the ruck. I'm getting brassed off with you following me."

'To which he replied, "I'm sorry. I can't. Jack has given me specific instructions to follow you, tackle you and be in your face all game. And no-one disobeys Jack." But by the end of the first half, the situation was becoming totally tiresome, and I told Charlie if he didn't get off my back, he'd be on his.

'It goes without saying nothing changed. Charlie came in for a particular big hit on me, but I was just a little quicker and unfortunately my self defence mechanism beat Charlie to the big hit. My elbow caught Charlie square on the jaw. Charlie went down and I got my marching orders.

'I felt really hard done by and after the game asked Souths secretary, Terry Parker, if I could have a chat with Charlie and see if he could give evidence at the judiciary to say I had made no contact with him of any consequential damage. I remember Terry looked at me very strangely and said, "Sure, you can if you wish."

'So I went into the changing room, saw Charlie, who had an icebag on his jaw, and went over to him. As I did so, he took away the icebag only for me to see a very swollen jawline. He could only talk in a muffled voice, which sounded as though he had his mouth full of cotton wool.

'At that instant I decided my intended use of Charlie would be fruitless. So I apologised and wished him all the best. Result? Ten-week suspension by Mr Jim Comans, the modern day Oliver Cromwell of rugby league. A very harsh sentence indeed.'

While Gray looks back on his banishments with equanimity, some take a quarter of a century to resolve.

At Wagga one Saturday afternoon on a Men of League visit, I sat with former Souths fullback Eric Ferguson at the bar of the Turvey Park Tavern and tears welled in his eyes about an incident that occurred in the late 1970s.

Ferguson had slipped into the bar quietly, dressed in a black singlet, showing off his broad shoulders and flat torso. He worked through the week in bush locations and late Saturday afternoon was his own, his down time. The regulars chatted with him, many deferring to the fit Aboriginal, a respect which is still, sadly, unusual in rural Australia.

He punched me gently in the ribs when we recalled a trial game between Souths and Wests when Sloth (Wests prop Bruce Gibbs) fell on him, dislocating Eric's hip. Ferguson's rebuke was more gentle than Jack Gibson's, then Souths' coach, who told me after the game, 'Your big, fat, heap of shit put my best player out for eight weeks.'

Ferguson explained how rugby league had largely detoured him from a life of crime. 'I grew up in Griffith with the Trimbole kids,' he said of the sons of Robert Trimbole, the drugs czar rumoured to have masterminded the assassination of Donald McKay, who was leading a campaign to rid the Riverina of marijuana.

'I got in a brawl in Griffith one night,' he said. 'There were five white kids and one black. I was the only one charged.' Fortunately, a decent detective intervened, organising for Ferguson to leave town and play in Newcastle. But the injustice of another brawl, one which cost him only half the time off the paddock as the Sloth incident, still troubles him.

Despite us being in the most macho of environments – a country pub on a Saturday arvo with beer flowing and the sound of races from the radio, with ten former rugby league internationals over near the window – Ferguson allowed emotion to overtake him.

'I was sent off after a brawl at Belmore and so was [Canterbury half] Steve Mortimer,' he said, still clearly upset. 'It was the only time in my life I got sent off. I got four weeks. It was explained to me that Mortimer, as an international, had to get four weeks, and they had to balance it up with four for me. But I was largely innocent.

'Mortimer came up to me later and said he knew I was from the bush and invited me pig shooting, but I told him where to go. If he came into this pub now, I would belt him.'

It struck me as ironic that this discussion, in mid-November 2005, would take place in a tavern named Turvey, the nickname Mortimer was given when he arrived at Belmore from Wagga as an 18-year-old. Even more ironic was the visit by Mortimer to the same pub, six weeks later.

'I went to the Turvey Tavern two days after Christmas with my son, Andrew,' Mortimer said when I relayed the Ferguson story to him. 'I saw this bloke standing there, and I said, "I know you." He said, "You should because I'll never forget you. You got me sent off."' It was Eric Ferguson. 'We had a talk about it and bought each other a beer.'

Mortimer agrees justice was unkind to Ferguson, who appeared to be playing the role of peacemaker in the brawl. 'He held both my hands down by my side, so there was nothing I could do but head-butt him,' Mortimer recalled. 'I probably knocked myself out.'

Mortimer, a one-club man, epitomises rugby league. His nose even resembles a football – scraped and reddish and swollen at the bridge. When the time came for him, as a 32-year-old, to exit the game as a player, he behaved with the quiet dignity to which Shakespeare's Malcolm referred. He had lost the Canterbury captaincy in early 1988 when his lifelong struggle with asthma, together with a virus, got him down.

'It took me about six weeks to be 100 per cent right again, and I came on in the next four games as a sub and played well by creating a few tries,' he said. 'The media put pressure on the coach [Phil Gould] as to when I would be selected as a starting half, making it hard for him and me and perhaps put a wedge between us.

'I finally got back into the starting line and played a few games before [St George's] Wally Fullerton Smith accidentally broke my arm about four weeks out from the finals. From there it was rehab in the hope I would be available for the grand final, and I told the coach I would be available to come on as a sub again. As it worked out, I was. The team was travelling well and we had Balmain's measure, particularly after Ellery Hanley head-butted Baa's [Terry Lamb] elbow late in the first half! I wasn't needed but, with ten minutes to go and the game well and truly won, an order came down to take the field, to which I said, "Give a young bloke the experience."

'Then the order came down again that Bullfrog [chief executive Peter Moore] backed up the coach's orders. So I took the field, realising this was my last game for the Dogs.'

BAD BOYS, BONDING AND BUSTED BODIES

The pain I felt that day could not be considered in terms of mere physical hurt, or the ache of injury. It was beyond measure and metaphor, almost beyond words.

Foolishly, I elected to take a double dose of it that Friday morning in December 2005: visit the grave of my son, Paul, who died of a rare heart and lung disease when he was 15, and call in on Jack Gibson, who was suffering from a combination of health problems, including Parkinson's disease. Both reside in 'the Shire', as Cronulla people insularly call their region – Paul in Sutherland Cemetery and Jack in a blue, cement rendered fortress overlooking Port Hacking.

Ron Massey drove me to both locations, even waiting while I bought a huge bunch of the Australian flowers Paul loved. Rugby league friendships endure in a way men working on an assembly line, or in an office, or even in an iron and steel mill do not understand. Perhaps it's the shared camaraderie of physical and mental pain, or the mutual understanding that winning and losing are often the result of forces beyond our control – a referee's whim, a wicked bounce, a gust of wind, even a fresh coat of paint on a crossbar.

Ron was in the kitchen with Jack's wife, Judy, when Jack walked down the stairs, taking careful steps, as a man might take slow, measured sips of a long glass of water. It was clear that physical and mental discomfort followed him everywhere, like another man's shadow. Although immaculately dressed, as always, he had lost weight.

At the height of his power and influence in the game in the 1970s, Gibson was always imperious, sometimes impassive and, to some, impenetrable. He brought to mind Shakespeare's words in *Julius Caesar*: 'He doth bestride the narrow world like a Colossus; and we petty men walk under his huge legs, and peep about.' He was a man close enough for people to shake his hand but rarely close enough for anyone to sling an arm around. But on this day, he looked frail and vulnerable, as if he acknowledged he needed family and friends to invade his personal space. His voice was soft, almost gentle.

I had been warned he would not remember me, but when he called me 'brother' and later 'Roy', an enormous wave of pride and relief washed over me. After all, when I'd seen him at a Team of the Seventies function at the Opera House months earlier, he had seemed deaf to the best of wishes. At reunions the participants tend to revert to their old pecking order, no matter where the years have taken them. At this particular reunion, some team-mates did not actually recognise each other. Some had blown up so much that they looked like helium balloons after the gas had been left on too long. But everyone recognised Jack. He was top of the order, and it was through him that we summoned our dormant memories. Paradoxically, we couldn't be sure he knew us. However, on this Friday morning at his Cronulla home, he was, according to Massey, having 'his best day'.

Bad Boys, Bonding and Busted Bodies

We first sat down on the balcony overlooking the in-ground pool on a lower deck, but it was too sunny and we moved inside to the comfortable lounge chairs adjacent to the huge oil painting of Jack that captures the authority that summoned so much respect. The painting is so good, you can't understand why it didn't win the Archibald Prize. But, as Massey explained, it was done from a photograph.

Nearby is his desk from which he wrote letters in a copperplate style that would make a royal calligrapher envious. In fact, handwriting is both a family trait and a point of pride. While talking to Jack, an amateur genealogist called by, a woman interested in tracing the Gibson family tree. I mentioned Jack had once told me the story of his father, who fought in the Boer War, writing a letter while in camp in South Africa. The orderly sergeant remarked how the handwriting was incredibly similar to that of a soldier by the same name, in the next tent. It was his own brother, Jack's uncle. The brother had left Australia to chase the American gold rush and enlisted in the war effort from California.

The Boer War discussion ignited something in Jack's memory, as if order and logic surged in where disconnected memories once pooled. He nodded knowingly, looking almost relieved, like someone who had solved his own private equation.

Our conversation drifted, as it inevitably does, to football and arguably the most savage hit in the history of the game. Massey, who has played and watched football since the end of World War II, still says, 'It was the biggest hit I've ever seen.' It occurred in a trial match at Redfern Oval between Jack's Souths and my Wests in the pre-season of 1979. Charlie Frith, Jack's forward recruit, had come down from Roma on the recommendation of the late Bob Bax, a coaching legend in Brisbane.

Bob had told Jack, 'This bloke will hit telegraph poles.'

Earlier in Brisbane, Charlie had wiped out Bob's best three players by half-time. He didn't make a tackle in the second half and was dropped to reserve grade. The stupid officials at Charlie's club didn't understand that his zero tackle count was because no-one ran near him after the interval. Bob was as anxious to get Charlie out of Brisbane as he was to find a new forward for his old mate Jack. He rang Souths, Charlie made the move and debuted against Wests. At one point in the game, Wests received a penalty, found touch and prop Bill Cloughessy positioned himself to take the ball up.

Most top footballers have an in-built radar, a capacity to detect trouble before it arrives, and Les Boyd had an advanced early warning system. He spied Charlie out of the corner of his eye, zooming in like a missile on Cloughessy. Boyd yelled out to Cloughessy to duck his head, meaning for him to bend at the waist and tuck his head into his shoulder. But Cloughessy, tall and blond like Dolf Lundren who played the Russian, Ivan Drago, in *Rocky IV*, prided himself on his erect carriage. He persisted in running forward, shoulders back, ball clamped to his chest, head high on his broad neck like a globe of the world set on its standard.

Frith's hit was so mechanically precise, it seemed to emanate from an engine house in hell rather than the domain of weight room kinetics.

Charlie was tall, with huge shoulders, and the point of his right shoulder caught Cloughessy flush in the mouth. The Wests prop slithered to the ground as if he was a crash test dummy colliding with a brick wall. He dropped like an empty suit of clothes. The suddenness was almost cartoon-like: Wile E. Coyote squashed by a falling anvil.

Cloughessy lay motionless, face down, and when they rolled him over, his teeth fell out with his bloodied mouthguard, molars cascading onto the grass. Souths international back-rower, Paul Sait, began retching but had recovered when Charlie asked, 'What if I've killed him?'

Sait, never one to show even team-mates sympathy, said, 'Kill another one.'

The versatile Sait was at the Team of the Seventies reunion. Nicknamed 'The Sneak', according to Massey, he created mayhem on the field, yet rarely attracted the attention of referees because he never reacted either to illegalities he received, or those he committed.

Once, in an intra-club trial at Souths, lower grade forward John Dykes hurt Sait in a tackle, forcing the international off. A season later, in a similar trial, it was Dykes who ended up in the dressing room. When asked what happened, Dykes simply said, 'He got me.' No-one needed to ask who.

At the reunion, foolishly held in the Sydney Opera House foyer with no seating, Sait, troubled by arthritic ankles, was forced to find a low ledge on which to sit. He missed much of the conversation between the standing groups, including Rod 'Rocket' Reddy, who, indicating in the direction of Sait, said, 'That Paul Sait was one of the dirtiest players ever.'

It was an occasion where those listening felt like calling Sait over and saying, 'Kettle, meet Pot.' Rocket complaining about a player committing undetected illegalities is akin to Pavarotti complaining about the meagre pasta portions at an up-market Paris restaurant. He has a point, but he is the wrong person to make it.

After the Frith hit on Cloughessy, the Souths–Wests trial game may as well have been abandoned for all the value it gave to grading the players. Football is best – and most safely – played with heedless emotion, yet after the hit, everyone on the field seemed to be holding back. They went through the motions like men who had become aware of some unfamiliar fragility deep in themselves – far beneath muscle and bone, ligament and tendon, where they may not have detected any vulnerability before.

I only ever saw that dramatic shift in awareness once again – the day news reached the Sydney Football Stadium that the Princess of Wales had died. Footballers tend to believe they are invulnerable, yet when they heard that something as divinely attractive and youthful as Diana had been destroyed, they knew the privileged person's exemption from the laws of real life had finally been proven illusory. They suddenly became aware of their physical frailties, or no longer believed in their indestructibility, and they held back.

It's difficult to measure hits. Is it done by the number of broken bones inflicted? Or by the ending of someone's career? There is no human Richter scale for hits. You can no more define impact with a statistic than you can declare Don McLean's 'American Pie' a classic because it is 8 minutes, 31 seconds long. In football, as in music, hits succeed because of the impression they leave on the spectators and the participants, and the Frith hit endures in the minds of all who witnessed it that day in 1979.

Jack followed the conversation but sometimes rubbed his hands across his head, as if trying to coax answers from a fuzzy crystal ball. But the recollection of the Frith hit energised him. He turned to Massey and asked him to name the Wests player hit. So we talked more Frith stories, including the way he acted like a traffic light in halting the opposition attack.

When a ball carrier approached the Souths defensive line, the Rabbitoh players would yell out 'He's yours, Charlie', even when the attacking player was 20 metres away.

'Fair dinkum,' Souths John Peek would later tell Massey in the dressing room, 'the bloke with the ball would stop and have a look for Charlie.'

Massey declared Frith 'the best hitter ever' and Jack glanced over at his oldest friend, the man who translates for him, and nodded agreement. But I felt some residual need to boast about my own player – Cloughessy – the honest shipwright who built wooden sailing craft, working with his hands as if he was keeper of an ancient flame, ennobling an honourable trade. Cloughessy subsequently displayed as much courage as Frith had exhibited commitment. After all, his actions post-match would have endeared him to Gibson, whose core philosophy is that the game is tough enough, even violent, without any of the cheap shots.

I didn't expect to see Cloughessy for a month after he was taken by ambulance to the nearby dental hospital. Yet there was wonder on the faces of the Wests players when they reported for the next training session at Cronulla beach. It was only about 36 hours after the hit and I was facing them, looking into the sun, as they stared past me to a figure walking along the beach. It was Cloughessy. He had signed himself out of hospital and, despite an aching mouth and a brain still disco dancing, was ready to run up sand hills. Jack seemed to understand Cloughessy's resurrection, but it was Frith who evoked more echoes.

Massey told about the apparatus Souths had to measure the strength of grips. Frith busted it. He now owns two cattle stations, one in his hometown of Roma and another in the Northern Territory. He likes everything big – big hearts, big cars, big properties, big states. While no-one has ever seen him bench press a horse, he has been known to turn a bull. A massive Brahman was once caught in a cattle race, its head wedged between the wooden railings, facing back the other way. No-one could dislodge it until Charlie nonchalantly climbed into the race and jerked the bull's neck free.

Holiday makers at Broome's Head on the NSW North Coast swear they saw him pull a 100 kg man by the wrist from the ground floor of a beach house onto a balcony. Charlie spied the man leaving a Christmas drinks session early and, when the guy protested that he wasn't prepared to climb the stairs to rejoin the party, Charlie leaned over the railing, took the man's wrist and hauled him back to the festivities.

It is a metaphor for what Gibson did to a thousand careers.

When Parramatta, which he coached to three premierships, chose their best team ever, chief executive Denis Fitzgerald petulantly opted not to name a coach. Player opposition was so profound that Gibson's name was added the following year.

While we spoke, Jack fiddled with an ancient bundle of personal cards, held together with a rubber band. But finally he said something that helped wash away some of the incredible ache and sorrow I felt that day. He made a confused comment, perhaps in reference to the times I visited him and helped frame his public position on major issues, such as his opposition to the legalisation of drugs. 'A man with your knowledge would want a cup of coffee,' he said, and I gloried in his saying it.

A story Ron Barassi told me will help AFL people understand Gibson's standing in rugby league. 'One night at [North Melbourne] training, I divided the group into two, 60 metres apart,' he said, fixing the scene in his mind's eye. 'I'm in the middle. The blokes are running the ball past me, doing drills. All of a sudden, I'm flattened. I was knocked rotten. Your first instinct is to get up straightaway, and I see Sam Kekovich running to the other end.

'*It must have been Sam*, I thought. I went to him.' The vision of Barassi pacing downfield, chin up like a fighter jet poised for take-off, arms about to flap in fury, must have been frightening. '"Did you do that on fucking purpose?" I asked. He said no. Well, I was stuffed. I couldn't do anything.'

If Barassi was confronting, with his chin jutting out like a bonnet emblem in search of a collision, Gibson had that 'don't mess with me' glint in his eye that belonged in a Clint Eastwood movie. Maybe you could argue there was only one Kekovich and, had he existed in Jack's rugby league world, the incident would have been replicated.

The uniqueness of Kekovich was further demonstrated during the summer of 2005–06 when the board members of the Advertising Standards Bureau met by phone hook-up to debate a commercial in which Sam, the former star of the ABC TV show *The Fat*, played a spokesman for the lamb industry. A number of complaints had been received about the advertisement, claiming it vilified people on the basis of religion, sex, age, ethnic background, even appetite. Basically, the commercial took a shot at anyone who didn't plan to eat lamb on Australia Day. Sam even lambasted cricketer Shane Warne for speaking on a mobile phone to an 'English trollop', saying there were plenty of 'Aussie sheilas' who'd like to take on his 'middle stump'. However, the board, of which I was then a member, dismissed the complaints on the basis that the unique Australian humour overrode any perceived slights. Another board member is John Brown, the former Federal Minister for Sport, Recreation and Tourism. I remember him ending the teleconferenced meeting with the words, directed at me, 'Kekovich would have made an ideal member of that Wests pack you had at Lidcombe, Roy.'

Maybe Sam would have taken the odds to flattening me the way Les Boyd once hipped my predecessor at Wests, Keith Holman, during a training drill. 'Yappy', a quarter of a century older than Boyd, prided himself on his fitness and insisted he tackle each forward in turn. Big props like Dallas Donnelly couldn't help but cushion themselves into the tackle, but when Les's turn came, he swivelled his massive hips a quarter turn at the moment of impact, sending Keith cartwheeling across the turf.

No action was taken against Boyd, but Barassi did eventually sack Kekovich. 'He could have been one of the greatest players ever, but he didn't work at his game,' Barassi said of the man who can read a 500-word long diatribe off an autocue without once blinking. 'He's a very funny bloke. I interviewed him once [in Barassi's later capacity as an emcee] and I asked him where his ability with the English language came from. He said, "I do the crossword every day, and I look at the dictionary the next day for words I missed. I study their explanations. That's how I became good with words."'

Barassi admires his effort with language, wishing he had applied the same diligence to football, which obviously came more easily.

Despite the greater longevity of AFL players, they don't seem to suffer physically in retirement as much as rugby league men. This is despite the fact that the top AFL men play 100 more games. Rugby league has only a handful of 300-plus games men, whereas AFL has two 400-game players. My observation of the mobility of ex-AFL footballers at the functions I've attended is that the leaguies suffer more, probably as a result of the brutal tackling. But the incidence of knee and hip replacements and degenerative arthritis among retired AFL players is far greater than the general population.

A study in 2003 by a team of orthopaedic doctors and physiotherapists found retired players suffered a significantly higher level of hip, knee and back injuries and required surgery at a younger age than the general population. The study of 413 elite former players revealed 10.6 per cent have required hip replacements and 4.1 per cent knee replacements, compared to 1.5 per cent of the general population aged over 35 who have had either operation.

Still, most of the respondents in the survey claimed that, given the opportunity to relive their careers, they would do it all again because the social and financial benefits outweigh the financial and physical costs of injury.

Swans medico Dr Nathan Gibbs, a former first grade rugby league player, says, 'No similar study has been done in the rugby codes. Anyone who plays a significant number of years of AFL or league is guaranteed to get premature arthritis in one or more of the lower-limb joints. There are no ifs or buts. Everyone will get it.'

Multi-premiership player and coach David Parkin seems as if he could still play in a pick-up game with men half his age. After all, he was ambushed by a group of young hoods when he was in his late 50s and managed to connect a few blows.

'I went to a Friday night game at the MCG in '98 and left at half-time,' he recalls. 'I was walking to my car, past four or five young blokes who'd been thrown out for liquor or drugs or something. They were mucking around and gave me a bit of lip. I kept walking, but I could hear feet behind me and stepped to my left as one of them hip and shouldered me. When I spun around there were three onto me like a shot, 15- to 16-year-olds.

'I took a few blows between whacking them back and getting into my car. They began belting the car, kicking it, and I rang 000. The cops were there within three minutes, a divvy van, but the kids scattered as it approached.'

He offers the refrain of many an old footballer, 'I couldn't fight my way out of a wet paper bag', before adding, with a hint of old-man pride, 'I got a few in.'

Parkin also tells a story that demonstrates the enormous risk players take with their future health, simply to achieve personal goals. By way of explaining the toughness of Ted Whitten, the only

AFL player to challenge Barassi for the title of 'Mr Football', he says, 'He could play and mete it out. He broke my neck. I was piddling the ball towards goal and he whacked me. I got pins and needles in my arms and went to an orthopaedic surgeon, who told me I'd broken the seventh cervical in my neck. He said I should stop playing, but I'd been picked for the first time in an interstate match.

'It was 1965 and we were playing South Australia, and interstate matches were big things in those days, like rugby league's State of Origin now. South Australia's No. 1 player was Neil "Knuckles" Kerley. He was a super player who became a champion coach. Anyway, the doctor told me to pull out after the first minute so I could get a Vic jersey. But I got belted in the first minute and kept playing.

'Ted Whitten, the bloke who had broken my neck a week earlier, said before the match, "All right, young fella, don't worry, I'll be looking after you." Funny thing is I never felt my neck again [as pain] after that hit. A bloke called Pascoe got me, and I woke up 26 hours later in Royal Adelaide Hospital. I was crook for a week but I played the week after that.'

Parkin's major medical problems in his senior years have not been football related. An inner ear problem, resulting from a build up of fluid, forced him to skip many training sessions and prevented him flying to interstate games during his second time back as coach of Carlton. It's another story that demonstrates the curious bonds forged by illness and injury at football clubs and reflects the way men cover for each other.

'My successor [at Carlton] was Wayne Britton,' Parkin commented as he scurried to the library of his Hawthorn home, returning with record books. 'He coached the team in 1998 when we finished 11th and I was crook with the ear problem. In '99, he coached them again and we finished second [losing the grand final]. It's my name there [on the runner's up medallion] but he coached them. In 2000 we finished third and he coached again. They came sixth under him in 2001 and 16th in 2002, but the reality is he came second and third during his career.

'He was a good coach, but what he wasn't good at was representing the club. If you are not a good promoter, if you can't promote yourself when the club is going badly, you'll get done in.'

There is no Old Footballers' Home, no refuge for the wincing, hobbling wounded, no place the poet Charles Kingsley referred to in 'Young and Old':

> When all the world is old lad,
> And all the trees are brown,
> And all the sport is stale lad,
> And all the wheels run down,
> Creep home and find a place there,
> Where the spent and maimed belong,
> Pray god you'll find a face there,
> You loved when all was young.

The two oldest Kangaroos in NSW, Fred de Belin, who played with Balmain, and North Sydney's Nevyl Hand, found a home of sorts on the banks of the Murrumbidgee River. Both were 1948 Kangaroos and lived in the NSW town of Cootamundra, and they would sit and fish together once a week, inseparable for an afternoon, as if they somehow shared a heartbeat.

But Fred died in February 2006, leaving his mate, Nevyl, as the second oldest living Kangaroo in Australia next to 93-year-old Queenslander Harry Robison, who toured in 1937–38. The pair were as alike as fire and water, humble Fred and outspoken Nevyl, but everyone in the town left them alone to their memories when they sat together fishing.

People in country towns understand the pull of football, aware it churns on relentlessly like a great ocean current, its control on you greater beneath the surface than above. Fred and Nevyl were just two old corks who bobbed to the surface once a week to talk, probably most of the conversation focusing on their battered bodies.

Professional football is a notoriously joint-shearing, disc-popping, nerve-numbing, tendon-tearing occupation that has grown even more dangerous as players have become bigger and faster, challenging the laws of physics. Everyone aches in the usual places – back, knees, neck, hips, ankles, shoulders.

US studies have demonstrated that an athlete who suffers an injury to a major weight-bearing joint, such as the hip or knee, is five to seven times more likely to develop degenerative arthritis than an average member of the population. Even in the absence of injury, constant jarring of the joints during games and training, including the weight room, all but guarantee that former players will be caught in the ganglia of chronic, maddening pain.

Despite the message of the anti-obesity ads, sitting on a couch watching football may be healthier than playing it, at least on a professional level.

Massey says, 'Every reunion I go to, everyone's got hearing aids, or are limping, or both.' Reunions have become a gathering of men with liver-spotted hands and barren scalps, old players doddering arthritically with busted knees, numb and bulbous ankles, and artificial hips.

Everyone wants to talk about the Good Old Days, a significant acronym since it spells GOD. They had to be good, considering this was a time before clogged arteries and enlarged prostates, an era predating passive smoke and pills to keep you excited and erect. Reunion humour is often of the gallows variety.

At Wests' 2005 reunion, former winger John Mowbray, who'd had a leg amputated following a medical disorder, said to bald former international centre Peter Dimond, 'What happened to your hair?'

Dimond replied, 'Fell off, like your fucking leg.'

Anyone with Parkinson's is certain to be a butt of jokes, like the ones from former international John Peard. 'The Bomber' is likely to call an ex-player with an involuntary shake James Bond – as in 'shaken, not stirred' – or say, 'Don't clap yet, I haven't got to the punchline.' Remarks like this in the wider community would be interpreted as cruel and disrespectful, but sportspeople understand laughter is often the best medicine.

This was very apparent to me when covering the Sydney Paralympics, where the athletes referred to each other in irreverent and politically incorrect slang. 'Shakey' is a common nickname for someone with a neurological disorder; blind athletes are called 'blinkies'; and many Winter Olympians are called 'hoppies', even those who don't ski on one leg.

They joke 'legend' should be pronounced, 'leg-end'.

It's a perverse purgatory where the paralympian, or the permanently injured footballer, must exist in a netherworld, neither damned by physical limitations nor delivered by their fierce spirit. How else do they manage – these elite triathletes or footballers who, having achieved almost perfect control of their bodies, then lose it to a truck, tackle or disease?

Some reunions of old team-mates can be sorrowful. Former Manly international second-rower Allan Thomson, small by even 1960s standards, is now in a hospice in Newcastle, suffering frontal lobe brain damage, only a quarter of a century after his one-year term as coach of the Sea Eagles in 1980.

Ray Brown, the hooker who transferred from Wests to Manly, vouches for Thomson's strength, saying, 'He once told me to come down to training 45 minutes early because he wanted me to play in the front row, and he thought I wasn't tough enough. He threw me around like a rag doll. He was a 40-, 45-year-old man and I was 22.'

But Thomson's toughness turned to softness when he was visited at the hospice by some of his team-mates and opponents, including former Wests hard man, Noel Kelly. Kelly rested his hand on Thomson's shoulder and Thomson placed his on Kelly's, volunteering only one tortured, semi-coherent word, 'friend'.

Thomson's relentless, self-sacrificial style of tackling on the field carried over to his job as a bouncer at the Royal Antler, a tough Northern Beaches pub that gives lie to the myth that there are no Fibros near Manly. Former Wests winger Jon Clarke worked with him at the pub and recalls, 'He was once king-hit by a Maori with a giant, tattooed right fist and fell to the ground unconscious. I "harbour bridged" [coathangered] the Maori and he fell to the ground. Before I could dive on top to punch the shit out of him, Allan had already come to and was doing it.'

His nephew Ian, also a Manly international, says Allan's refusal to submit is family lore. 'He once rode a fixed-wheel bike from Newcastle to Sydney at the age of 12 to collect a set of weights from Jim [Ian's father, who played for Balmain]. Five set off on the ride, but by Swansea, Allan was the only one still going. He returned with the weights strapped to the handlebar of the bike.'

Bomber Peard, an entertaining after-dinner speaker, despite suffering a stroke brought on by pushing himself one morning at a weights session while on a Legends trip to north Queensland, tells perhaps the best story demonstrating the bonds brought by injury.

While on a World Cup tour to Great Britain in 1975, Peard's mate, John 'Canon' Quayle – later to become chief executive of the NSWRL – dislocated his shoulder in a match against Wales. 'His shoulder was sticking out his back like a hunchback,' says Peard of Canon. 'He was in great pain and bandaged up like a mummy and kept moaning he wanted to go home. I kept saying we've got to go to France yet. This is the trip of a lifetime. "You can't go home now." I told him I'd go up to his hotel room and check every 20 minutes, but I got tired of trooping upstairs from the bar, so I asked Tommy [Raudonikis] to check on him. About 5 am in the bar, I said to Tommy, "How's Canon?" Tommy said, "Shit, I've forgotten all about him."

'I went up to see him and he was moaning and even more insistent he wanted to go home. But I kept him there, looking after him. You become great mates when someone is bandaged up like a mummy and he needs his room-mate to wipe his arse.'

If Raudonikis was oblivious to Quayle's pain, he wasn't backward in inflicting it on others in the name of bonding. One Christmas Eve, my car was stolen from outside a Penrith shop. My son was sitting on my shoulders, kicking his heels into my chest as he looked through the shop window, saying, 'Dad, there's a man pinching our car.' Foolishly I ignored him until I saw the thief pull out and drive away, ending our planned holiday in a caravan on the NSW South Coast.

Raudonikis immediately came good with his Ford Customline, insisting his family could get by with his panel van. However, late on Christmas Day, the police called to say a linesman on the old PMG, the precursor to Telstra, had found the car in bush near Windsor. Tommy drove me to the car. It was covered by bushes and missing almost anything a Phillips screwdriver could remove.

It was obvious the thief intended returning that night and removing engine parts. We towed the car back to Penrith, and Tom insisted I keep his car because our caravan park booking began the following day and it was impossible to replace the parts of my car in time. But first he bought a carton of beer and wanted to drive back to Windsor.

Why? I wondered.

'So we can sit in the bushes, drink the carton and bash the shit out of the bloke when he comes back for the car,' Tommy said, as if I should have thought of it first. Who knows what would have happened to the thief, considering what Tommy once did to a team-mate? Les Boyd and Tom went on the 1978 Kangaroo tour, where players would wrestle to overcome the boredom.

'We were staying at this four-star hotel in England where the fourth floor was actually the foyer,' Boyd recalls. 'We used to organise tag wrestle teams and strip down to our underpants and wrestle. I was teamed with Steve Rogers and Tommy with [Bob] Fulton. Everyone would sit around and have a beer while we wrestled. Players would push the lift button so people coming up could see it when the lift door opened.

'In the Leeds game, someone had elbowed me and I had no skin on my bottom lip. One day Tommy couldn't find anyone to wrestle him, so he came into my room and jumped on the bed and started wrestling me. It got a bit serious and he hit me on the lip, taking away all the skin again. We got into it. There was blood from my lip all over the wall.'

The commotion drew fellow Kangaroos.

'They broke it up and Tommy came back about 10 minutes later, bawling, saying, "You're my Wests team-mate." He could get very emotional.'

In fact, Tommy, Wests' captain, called me from England to apologise for the hotel altercation and was sorrowful.

Pain to Raudonikis was an interesting companion, something that aroused his contempt and his inexhaustible taste for challenge. The French call it *peine*, the Italians know it as *pena*, and in German it is *pein*. It's a simple word, but to a footballer who spends much of his lifetime suffering it, or inflicting it, pain sickens yet fascinates.

Some are curious about it, even the rush of numbness through their body after a big hit, the time-frozen second where they have no senses whatsoever. Only the catatonic or moronic are not touched by pain, but Tommy seemed impervious to it. His ears would sting and his teeth ache from a hit, and he could be gelatin from his eyeballs to his blood blisters, but he wouldn't show it. He could carry more injuries than an ambulance.

Pain to footballers is like the migratory habits of birds. Some, like the tern, can fly for three years before landing. Others can merely hop from tree to tree. I was reminded of this when my wife, a bird-watcher, took me one winter to Broome. We tramped through ankle-deep mud to a bay where migratory waders were about to fly to the Northern Hemisphere. We watched as this giant flock did one final sweep of the bay before departing, but I noticed a small number land, deciding at the final moment that the journey was too far.

Some footballers are like that.

Boyd's pain threshold was lower than Tommy's, but his sense of revenge greater. 'Tommy drinks tea and he'd put the spoon in it, making it hot,' he remembers. 'Then he'd put the spoon on your neck. He did it to me one day, giving me a big blister. So I went to the urn and got half a cup of hot water and poured it on his foot.

'In 1981 we were on a tour of New Zealand and staying at a hotel in Auckland. There was a pizza parlour a few doors away run by two Russians. One was a giant of a bloke in his late 30s but with a big, pointy nose. He used to come into the lounge bar after work and have a beer. One night Tommy came back and we were all talking about broken noses. The Russian skited his wasn't broken and no-one had ever been able to do anything to it.

'The next minute Tom grabbed him by the crotch of his pants, up-ended him, walked him over to a table and then smashed him headfirst into a table, breaking the Russian's nose and the table as well.

'Tom Bellew, the manager, started to panic. The Russian shit himself and walked out.'

Maybe Tommy's Lithuanian background would have had something to do with it, the Russians having marched into his father's homeland. Afterwards, Tom sat alone, fuming in the bar, retreating into himself, a little like a puffer fish when a threat has receded. He repeated the Russian's boast, muttering to himself, 'I'll break his fuckin' nose.'

Raudonikis relished the savagery of the battle, the world of stripped-down pain, where things are never quite straightforward, often a little bit skewed, where collisions are embraced, where hitting is a form of chatting. When struck with a full can of beer before a NSW versus Queensland game at Lang Park, he licked the blood as it trickled down his cheek and asked a team-mate, 'How fuckin' good is this?' He completely changed the course of another State game, coming onto the field as a replacement like a berserker in Norse mythology, spreading death and destruction.

Even those who played football at the lowest level recall a perfectly executed tackle, hearing a guy wheeze as the air left him, the little moan as snot ran down his face. Even soccer players relish the memory of a good tackle, the surge of adrenaline going from the toes to the top of the head. Ray Richards, who played for Australia in soccer's 1974 World Cup, remembers: 'I slid into a guy and he did a complete cartwheel in the air. Afterwards team-mates said, "Rugby league supporters would love you for that." A neighbour of Richards once showed him the English translation of an interview with Pelé in a German newspaper. Pelé said he recalled the game where Richards marked him.

'Pelé said he couldn't wait until the game was over,' Richards says with pride.

*

No chapter with this title would be complete without the story of the Storm's Robbie Kearns and Canberra's Bradley Clyde, busted while on a bonding exercise with the NSW State of Origin team in 1999.

Anxious to keep the lads out of the pub, teetotaller coach Wayne Pearce took the team on a horseriding expedition to the Blue Mountains. Unfortunately, Pearce lost two of his best forwards for the series that day and endured recriminations and malicious mockery. Unknown at the time was the role of the erratic and irrepressible Terry Hill.

Kearns reveals, 'Everyone was a bit "how are you going" about the horse riding, especially after being out the night before. I'd never been on a horse before, and I jumped on one twice my size and thought, *shit*. But the bloke in charge assured us they were only trail horses and would stick behind each other.

'He divided us into two groups, and I went with the casual walk group while Terry Hill and others went with the galloping group. We went the short way and they went the long way, and we met in the middle of this big opening. The gallop group were all giggling and their horses all puffing and panting, and the walking group looked like death warmed up.

'Terry Hill yelled to the bloke in charge, "Where are we going next?" He pointed to a fence about 500 metres away, and Terry Hill gave his horse a kick in the guts and said, "See you there."

'All the horses were trained to follow. I remember going flat-out down a hill next to Matt Geyer and Choc [Anthony Mundine], giggling but petrified. We got to the fence. All the horses stopped and we were freaking out. One of the people in charge said it was "not on" to do what Terry did.

'Then Terry asked where we were going to next and the guy pointed, and Terry took off again. Away we went again in single file through bush and rock. All I remember is going down a dip and up the other side.

'I learned later that one of the boys had let his foot slip from the stirrup and pulled up. My horse overtook it like a car. It went right, then left, but when it went left, I kept going right. I don't remember anything until being on the X-ray table at hospital an hour later. The fall cracked my helmet and my collar bone. Bradley Clyde fell off at the same time but got dragged and did the ligaments in his shoulder. I missed ten weeks.'

To Pearce, it was as if the terrible day rained down all its doom on him. It evoked the essential apocalyptic text in poet WB Yeats's 'The Second Coming', the famous line that has long puzzled scholars with its imagery: 'Things fall apart; the centre cannot hold.' Centre Hill did hold his horse, although Pearce could not hold the team together afterwards, and the Origin campaign was doomed.

Kearns, under considerable pressure to take legal action, declined. 'I knew if I didn't behave like a nark, the game would look after me, and it has,' says Kearns, now an assistant coach at the Storm.

A dressing room is possibly among the most effective social experiments in modern society, a sanctuary of shared expectations in which unity of purpose almost always dominates differences in race, nationality, income, family background and positions on the field.

A sign posted in many baseball clubhouses in the United States sums up the exclusive culture: 'What we say here, what you see here, let it stay here when you leave here.' (This particularly applies to injuries, for fear opponents will learn of a physical problem a player may be carrying into a game.) Nor do players speak when someone is hurt. The air inside the room can be as still as a cave, as the ego thrashes with the villain of pain.

It's a place where ordinary emotions, like disappointment, frustration and loneliness, are quadrupled. Team-mates can often only sense, or guess, the agony of the injured footballer as he confronts the complex equation of play equals pain in a frightening struggle of self interrogation. Some, like Raudonikis, can play with broken thumbs, grabbing opposition jerseys as if their hands were forged of steel. St George half Billy Smith had a cut in his calf in a game on a Kangaroo tour so deep the bone was visible. 'Just pull the sock up and tape the top to my leg,' he told the trainer. 'I'm not going off.'

Some scheme against pain, or use it to experiment with their own private envelope of tolerance, while others succumb. Only in their final years do some players gradually slide into that grey area populated by non risk takers, hypochondriacs and 'last minute withdrawals'. To most, pain on the football field is like being in a giant cowyard. Walk in the first time, you smell the cow shit. Stay there for five minutes and you don't notice it.

Kiwis appear especially impervious to pain. During a Test match between Australia and New Zealand in Melbourne in the early 1990s, a Kiwi forward twitched violently after a tackle, as if his body had been shot with a giant volt of electricity. Afterwards at the reception I was paged to the phone. A neurologist was calling from Sydney during the delayed telecast of the game. He was seriously concerned at the player's symptoms. I was the only person he knew who he thought could convey this message to the team's management. I approached the Kiwi's halfback and relayed the doctor's concerns at the twitching. 'Don't worry,' the half said, 'he does it all the time, goes like that when he fucks.'

Trainers have fascinating stories to tell about pain and how players manage it. St George's long-term trainer, John 'Snow' French, says the most memorable injury he treated was when the Dragons' giant Tongan, John Fifita, was knocked out. The first team-mate to the scene was prop Pat Jarvis, who had embraced L. Ron Hubbard's Church of Scientology and genuinely believed faith could heal all injuries.

'Pat is lying beside Johnny on the ground, saying, "You're the King of Tonga. Nothing can hurt you,"' Snow recalls. 'The only way I could get John to hear what I wanted to say was to get down on the ground myself and yell into his other ear. So there we were, the three of us, all lying down together in the middle of the field like idiots.'

Rugby union has its stories of fabled players who insist on enduring despite pain. Against France in 1986, Wayne 'Buck' Shelford of the All Blacks suffered a badly torn scrotum, although most males would say the adverb is superfluous. With the French TV camera broadcasting the ad hoc procedure, Buck was sewn up on the touchline and returned to the relative safety of the field.

Lest we accuse the French of being voyeuristic, it should be remembered NSW doctor John Orchard was televised suturing the cut foreheads of Blues players with a staple gun on the sideline during a recent State of Origin match. The vision, shown to millions, horrified league officials, who insisted Dr Orchard perform future operations under a blanket.

Dr John Bartlett, a leading orthopaedic surgeon and consultant to Collingwood, recalls a finals match at the old VFL Park at Waverley where the club's key player, Ronnie Wearmouth, was injured. Wearmouth, a champion rover, had kicked five goals in the first half but entered the dressing room with a rapidly closing eye. The club doctor, unable to improve Wearmouth's vision, called Dr Bartlett over, and the possibility was raised of nicking the bruised area to remove the built-up fluid.

'It worked for Rocky,' Dr Bartlett recalls the club doctor saying. The player gave his permission and the slice was made, but it made no difference according to Bartlett. 'Ooze just trickled out.'

Former Wests players still joke about the occasion club doctor Bob McInerney sewed the eyelid of a player to his eyebrow, meaning the eye was perpetually open. Admittedly, it was a very exciting game and Dr McInerney was keen to return to the action, but he good naturedly took the barbs about his errant surgery.

When it comes to barbarism, nothing on the field, sideline or in the dressing room compares with the Welsh-loving rugby fan who promised, in front of fellow drinkers in a bar, to 'cut my balls off' should Wales beat world champions England in a Six Nations match. When Wales *did* unexpectedly win, Geoff Huish made good on his word and cut off his testicles using a pair of blunt wire-cutters. He returned to the pub, shouting to patrons 'I've done it' and passed out. The severed anatomy was put in a pint glass until an ambulance arrived. Huish, who can no longer have children, should have been cognisant of the T-shirt that reads, 'Rugby: It takes leather balls'.

Male genitalia are a common topic of conversation in a dressing room.

When John Bailey was coach of Wests, there was considerable excitement when English superstar Ellery 'Black Pearl' Hanley was signed to play for the club, particularly for the first game of the season at Campbelltown. 'There were TV cameras everywhere,' Bailey says, 'They were standing on each other's shoulders, trying to shoot in through the high windows of the dressing room. It was packed. After the press conference, Ellery and I went back into the dressing room. It was still full of people. Ellery had a towel around him and sat down with a couple of journalists. No-one left. He went into the showers. The whole crowd surged towards the showers. They were lined up along the edge of the tiles, you couldn't have got them to stand straighter if you tried. They were there to see his cock.

'Dave Woods, a prop forward, left the showers and said, "I can't stay in there with that."'

The patronising academics will suggest that this is a sign of latent homosexuality. Not true. It's just a status thing. It begins even before the player comes to grade.

A Melbourne professional couple, who invite rookies from their AFL club around to their home for meals, once found it difficult making conversation with a truculent young recruit. While turning the steaks on the barbecue, the man of the house enquired politely of the lad's junior career. 'Anyone who wore his Speedos in the showers, I'd piss on,' was his opening remark.

In football, big is good. Big kicks, big tackles, big pay cheques. Footballers are like Americans who like big cars, big buffets and big heavyweight boxers. Rugby union footballers who call someone 'Bushman' do so from their knowledge of the physical endowments of the tribes of the Kalahari desert rather than anyone's skill in the scrum. When St George appointed a woman doctor, my predecessor at the club, Harry Bath, lectured the players about dressing room propriety, insisting they wrap a towel around their waists. One well-endowed player challenged the edict immediately. He strolled naked towards the doctor with his injured right thumb hanging loosely in the vicinity of his groin. 'Can you strap my thumb?' he asked Dr Jenni Saunders.

'Certainly,' the doctor replied. 'Which one is your thumb?'

The preoccupation with penis size exists beyond the closed locker-room of the football world.

Twenty-five years ago, when an international, who later became very prominent, was photographed in the shower at Brookvale Oval, snaps of him were selling for $1 each in the Time and Tide Hotel. Homosexuality has nothing to do with it. It's all to do with status.

This is not to say that some players don't harbour fears of homosexual approaches. AFL great Tim Watson, now a Channel Seven broadcaster, told a delightful story at the annual Essendon Women's Network grand final lunch about his first contact with his hero, brutal Ronnie Andrews.

Watson was Essendon's youngest recruit to the top grade, a mere 15-year-old when he played his first game. Andrews was an uncompromising veteran. Apparently the coach was keen to introduce New Age integration drills where the players would lie on their backs, feet to the centre and arms extended, forming a circle, like an oversized daisy.

'We were told to reach out and hold the hand of the player on either side,' Watson, who retains a boyish handsome face and a smile some would call sweet, said to an audience of 1,000 women. 'I reached out and held the hand of the player on my left and he grasped it. On my right was my hero, Ronnie Andrews.' It was his big chance to commune with his idol. 'I reached out for Ronnie's hand and he said, "Fuck off, gay boy."'

When one of rugby league's top players, Ian Roberts, came out, it was no big deal. During one game at North Sydney Oval, a prop, noticing Roberts bleeding from his forehead as he moved to pack into a scrum, told the referee, 'Get the poof out of the front row.'

But that was during the hysteria over AIDS, before the introduction of the blood bin. If anyone ridiculed Roberts, it was not long before a team-mate reminded him of Roberts's vengeance on Balmain's Garry Jack as the pair once walked from the field at half-time.

One of Jack's team-mates had called Roberts a name and his eruption of fury on Jack was reminiscent of boxer Emile Griffith's assault on Benny Paret for a similar affront, which killed Paret – a flurry of fierce combinations that made beef carpaccio of the face of the Balmain fullback. Roberts had skin stretched so tight on his super-fit body, if you plucked him with your finger you'd swear he'd make a sound like a harp. Talk about limp wrists with a knockout punch!

Roberts was able to tease team-mates, rather than the reverse. Once, when he was playing in Townsville, the team convened to discuss the talents of the opposition. It's a regular thing – players and coaches pooling ideas. One of the Cowboys was unimpressed with the skills of an opponent under discussion.

'If he's a good footballer, you can fuck me,' the Cowboy said.

Roberts, feigning effeminate traits, said, 'I think he's a good footballer.'

Roberts is the only top-line footballer or cricketer in Australia of any code to come out. It's odd because what sport does best is break down barriers and bring people of all creeds and colours together. Remarkably, no bat or ball or fist or foot has smashed through this wall except Roberts.

In the United States the official representation of homosexual men in professional male sport is zero. While homosexual men are thought to compose anywhere from 2.5 per cent to 10 per cent of the general population, among the 3,500 or so men active in the four major pro sports in the US – football, baseball, basketball and ice hockey – not a single gay is 'out'. The few professional athletes who have revealed their sexuality have, significantly, done so in retirement, long after they've stopped picking up sponsors' dollars.

It's not fear of losing regard of team-mates that keeps gays in the closet. Nor the physical responses from opponents. The main obstacle to gay footballers coming out is the hassle. You can't be half out. Coming out implies coping with a million requests from journalists for 'serious' interviews to appearances at gay rights lobbies. A female AFL journalist basically accused me of lying when I told her I didn't have Roberts's mobile phone number. Her attitude was possibly a reason Roberts kept it a secret.

The punishment exacted by the man who dominates is not the most frightening emotion to the footballer. It's the weakness of the one who submits. The inner doubt he won't aim up. That's the fear that must be locked in the closet. Few admit to that moment of submission on the football field. Warwick Moss, the man who once hosted the Channel Nine show *That's Incredible*, offers a rare insight into the occasion he was a late addition to the NSW team to play the All Blacks in Sydney in 1967.

Moss, a centre, received the ball on the halfway line and sprinted clear until, as he says, 'I saw him – Colin "Pine Tree" Meads, the All Black man mountain. He was loping across from the back of the scrum. The man who had just the previous year almost ripped Ken Catchpole's leg from his torso; the farmer from Waikato; the man known for wrestling rogue bulls into submission; the most fearsome lock forward in the world . . . arms spread from touchline to touchline, with a grin from ear to ear.

'That was the moment. That was the split second. I had the skills. I'd practised them in the backyard for years. I could have stepped left. I could have stepped right. I could have ducked under one of his windmilling arms. I could have kicked over his head, regathered and scored under the posts . . . On the other hand, I might have been caught around the neck by his little finger, which was as thick as my wrist.

'To my left I could see the blond hair of [fellow centre] Phil Smith, way inside. Behind him, and unknown to Phil, three salivating All Blacks converged, ready to pounce. It was Phil or me. My death or his . . . I threw a long, looping pass, his eyes wide with anticipation. Then he disappeared in a swirling cloud of dust.

'I think he turned to rugby league the following year. I carried that guilt with me all these years – a coward in the heat of war. My shrink reckons it's got a lot to do with some of my problems.'

Occasional brutal drills are done at training in order to intimidate the naturally non-aggressive into developing 'mongrel'.

Former AFL coach Robert Walls was involved in an episode in Brisbane where a player was subjected to vicious punching by team-mates in order to force him to be aggressive. Similarly, at one Broncos training session the man in charge, a former heavyweight boxer, took talented but timid Bradley Meyers, Brisbane's red-headed Origin second-rower, into the ring. The merciless punishment sickened many who saw it, forcing them to look away and cringe.

Former international centre Chris Johns, later a senior executive with the Storm and Broncos, says, 'Meyers had been knocked out in an earlier game. A big hit. The Broncos trainer got him in the ring to try and toughen him up. He called it trying to build courage, I call it bullshit. He was an Australian champion and Meyers couldn't hold his hands up. He pummeled him. Meyers had the greatest untapped potential I've ever seen, but he's now playing in England.'

High incomes, peer group pressure, the constant measurement of body fat percentage, breathalysers in the dressing room and the banning of marijuana have all conspired to drive footballers to more extreme forms of escape, like cocaine and ecstasy.

Unlike marijuana, which stays in the body for around 14 days, or alcohol that puts on weight and can be measured by breath tests, the new social drugs are out of the system in 24 hours and leave no odour. Reports of players in nightclubs, each carrying a bottle of water, high on eccies or coke, are manifold, particularly following a big Friday night match when they want to stay up or shut out a loss. But the drug testers don't always swab for recreational drugs, particularly if it is an out-of-competition test. Occasionally they catch a player when they report unannounced to an early morning training session, but to be effective, they would need to set up a sampling session outside a bar.

Recently retired players claim usage is epidemic.

While there were complaints from management about binge drinking on the 2005 Kangaroo tour, on an earlier tour a team captain went to the coach and demanded to know what he intended doing about the use of social drugs. At Sydney Casino, following a legends match, one of rugby league's best players was castigated by a pair of the code's recently retired greats for being high on cocaine.

Even allowing for Australia being a decade behind the US in social trends, our football codes introduced testing earlier than some of their major sports, such as baseball. Our incidence is not like America's problems with cocaine in the 1980s, where one baseballer would slide headfirst into a base so as not to disturb the vial of powder in his back pocket.

At a Christmas drinks party in 2005, Quayle reminded me of my role in drug eradication while coach of St George in the mid-1980s. I had become puzzled by the vagueness of some players. I remember saying to one, 'You look like you're playing in a fog,' and he shot me a look that said, 'You know something.' So I asked the club doctor to take a urine sample of every player who reported for a Monday morning medical.

Maybe it was an invasion of privacy, but there were three positives for marijuana and all three had their contracts cancelled immediately. One of the players, a tall, young, promising forward from the country, said as he left the committee room at Kogarah, 'When word of this gets around NSW, you won't have a player come to the club.'

I remember saying, 'I'll take a risk on that. At least parents in the bush will know their kids won't be on drugs if they come to St George.'

The players were never identified, but word did reach other clubs.

In 2005, when the AFL attempted to block marijuana from being on the banned list of WADA, the World Anti-Doping

Authority, rugby league was able to say its incidence was so negligible that the code had no problems testing for it. While steroids have also been all but eliminated, the temptation for the marginal athlete is ever present.

Athletes have been searching for an edge since the ancient Greeks ingested herbs and hallucinogenic fungi and the Roman gladiators swallowed strychnine. Tour de France rider Tom Simpson, who died while high on amphetamines in the 1967 race, once said, 'If it takes ten to kill you, I'll take nine.' In 1984, 198 world-class athletes were asked if they'd take a pill that would guarantee them a gold medal, even if they knew it would kill them in five years. Fifty-two per cent of them said yes.

Many football officials are convinced there is a link between drug use and mental illness. Professional teams have shown concern at the rising rate of youth suicide. When the players from Australia's most recent Super 14 team, the Perth-based Western Force, voted on which charity to support, the decision was almost unanimous. They chose Youth Focus, an organisation dedicated to assisting teenagers suffering from depression.

Nor do footballers continue to hide their problems with the 'black dog', a term Winston Churchill used when describing the dark moods that descended over him like a brooding, debilitating cloud. Churchill shared the problem with Ernest Hemingway, van Gogh, Peter Sellers, Johnny O'Keefe and Newcastle's Andrew Johns. 'Joey' can play football like Hemingway could write, van Gogh paint, Peter Sellers act, Johnny O'Keefe sing and Winston Churchill orate, but they all suffered dark days.

The three-times Dally M winner, who has a couple of litres of zany in his blood, has acknowledged that he rides an emotional roller coaster. 'I ride the emotions on the field,' Johns said, conceding he flips from bright, expansive highs to dark, despondent lows. 'The worst thing is I show them.' But off the field, the lows send him into a cocoon, provoking a silence so leaden and sullen, all the world's clocks appear to have stopped. Even in public, head down, eyes refusing to make contact, he can wear the uncomfortable look of a man fighting an infection that won't go away.

'I don't know why they last,' he said, laughing. 'They just drag on. I don't know why it is.'

In 2004 the dark days lasted weeks following his knee collapse at Parramatta Stadium. 'When you're injured, you don't feel part of the club, especially me getting paid a fair chunk of the salary cap,' he said, his voice as flat as a dial tone. 'The guys were struggling, there was a lot of injuries and there was me in the grandstand, eating a meat pie, watching.'

Phil Gould, as NSW coach, pulled Johns from a bout of lethargy in an infamous finger-pointing incident outside a Bondi hotel. 'Gus gave me some home truths,' he admitted. 'I was going through a black period. We were struggling at Newcastle and there were a few things happening. When you're in my position, a lot of people don't tell you the truth about how you're playing.'

When asked what Joey is really like, the words of Charles Dickens come to mind: 'A wonderful fact to reflect upon is that every human creature is constituted to be that profound secret and mystery to every other one.'

Joey is such a mystery, he is a secret even unto himself. The total Joey package comes with a warning: he's made a career out of shining brightest when most eyes are on him. His partner, Cathrine, is Welsh and went to university in Manchester where she was exposed to David Beckham's heavily scrutinised world. Yet she is continually astounded by the off-field theatre of rugby league. 'She can't believe how big a soap opera the game is,' he said. But in an era where footballers are paid like rock stars, don't they expect the same attention?

During a one-day cricket match between Australia and South Africa at the SCG, I discussed these matters with iconic English TV host, Michael Parkinson. He recalled his first meeting with Beckham, who, like Johns with the leather in his hands, can do things with a soccer ball that makes you wonder if he has it on a yo-yo.

It was at the BBC's London studios that Parkie met Beckham, the footballer wearing only a pair of shorts, leading Parkie to say, 'He's even better looking in person than on the screen ... those flashing white teeth, and a lovely chap as well. He knocked on my dressing room door, explaining that his shower was knackered and wanting to use mine.

'When he finished the shower, he stepped out into the corridor, wearing only a towel, and coming towards him was one of the BBC's senior PAs, carrying a stack of files. She got such a shock at seeing Beckham wearing nought but a towel, she dropped the files, which scattered across the floor.

'Beckham, nice lad that he is, tried to help her pick up the files while still clutching the towel.' Parkie watched the action from his dressing room door and, when Beckham continued on his way, waited for the flustered PA to pass.

Still blushing, she rolled her eyes ceilingward, turned to Parkie as she passed and said with mock disappointment at the missed opportunity, 'And me a married woman!'

If England treats Beckham like royalty, it's worth recalling how rugby league treated royalty three decades ago. It's a story that also reflects the fun in the dressing room, before coaches replaced beer with watermelons as post-game sustenance. The 1970s was a time when dressing rooms were a cross between *Animal House* and *Animal Farm*, monuments to the twin propositions that anything goes and some footballers were more equal than others.

John Gray, who was brought from England to Australia by North Sydney, says, 'By 1977, Norths had bought some good players, and the team and club were full of confidence for the season. This confidence was justified straightaway when the club reached the final of the Wills Cup pre-season competition, which was to be played in front of Her Royal Highness and Prince Philip.

'We arrived early for the game and really had too much time on our hands in the dressing room. We had a sponsor for the day, which was FLICK, the pesticide control group. Their name had been put on the jerseys, both front and back. Whilst my jersey was lying down, it fell at an odd angle, which reminded me of a particular word, beginning with F and ending with K. With two pieces of white tape [joining the L and I], the world FLICK became something different. We had much amusement in the changing room over this fact. As the mood changed going towards the game, I had forgotten I still had my pieces of white tape on the jersey.

'Bill Hamilton, who was captain-coach, had called the troops together for a final rev-up and, "Let's go and show them what we can do." As he led the team from the changing room, he gave instructions to Bobby "Bear" Saunders [club CEO] to put his false teeth in his top pocket.'

'Bobby was to collect them at the conclusion of the game and bring them to Bill when we were to be presented to the Queen. Folly – we still had half-time [when the teeth could be secreted elsewhere]. Throughout the game, my jersey bore the correct logo on the back and my spontaneous but forgotten logo on the front. Nothing was mentioned and I even went up in front of the Queen and Duke wearing the same.

'I had an amiable chat with both, explaining how I had seen them in a cavalcade outside my home when I was 5 years old and waved a flag along the streets to Coventry Cathedral for its consecration. Did they remember me? Apparently not. I also mentioned that I had to come 12,000 miles to actually meet them.

'A very gummy Bill Hamilton did the introduction of players to the HRHs minus his front teeth. They had somehow ended up in [second-rower] Bruce Walker's pocket. Bobby Bear got an almighty bollocking from big Bill for not taking more care of his teeth.'

A photograph of Gray, chatting to the Queen with the changed logo very visible, hangs on the wall of his Lavender Bay unit.

BAD BOYS AND BRAWLS

A quarter of a century after receiving the equal longest suspension in rugby league history, Bob Cooper slid a video tape into a recorder, sat down in a soft, brown leather armchair at his Sydney home and watched the punch that changed his life.

Weighing 145 kg and over two-metres tall, the former Western Suburbs second-rower, nicknamed 'Longback', looked like he could still inflict the same damage he did that July day in 1982 at Wollongong Showground – three Illawarra Steelers prone on the turf after the wild exchange, one with a broken jaw, another with a smashed nose and cheekbone, and a third heavily concussed. It was the first time the 53-year-old had watched the video since Jim 'Hanging Judge' Comans suspended him for 15 months, effectively ending Cooper's career, who played for NSW in the opening State of Origin game in 1980.

'We take a tap and [hooker] Arthur Mountier gives it to Max,' said Cooper, providing his own commentary of the one-camera coverage of the Magpies–Steelers match, then only 90-seconds old.

'Max' was second-rower Paul Merlo, so named because he resembled the character in Mad Max, a very popular film at the time.

'[Greg] Cook [Steelers prop] goes at Max with his right elbow cocked and I race in, bringing my knee up,' he continued. 'No punches are thrown yet, but there are plenty of arms swinging around.'

The camera inexplicably swings away from the action to show players in front of the ball. 'Everyone is looking back,' said Cooper, pointing to the screen where players were staring at action off camera. The camera returns to the brawl, now involving about five players.

'Cook throws the first blow – a right hand,' Cooper recalled. 'He belted me first off. It was a good one.' Cooper watches as he spins out of the melee, a long stick propelled by a churning tyre. Cook's head then disappeared momentarily in the thicket of arms, only to emerge level with the waists of the others.

'I pop out of the action and then I see Cook's head just sitting there,' Cooper continued. 'I go *whack* and hit Cook's head. Then I saw [Lee] Pomfret and hit him.' The tape showed Pomfret, a slight winger who had come in from the blind side, standing on the edge of the melee, meekly attempting to separate players. Cooper's swinging right fist sledgehammered Pomfret's face.

At this point, Cooper turned the machine off and asked my opinion. I had brought Cooper into first grade at Wests and was coaching St George on the day of the incident, meaning we had never discussed his suspension.

'You were entitled to have a go at Cook, but you should never have gone near Pomfret,' I told him. Cooper dropped his head in a gesture of embarrassment and agreement.

'Spot on,' he said, according me the same authority that existed nearly 30 years earlier. It was as if the years had spooled back to 1977 with the same speed the cassette had rewound, preserving the coach/player roles. Relationships, forged in the heat of competition, tend to endure, provided the input of honesty has been equal on both sides.

'Cook deserved what he got, but it was a cheap shot to hit Pomfret,' he conceded. 'I knew I was in trouble. I walked away. I only threw two punches. Still, they were good punches.'

But didn't he hit a third player?

'This is the first time I have ever heard of another player,' Cooper said. 'I shit myself as soon as I hit Pomfret. I walked away after I hit him. I knew I had hurt him.' So we played the tape again, taking it past the Pomfret hit, and watched as the melee, which now involved all but three players, began to resemble a windmill at high speed.

'Yeah, I could have hit that bloke there,' Cooper said, standing up to indicate a player on the screen, Scott Greenland, who was wearing a scarlet jersey with No. 9 on his back.

'This is the first time I ever knew I hit a third one,' he said, genuinely surprised.

Referee Chris Ward sent both Cooper and Cook off, pointing down at Cook lying sprawled on the turf with a bloodied nose and drooping jaw. Wests received a penalty from the incident because, as a touch judge said in evidence, Cook's cocked elbow ignited the conflagration. However, Cooper was 'third man in', meaning he joined the initial dispute between Merlo and Cook, a no-no at the time.

Brawls were like bushfires in the late 1970s and early 1980s, and judiciary chairman Comans believed the third man was the bolt of lightning in the dry forest, the spark that turned everything dangerous, although most players at the time believed in the axiom, no-one is ever seriously hurt in a brawl.

The parchment-faced Comans, a man with the pulse rate of a fish, made it very clear he would heavily punish anyone running to join a one-on-one contest, and the damage Cooper inflicted certainly disproved the 'no-one gets hurt' axiom. But the team ethos insists a player must look after his mate, even though the rugged Merlo was capable of caring for himself.

Two years earlier, I had sat in the Penrith grandstand watching a similar incident. Wests' John Ribot was making his debut on the wing, after playing his entire career as a back-rower. A last-minute withdrawal by one of the first grade wingers and the inexperience of the two reserve grade flankmen meant it was necessary to take a punt on playing Ribot out of position.

But it wasn't a huge gamble. Ribot was very strong and fast, and his only weakness was a tendency to lose concentration in the forwards, rarely a problem for a winger given the amount of ball they received in those days.

Ribot was marked by John Ryan, a stocky former rugby union international winger, and it soon became apparent that Ryan was frustrated by the ease with which the rookie flankman beat him to score a try. Ryan's pent-up fury boiled over, and he raced infield in the first half and whacked Wests' diminutive halfback, Alan 'Bloodnut' Neil. Ribot responded to this attack by his opposite on his smallest team-mate with a right hook that felled Ryan.

Penrith coach Len Stacker shot from his position in the stadium as though an ejector seat had activated beneath him. He sprinted onto the field to remonstrate with Ribot as players milled around, pushing and pulling. Referee Jack Danzey blew his whistle furiously, growing redder in the face by the second, ordering Stacker from the field.

I remember thinking to myself, *This is the beginning and the end of the game's next great winger. If Danzey sends Ribot off, Comans will give him life, because he seems to enjoy making headlines out of the third man in.*

But Danzey was a former player and you could almost see the cogs whirring inside his head. Perhaps he put himself in Ribot's position, asking whether he would do the same himself. Fortunately, he lectured Ribot and left him on the field, awarding the Magpies a penalty and Ribot the opportunity to become Australia's next winger and travel to England and France with the 1982 Kangaroos.

Stacker, now retired from a position as welfare officer in the NSW Justice Department, remembers his rush onto the field and is still incredulous that he was never punished. 'I don't know how I got away with it,' he says, before adding rhetorically, 'You know why I got away with it? Because Jack Danzey was such a good bloke. I used to get so emotional, mainly because I wasn't much older than the blokes I coached. If they were in a blue, I wanted to get in it with them.

'At half-time, I thought, *I'm fucked from here*. After the game, I went to the referees' room and said to Jack I hoped he wouldn't hold it against me. He said, "The matter's forgotten."'

Stacker is still amazed no-one from Wests, the media or the NSWRL ever protested. 'Imagine the outcry if it happened today?' he says in genuine disbelief.

Ryan, who was Penrith's captain, met a tragic fate. 'He was up to his eyeballs in debt from gambling and he committed a series of armed robberies while playing for us,' Stacker says. 'Yet I had no inkling of it at the time.' Detectives interviewed Ryan and presumably the evidence they tendered forced him to retire immediately. A short time later, he hanged himself.

After watching the video of the 1982 Wollongong game, Bob Cooper and I had lunch at his huge Queensland-style house, once a grand 1920s motorboat club, overlooking Port Hacking. Colleen, his wife, made grilled asparagus and cheese sandwiches and served tea in a silver pot, prompting Bob to comment that he didn't usually receive this treatment.

During the 20-minute drive to their home, he spoke of his daughter who had recently returned home to live, despite having to make the long journey each day from Sydney's southern suburbs to her job in North Sydney. She had recently ended a six-year relationship with a guy, and it was clear from the extent of the bathroom renovations that both parents were intent on making her welcome. But talk at the table soon reverted to football and Colleen disappeared, only to return with a portfolio of newspaper clippings, tapes and magazine articles, all carefully labelled.

In 1982 Bob was out of favour with first grade coach Terry Fearnley and had been in reserve grade prior to the Illawarra match. One second-rower withdrew during the week and Cooper was ignored. Another pulled out the day before the Steelers' match and Cooper was elevated. It's a rarity for two from the same position to withdraw, and it proved to be both a chance and a curse for Cooper.

'I didn't train with the side, but I saw it as an opportunity to cement a place,' Cooper recalled. 'All the players went to an outer field to warm-up, but I was delayed and about 50 metres behind them as I walked out. The Illawarra players were coming back from their warm-up and they had a go at me. "We're going to get you, Cooper. We're waiting for you." I took no notice. I didn't respond. I kept on walking.'

Newspapers at the time reported the Steelers being angry because Cooper had been exonerated by Comans's judiciary after a first-minute, round-one incident against their reserve grade team.

Cooper was not a violent player – it was never his instinct to fight – and Wests' captain Tom Raudonikis would implore me to stir Cooper up in the dressing room before a tough match. This was a time when temper and taunting were abided, because they represented the insistent twitching of an exposed nerve, the dark nimbus of aggression that hovered above the game.

That day in Wollongong, the pain of being ignored by Fearnley, the instinct for survival coming so soon after the Steelers' pre-match threats and the elbow to his mate, Merlo, clearly boiled over.

'I was ropeable when I walked off the field,' he remembered. 'I'd gone in to help Max and got into massive trouble. When I got in front of the grandstand on the walk to the dressing room, a spectator hit me on the head with an umbrella. Thank God I didn't react to it.'

Cooper was unrepresented at the hearing, a stark contrast to today when an army of club officials, lawyers, expert witnesses and the player's own manager accompanies him. Cooper pleaded guilty with provocation as his defence. 'I was hung, drawn and quartered before I went in,' he said.

Comans had a cosy relationship with senior media, whom he indulged by calling 'gentlemen of the press'. Before the hearings began, he often inquired of their level of comfort. Given the small room on the fifth floor of the NSW Leagues Club and the degree of interest in the case, comfort must have been in short supply. It was smaller than your ordinary dentist's waiting room and, under Comans, typical of the atmosphere in one. The air inside the windowless space didn't move and was noticeably undisturbed by conversation.

'There were fifteen reporters there,' Cooper said. 'It indicated they knew something was going to happen.'

Comans made it clear he acted only on Cooper's punch on Cook, meaning a 15-month suspension for one punch was as staggering to the general rugby league community as the initial blow was. Furthermore, Cook was the aggressor and summoned to appear at the same hearing as Cooper.

The then secretary of the Steelers, Bob Millward, recalls, 'I went to the judiciary and told Mr Comans that Cook was unwell. He had concussion. Comans said he couldn't play until he appeared.'

However, the Steelers submitted a report on the match, listing four incidents, three of them presumably involving Cook, Pomfret and Greenland. After the hearing, they withdrew the report. It would seem that if the suspension hadn't satisfied the Steelers, they intended to cite Cooper on the other incidents.

'Comans was a cunning old bugger,' Cooper said. 'You'd have to assume maybe he had other avenues to get me if there was some slip-up at the hearing and I got off. He kept Pomfret out so he could come back at a later stage if he had to.'

An audio tape of the hearing reveals Comans to be ponderous, his mind moving at the speed of cold honey. His shorthand proved inadequate in his summing up, confusing pre-match evidence with events in the match itself, quoting metres when he meant minutes. Yet when he delivered his verdict, it was so clinical and concise. It appeared as if it had been written in advance.

He described Cooper's attack on Cook as 'unnecessary', 'vicious', 'utterly despicable' and undermining 'the moral wellbeing of the people of the city of Wollongong'. He told Cooper, 'Acts such as these must be obliterated from the game, and I'll begin by obliterating you.'

'I still remember him looking at me above his glasses,' Cooper said. 'He pounded me with accusations that I was no good for the game. The tirade was savage. He reduced me to tears. When he said he was going to suspend me till the end of the season, I thought, *I can get through this*. But when he said he was going to suspend me for the next season too . . . well, hell.

'I walked away shattered. I got in my car and called in at McDonald's at Sylvania on the way home. I got a burger, and the bloke who owned the joint came over to talk to me. I had to tell him to go away, I was so shattered. When I got home, the phone started. It had been on the news. Mum called. She was crying. Dad had died when I was 15. One of the things I regretted is he never saw me play.'

Although media reports described the faces of Cook and Pomfret as though they had been painted by Goya, Cooper always suspected the injuries he inflicted were not as serious. 'I thought I only threw two punches and, hence, I was never sure of the damage I caused,' he said. Certainly, there were whispers one or both players could have returned before the end of the season, but the strategy was dismissed because it would have suggested Cooper's suspension was excessive.

Millward maintains the damage was real and lasting, saying, 'Pomfret had a smashed nose and a cheekbone broken on both sides. I visited him in hospital and he had a screw through his nose, and Cook had a jaw injury. I'm sure they both came back and played again that season.'

They didn't. Cook played only three games the following season and Pomfret had lost all confidence, not able to make first grade in the local Wollongong league. Cooper appealed his suspension to the NSW Supreme Court and was represented by barrister Steve Finnane, a former rugby union international who, as related later, left a trail of broken jaws. The two jaw breakers lost the case, the court ordering Cooper to pay the NSWRL's legal expenses of around $10,000.

Chief executive John Quayle never pursued Cooper for the money, aware the Wests second-rower was a sacrificial lamb in the code's clean-up campaign.

'I ran into Comans once in a toilet in the city,' Cooper recalled. 'We were both having a piss. He looked up at me and I looked down at him and nothing was said.'

Cooper played Aussie Rules for a year and signed with North Sydney in 1984 for the biggest contract he ever earned. But he was gone soon after. 'I popped my elbow and dislocated my shoulder,' he said. 'I put my hands up.'

Although Cooper was a victim of a campaign to stop a worrying trend towards violence in the game, he benefited by anticipating another trend in an unlikely area.

While working as a salesman, he foresaw the mounting protests of the environmentalists to control waste and invested in recycling used water and oil. The liquid waste business in which he holds a one-third interest now employs 45 people, including his two sons.

Colleen and Bob missed the win by his old club in the 2005 Grand Final because they were holidaying in Sorrento. 'I'd made arrangements with my mates to text message me every few minutes with the score,' he said. 'But I got so excited, I went looking for a pub which might show it. It was about 10 am, and finally I found this old English-style pub with two screens showing it. The only bloke watching was this young bloke and, boy, was he happy. We bought him beers all morning.'

As the grand final went live to Melbourne at 8 pm, I couldn't understand why only one pub would show it . . . and at 10 am in Sorrento, presumably the town on the Mornington Peninsula.

But Longback was talking Sorrento, Italy.

He may have changed his tax bracket and his address but not his working-class attitude. Despite the wealth that allows him to travel, the specialist Italian cuisine may have been wasted on Big Bobby, just as the tastebuds of a couple of Steelers were destroyed by his fists.

Fans have long held a fascination, a voyeurism, with violence. Consider the opening minute of *This Sporting Life*, the English film starring the brilliantly cast Richard Harris and the haunting Rachel

Bad Boys and Brawls

Roberts, one of sport's best movies. It shows a fist flying from the second row of a Wakefield Trinity rugby league scrum, crunching the face of an opposing player. But this preoccupation with violence also exists in polite circles, even in Melbourne's gentlemen's clubs.

The Melbourne Savage Club, a four-storey stone building near the bankers' district, caters for judges, barristers, politicians, artists, journalists and businessmen with eclectic interests. It holds an annual sportsmen's lunch in the lead-up to the AFL grand final and always attracts former top coaches and players.

The 2005 head table had a particularly illustrious group, including: Ron Barassi; Bob Davis, Geelong's last premiership coach; four-time grand final-winning coach David Parkin; and former Richmond coach, Tony Jewell. AFL historian and academic Professor Geoffrey Blainey sat under a caricature of Percy Peppin Cook, the club president from 1930–33. The drawing has Peppin dressed in the loincloth of a cannibal chief, his giant gut hanging over a huge pot of human heads that he is stirring. Cook had an uncanny resemblance to Bob Menzies, who was the club president for 15 years, almost all of them during his prime ministership.

The Savage Club is not named after cannibals, although weapons of South Pacific wars decorate its walls and ledges, gifts from resettled territorians who assume this is the case. It is named after Richard Savage, an obscure English poet who killed a man in a duel, a symbolism that gained even greater relevance as the afternoon unfolded.

Political correctness has rarely been an issue at the Savage Club, as the questions from the emcee to the coaches demonstrated. They focused on violence, exposing once again the veneer of respectability that spreads as a thin blanket over the game.

The Swans' place in the 2005 Grand Final provided the opportunity to raise the 1945 'Bloodbath' Grand Final played between Carlton and South, aka the Blues and the Bloods.

The match was played at Princes Park, the only one staged there because the MCG then housed American troops. Falling in with the theme, Davis told how he once instructed a player, 'I want you to get ferocious in the second half'. The player responded, 'What number is he?'

The stories of the coaches had become as perfect as parables, measured out for pauses and appropriate reactions at appropriate places. It was obvious they had been told and retold, sharpened every time, like an old cutthroat razor that still drew blood. The Chatham House Rule applies at the Savage Club, but all the coaches later agreed they could be quoted. The audience, including many from the top end of town, gobbled up the tales of men who could once turn the brains of others into tapioca and whose fists had been known to turn faces into steak tartare.

Jewell spoke of the time his coach at Richmond declared two weeks before the grand final that the team's only hope of winning was to get rid of Barassi, then playing for Carlton. The coach asked who was going to knock Barassi out.

'"I'll do it," I told everyone, then immediately wondered why I had volunteered,' Jewell recalled saying. 'Then followed two weeks of sleepless nights as I thought about the retribution which would come my way. I even dreamed about it. Thank God Carlton lost the preliminary final, because we ended up playing Geelong.'

This offered the opportunity for the emcee to ask Barassi, 'Have you ever sent players out to knock an opposition player out of a game?'

Football coaches can be very hypocritical about violence. They draw an almost Jesuitical distinction between physical play (good, they say) and dirty play (not good, but not us either). There's a thin line between playing very aggressively and playing foul, and most want their players to toe right up to that line.

Barassi offered a little homily about being opposed to violence, and the truth is his record validates this. However, he did admit to sooling Peter 'Crackers' Keenan onto Don Scott, then a star ruckman with Hawthorn, a move that backfired. Barassi later verified it for this book, saying, 'Don Scott was terrorising our [North Melbourne] players, and I organised Crackers Keenan to oppose him at the opening bounce of the grand final. I told him to iron him out, or take him out, whatever you call it,' clearly showing discomfort, even with the terminology of violence.

'It was very much against my principles. Hawthorn got wind of it. Apparently someone heard us planning it. Don Scott was just about to run down the race to start the grand final and he got a message from a trainer. "The coach wants you to start in the forward pocket," was the message from the coach. Scott didn't start as ruckman, so it didn't happen.'

I asked Barassi the result.

'We didn't win,' he said.

There is an interesting postscript to the story that Crackers enjoys relating at after-dinner speeches. His opposing ruckman was Bernie Jones, a genial, gentle giant who had heard the plan.

'You're not going to do it to me are you, Crackers?' Jones nervously asked before the opening bounce. Crackers then sent the runner, Laurie Dwyer, to ask Barassi if he should persist with the plan. The message came back to abandon it.

Scott is an enigma; the first player to carry a manbag, he also terrified opponents. A fastidious dresser, he favours a yellow jumper, but the colour for surrender was never in his mind when he led the charge against Hawthorn merging with Melbourne.

David Parkin, who coached Scott at Hawthorn, shook his head at the mention of Scott, creating the impression the former ruckman is an entity only slightly less stable than nitroglycerin. 'He was quite strange,' Parkin said. 'We were playing a pre-season night grand final against Collingwood. When we were out on the ground, Scott said, "Get someone to centre halfback." I told him we've already got someone there. He said, "I'm going to knock Peter Moore out at the first bounce." Moore was a Brownlow medallist. 'I said, "You can't do that," and he said to get someone to centre halfback, because he knew he was going to concede a free kick.

'I didn't think he would be stupid enough to do it. The ball was bounced and thankfully it bounced right back to Don. I remember thinking *Thank God for that*, and I breathed a sigh of relief. Then, at the second bounce, he knocked Peter Moore out. Kinged him. We got beaten by nine goals, Collingwood were so incensed.'

Plans to ignite a brawl often find their way to the opposition camp. In 1984 the South Sydney rugby league team had a mad pack of forwards, including the Rampling brothers, whose role on the field was akin to that of the violent triplets in the Paul Newman ice hockey movie, *Slapshot*.

The Rabbitohs' coach was the late Ron Willey, and his best mate was a boxing trainer, Bernie Hall. Hall had enormous confidence in the role amphetamines play in elevating a sportsman's perception of his own skills, an asset when meeting opponents of superior ability.

My team, St George, was drawn to meet Souths in a semifinal match at the SCG, and the game was tailor-made for Hall's core belief. The 1984 Dragons could play football, but many couldn't fight.

The night before the match, we learned the Rabbitohs intended to start a brawl in the second scrum – it apparently would be too obvious to the referee to launch it in the first one. Souths' strategy reached us in a curious way.

An election campaign was underway and Graham Richardson, later a Labor senator and lifelong St George supporter, had been on a tour of inner city electorates. He had called in at Souths headquarters at Redfern but was due at Kogarah where it had been arranged for me to speak in favour of the local Labor candidate.

Gary Punch, the local Barton member, and all the faithful attended, but Richo carried special intelligence for the Dragons that evening: news of Souths' plan. I therefore had to concoct a plan to defuse their impending fury.

My instructions were to keep the ball in play, never kicking for touch, which would have meant play restarting with a scrum. It took some time for the first scrum to be packed because no-one dropped the ball. In the case of St George, fear motivated their ball security. The big cartoon wolf who had been licking his chops in anticipation of the fistic feat found himself lured into a trap by a sly mouse. When the second scrum packed, the Souths monsters almost collapsed into it, relieved to have a break.

But someone in a cardinal and myrtle jumper remembered the instructions to start a blue, and the Rabbitohs nodded to each other, like gangsters about to execute a hit. It was on. Even the Dragons' diminutive, peace-loving winger, Steve 'Bubba' Gearin, joined the action, surprising those who joked to him later that they expected he would extract a corner post and hide in its hole.

The brawl, involving all 26 players, raged across the field, pairs fighting, others attempting to break it up, only to find themselves having to trade blows with an opponent who had moved on after felling some unfortunate. It became a bar-room brawl, pure and simple, fought with bravery and savagery. It lasted eight minutes, longer than anyone I have spoken to had ever seen, and a low *boo* began, building to a solid roar. It was one of those sphincter-tightening moments. It embarrassed me, and a cold, guilty shiver went up my spine with the realisation violence can go too far.

Afterwards, with the Dragons winning and no player injured, I expounded to someone in the dressing room the catharsis theory of sport. 'Well, that's the end of the theory that fans go to games wanting to see their own pent-up, aggressive feelings acted out on the field,' I said. 'I never thought I'd ever see the mob boo a blue.'

The person with whom I was chatting looked at me with disbelief.

'Bullshit,' he said. 'The crowd booed when the officials turned the big screen off.' Apparently, there were two views of the action – a direct look at the brawl on the field and another via the cathode rays of TV, which showed close-ups of the fighting on a big screen. Some of the crowd, like me, fixed their eyes only on the direct action, but as the brawl progressed, most fans wanted to switch their view between the field and the screen and back again. The brawl appeared to satisfy a Neanderthal blood lust. NSWRL chief executive John Quayle had ordered the big screen turned off, lest the code be accused of condoning violence.

Football people have long been aware that fans are hypocritical over violence. Former Roosters champion Brad Fittler expressed it to me best while on a visit to Dubbo primary schools. Fittler attended school assemblies, standing on the stage with the kids sitting on the playground in their sunhats and uniforms, offering a 'Good morning, Mr Fittler' greeting in their singsong chorus.

Most of their questions focused on his injuries: How many of his bones had been broken? Had he been knocked out? Why didn't he wear a mouthguard? He answered patiently and with political correctness, even conceding it was folly to play without a mouthguard, which he explained away as impeding his ability to speak on the field.

That night we attended a dinner for rugby league-loving adults, and most questions, many directed at me, focused on the game's most explosive incidents.

Fittler said afterwards, 'The same people tonight asking questions about fights on the field are the parents of kids who asked me today about busted bones and getting knocked out. They don't want their own kids to play, but they are happy to see someone else hurt.' It was almost as if they'd give their kids $1 to see Van Gogh paint *Sunflowers* but would pay $100 to watch him cut his ear off.

If the players see this as unfair, the lack of justice is magnified when the authorities make sacrificial lambs of the men who produce record ratings for the six o'clock news when highlights of brawls are shown.

Or is it worse to exploit the violence for promotional purposes?

Les Boyd, upset that Channel Nine had used vision of his elbow to the head of Queensland's Darrell Brohman to hype a State of Origin match, rang Quayle to protest the double-standard. Boyd was a common factor in most of the huge brawls from the late 1970s to the mid-1980s and argues few are premeditated, most a product of the hype that builds in the dressing room. We discussed it, along with the upcoming wedding of his daughter, his son Grant's invitation to trial with Wests and the general wellbeing of his wife, Judy – still so attractive rivers stop and take a look – while driving to the Snake Gully Cup race meeting.

The meeting was at Gundagai, and he'd collected me at Wagga Railway Station after the XPT was an hour-and-a-half late from Melbourne. He doesn't like talking rugby league, preferring to watch Essendon matches on TV.

The Riverina is a duelling ground for both codes and, because publicans are fluent in rugby league and Aussie Rules, so are the beer salesmen. He gleefully seized on trivia I gave him about one of his customers, Col Lyons, the licensee of the Turvey Park Tavern, Wagga, a pub part-owned by Qantas boss, Geoff Dixon. Col is perhaps the only sportsman to win two premierships in Australia's main football codes on successive days. In 1961 he won an Aussie Rules flag on the Saturday and a rugby league grand final on the Sunday, both for Wagga clubs.

Lyons was best man at Dixon's wedding; Dixon's father, Arthur, started the Wagga Leagues Club. Arthur gave Steve Mortimer his first pair of football boots. Geoff Dixon's mother, Kate, once went out with with Haydn Bunton, the triple Brownlow medallist, when they both lived in Albury. When she moved to Wagga, she married Arthur, the Magpies captain-coach, therefore ensuring Geoff grew up a leaguie, rather than an Aussie Rules follower.

All this was conversational grist for Les when he next met Lyons and made a pitch to replace an opposition brand with his product. But I wanted to talk brawls and, as the green wheat fields flashed by, he reluctantly unspooled his mind to the past.

'The talk in the sheds sets it all up,' he said of the pre-match dressing room hype, where the ordinary can change to crazy in a heartbeat. 'Someone says we don't take a backward step, and it goes from there. It's rare for fights to be premeditated in the sense someone says to put it on at a certain scrum or when someone gets the ball. Most of the time something happens and it is on. Everyone half expects it. The moment something happens, people say, "Fuck this, let's get it out of the way now." That's why brawls almost always happen early. People are fresh and keen. If you can exert dominance in the blue, it shows you can dominate the game.'

Maybe that little summary of violence exhausted him on the topic, because he failed to turn up to a function a night later in Wagga where Men of League were guests of honour. Emcee Laurie Daley nominated Boyd and myself as the main act, no doubt to discuss the wild Fibros versus Silvertails battles, but as Laurie and I scanned the 500 guests in the Wagga hall that Saturday evening, Les was absent.

Later I phoned the man reviled for his so-called heartless attacks, and it seemed his 79-year-old mother was responsible for his no-show.

'She said she hurt her leg when she went out to feed the chooks on Thursday,' Les explained. 'When my brother and I hadn't heard from her, we went over to her house on Saturday. She had this big cut which required twenty stitches. When we asked why she didn't call us, she said she didn't want to bother us.' (A week later, while in Cootamundra for the wedding, the Boyd boys confided to me that they suspected their mother had cut her leg while chopping wood but didn't want to admit it.)

Boyd was a furnace with the potential to create magic or mayhem. Although he was not sent off during my two years with him at Wests, he was given a four-match suspension in May 1978 when he was cited on TV evidence for stomping on the head of a Manly player. TV cameras captured Boyd taking a quick glance at the near touch judge before lifting his boot and scraping his studs across the scalp of John Harvey. All of Sydney saw it on the 6.30 pm replay, and the authorities were obliged to act, taking the view of Shakespeare's Titania in *A Midsummer Night's Dream*: 'With thy brawls thou hast disturb'd our sport.'

By 1981 Boyd had shifted to Manly and his Magpie captain, Tom Raudonikis, to Newtown when the Sea Eagles played the Jets in a semifinal at the SCG. Highlights of this game, along with the Wests–Manly one, are compulsory vision at any of Raudonikis's speaking engagements, with close-ups of players turning each others' pusses into Picassos.

In the 1981 final, Newtown's Steve Bowden and Manly's Terry Randall were sent off following a wild brawl in the fifth minute. Bowden was dispatched for a flurry of blows to the head of Mark Broadhurst, a heavyweight champion of the South Island of New Zealand, along with Randall for kicking.

Another fight quickly followed, this time between the ex-Magpie team-mates. Boyd insists there was no prearranged signal for the violence. 'Newtown may have had a plan, but we didn't,' he said. 'We had blokes in our side like Bruce "Goldie" Walker, and they weren't really fighters.'

Boyd has heard the Newtown version – often told at celebrity nights – of how the action began. 'Bowden tells people that I started it with a punch from the second row in a scrum, but Newtown put the blue on,' he says. 'It had nothing to do with me. Tommy and Bowden instigated it in the scrum. Then, when Newtown got a penalty, Tommy took the tap. I came out of the line to tackle him. When I was about two steps away from him, he threw the ball away and started throwing punches. I got the blame. I did nothing. I came out of the line to clean him up and then he threw the ball away to fight.'

Bowden, now a successful publican, hosted a combined 50th/18th birthday party for himself and his son at Sydney's Stamford Plaza Hotel, Double Bay – the hotel where Bob Hawke lived after his prime ministership. Bowden's son was attending Scots College and many of the guests were parents of his classmates.

Bowden provided T-shirts with caricatures of him knocking out Broadhurst and big screens in the function room played the brawl repeatedly. Former Newtown players skolled Moët and a pile of room keys on a table were available for anyone who wanted to stay over. The ex-Jets, delighted at the presence of the Scots 'yummy mummies', occasionally took the opportunity – when a Scots dad headed off for a pee – to say to the wife, 'Reckon we should grab a room key, love?'

Among the entertainers were Reg Reagan and Jimmy Barnes. Barnes decided he had sung enough but changed his mind when Bowden wrote him another cheque for $20,000. The party was estimated to have cost $400,000.

As coach, I take responsibility for perhaps the only all-in brawl *before* a rugby league kick-off.

Entering the final match of the first round of the 1978 season, Wests and Cronulla were equal on premiership points at the top of the ladder and drawn to play at Lidcombe Oval. The home team traditionally ran out first and occupied its preferred end, and then the toss was made. If the visiting team won the toss and chose to defend the end where the home team was standing, the players would exchange positions.

I reasoned that no-one could be sent off before a game started, the 'bringing the game into disrepute' charge being an invention of a later age.

The Sharks had a talented young back and I suggested to Boyd that, should the teams swap ends, he nudge the player as they passed in order to unnerve him. After all, Boyd could scare flies off horse shit, and he was especially intimidating to players making their debut.

Unknown to me, a visitor to the game that day was Kevin Cashman, boss of Sunbeam, which owned Victa. Kevin was a Wests supporter but his daughters followed the Sharks. Neither team had a sponsor. The decision was made in the family car as the Cashmans travelled to Lidcombe that the winner of the match would have a Sunbeam company as sponsor.

The Magpies lost the toss and the trading places began, with the usual smorgasbord of insults as the players passed. Boyd's version of a nudge was a rib rattler, and suddenly it was on, as if the electricity was thrown on in a large neon sign. It signalled the unofficial beginning of the game, even before the opening kick-off.

Eventually referee Jack Danzey gained order and no-one was sent off. Wests won the match, took the premiership lead at the halfway mark and Victa was on the Magpies jumper for the start of the second round.

Following that match, the NSWRL decided the pre-match toss of the coin would be brought forward to half-time in reserve grade. As Manly's great fullback, Graham Eadie, told me at the wake following Robert Stone's funeral when this story was retold, 'Some players changed the game with their skill … You changed it with your mouth.'

If Boyd was the first player in a premiership game suspended on TV evidence (the May 1978 game), another player in that match has the dishonour of being the very first. John Gray, who played for Norths before joining Manly, was cited following a midweek televised match between Norths and Newtown in the old Amco Cup competition in May 1976.

The game was played on the night of a full moon, and a massive brawl drew a fierce reaction from the authorities because of the widespread publicity it generated. Norths chief executive 'Akka' Forbes used the full moon in his lunacy defence – three players were sent off and three cited.

'I played in the brawl that went around the world,' Gray says. 'There were twenty-five blokes fighting, except the Norths fullback, Mal McLachlan, who stood leaning against the goalposts with his arms folded. Because so many were involved, news outlets around the world picked it up. I picked on the smallest bloke there – Paul Hayward.'

Sometimes the scales of justice in rugby league have wicked ways of making amends without requiring retribution from the authorities as Gray, who had migrated from England, can attest.

'I didn't know Hayward was an ex-pug,' he says. 'He was so quick. When I threw one, he'd already thrown four. He was so fast, ducking and weaving. The only thing I could do was grab him by the ears and head-butt him. The hierarchy went berserk. They got the video of it and suspended four of us.'

Gray's story is similar to the last ugly brawl in international rugby league: Australia's Greg Dowling and New Zealand's Kevin Tamati fighting on the sideline at Lang Park in June 1985 after both had been sent to the sin bin.

Dowling, unaware Tamati had an undefeated career as an amateur boxer, made a comment about the Kiwi's fascination with sheep as the two props walked to the dressing rooms. Dowling copped the worst of the fistic fury, with both his face and his nickname changing.

'I used to have a pointy nose up until then and people would call me "Gonzo",' he is reported saying 20 years later. 'After that night, they started calling me "Dish Head".'

Gray agrees with Boyd that the dressing room hysteria sets the conditions for a brawl. But it would seem he believes these 'fellows of infinite tongue', as Shakespeare put it in *Henry V*, were mainly in the Wests room.

'When we played Wests, we'd hear the yelling and slapping from the other dressing room,' he recalls. 'We'd say, "Here we go again." We knew it was on.' The close proximity of the home and visitors rooms in the antiquated grandstands and the rival club doormen, often standing only metres away from each other, exacerbated the tension.

Referee Mick Stone was the man in charge of a 1985 Anzac Day match between Canterbury and Souths at the SCG. 'Peter Kelly set a world record for shortest time on the field,' he says. 'He beat the bugler off the ground. They played the Last Post and the two club presidents began walking off with the bugler. When they got to the touchline, I called time-on and Canterbury kicked off.

'Souths' Ross Harrington carried the ball to the 22-metre line and Kelly nailed him. I sent him off and remember looking to the SCG gate and seeing Canterbury president Barry 'Punchy' Nelson holding it open for the bugler, only to see Kelly race past him. Punchy thought Kel forgot his mouthguard and didn't know he'd been sent off until he saw him dressed in his suit at half-time.'

Stone's attitude towards Kelly changed after the tough prop retired. 'I'd sent him off a couple of times, and I didn't like him and he didn't like me,' Stone says. 'I often thought that of all the players I refereed, if I was walking up a dark alley one night and Peter Kelly ran into me, he'd give me a belting. But I ran into him at a pub out at Lapstone and he was very amiable, putting up his hand and saying of everything that happened on the field, "I did it."'

Kelly remembers the situation slightly differently. 'Every detail Mick said about the Anzac Day game is correct except for one fact. To this day, I'm convinced I was innocent over the tackle on Harrington. I hit him with the best tackle I've ever made. When I went before Jim Comans, he asked me my plea and I said, "Not guilty." He looked at me and asked for an explanation, and I said there was no blood. If I'd collected him on the head, there would have been plenty of damage.

'Comans asked me again and I said, "Not guilty." He asked me a third time, suggesting I produce another explanation. I was running out of things to say, so finally I said, "Generally, when I hit opposition players in the head, it makes a different sound to the one I heard when I hit Harrington."

'I got a four-week suspension. It wasn't the smartest thing I ever said.'

Rugby league's last major brawl occurred in a State of Origin match in Melbourne in 1995. Both the NSW and Queensland teams anticipated the fracas, but it was almost guaranteed when Blues coach Phil Gould made two last-minute replacements, relegating a pair of peace-loving forwards to the bench in favour of a duo of renowned tough men.

Gould's last words to the players as they left the dressing room were, 'If they pull the cat's tail, they get the full fucking cat,' strongly implying everyone should join a brawl if it erupted.

It did, entertaining the 50,000-strong Melbourne crowd.

Bad Boys and Brawls

When rugby union men discuss brawls over a beer, the 1975 Battle of Ballymore usually opens the bragging. Myth and legend surround the Australia–England Test series, but most agree the leader of the Australian forwards, prop Stuart MacDougall, started it and England's prop, Mike Burton, was the victim.

The eccentric Dave Brockhoff was Australia's coach and, once again, the 'no backward step' dressing room call probably set an avalanche of aggression on its inevitable way.

World Cup-winning Wallaby coach Bob Dwyer says, 'Australia kicked off and an astonishing thing happened. An England player caught the ball and an Australian player kicked him on the ground. Australia later said they were raking for the ball, but he definitely kicked him. There was stunned silence on the part of the Poms. They stood there dumbfounded. Then *whooom*, they were into it. The referee settled things down but soon after, at the next possible encounter, another brawl broke out. The referee threatened to send the next transgressor off.

'Micky Burton late tackled the Australian fullback and he was off. But Micky's tackle was innocuous compared to what had happened in the opening salvo. Brock's philosophy that no-one takes a backward step had been elaborated on. There were certainly a few steps forward.'

The 1974 British Lions had an emergency number to call on the field if an all-in brawl was required. Their call was '99', but Brockhoff has been accused of sending the players out to assault the Englishmen with a similar signal, 'Bondi Beach'. Brockhoff remembers a 'beach' call but denies there was a pre-match plan to use violent tactics. It is claimed in some rugby union books that ARU president Bill McLaughlin interceded when the referee could not extinguish the brawling in the Brisbane match.

McLaughlin allegedly sent Brockhoff a note, implying his career as Australian coach was over if the violence continued. Brockhoff counters by claiming McLaughlin and other officials were in the dressing room with the players before the match, implying that if mayhem was planned, they were witnesses.

However, the Australian team manager, Ross Turnbull, claims the circumstances have been dramatised. Turnbull's nickname is 'Mad Dog' from his days playing for Wanderers in Newcastle. It derives from 'Mad Dog' Vincent Cole, a character in *The Untouchables*, a popular TV show at the time. Turnbull dislikes the nickname, telling anyone who uses it, 'You can call me Ross.'

'The idea of an official entering the dressing room before a Test match was not conceivable,' Turnbull says of McLaughlin. 'I was the honorary team manager and Brockhoff was the honorary assistant team manager, and I simply would not have allowed them in the room.'

Nor does he believe there was any communication between the managers in the grandstand and the players on the field. 'I sat next to Brockhoff the whole of the match, which was a rare occasion because he was mad,' Turnbull maintains, an unusual admission considering his own nickname. 'In those days the coach couldn't go out on the field and address the team at half-time.'

Asked who started the brawl, Turnbull claims, 'MacDougall's boot was wavering around and I don't recall the referee warning him.'

Rugby union's worst brawl, according to Dwyer, occurred in France. 'South Africa played France in 1962 at the end of their tour of the British Isles,' he tells. 'The Springboks were undefeated and got the grand slam. They had a flanker named Martin Pelser, who had only one eye, or certainly only had vision in one eye. The opposition French prop or flanker stuck his thumb in Pelser's good eye. A brawl erupted and the referee settled it down.

'Then another scrum packed and the same thing happened, Pelser getting poked in his good eye. Another brawl erupted and the referee threatened to call the game off if it happened again. He didn't call it off but Pelser went off. He couldn't see. There were no replacements in those days, meaning they had to play one man short.'

Eye for an eye justice, as promulgated by the ancient Mesopotamian law-maker Hammurabi in 1780 BC, rarely applies in football. Football lore works like police law in some countries: crims are fitted for offences they don't commit, while escaping penalties for those they do.

Finnane, the barrister who defended Cooper, has been accused in a tome by a Welsh author of igniting the Battle of Ballymore, but he wasn't in the team, having injured his ankle in the first Test in Sydney. Not that Finnane's powerful right hand had to travel far to do damage. It was a short and untelegraphed 'goodnight'. American writer Damon Runyan, who once said of a punch, 'It only travelled six inches but was a thing of beauty,' would have approved.

Team-mates swear they saw Finnane pack cigarette foil between his knuckles, then tape his hand, in order to provide a uniform blow in the manner of a steel door blowing swiftly shut. He was involved in some close encounters of the worst kind.

'He possessed an unbelievably lethal punch,' Dwyer says. 'You never saw it coming. He was a very reserved personality, very quiet at training and off the field. I often thought that if I leaned close to him to hear what he was saying, I'd risk that right hand.'

Finnane certainly did some damage when he played for NSW against the touring England team that year. He disposed of three players: lock Bill Beaumont, now England's delegate to the International Rugby Board (IRB); Burton, the prop sent off in Brisbane who now runs international rugby tours; and flanker Steve

Callum, who was so impressed by Finnane's authority he joined Finnane's club, Easts, at the end of the tour.

Dwyer remembers the incident clearly. 'I have never seen anything like it. Beaumont shoved Finnane and Finnane split his eye like I've never seen one split. On came Mike Burton into the line-out with his sleeves rolled up and biceps bulging. Burton, who had been a renowned boxer in the armed services, jostled Finnane, whereupon, [Finnane] clocked him, knocking him off his feet.

'Later on in the game, Callum, on his first tour for England, stopped the ball from coming out of the line-out. Finnane decked him too.'

The incident for which Finnane is infamous occurred three years later in a 1978 Test match against Wales at the SCG when he broke the jaw of prop Graham Price, who was one third of the internationally acclaimed Pontypool Front Row, a club combination that was the usual Wales three. Photographs at the time showed Price leaving the field, blood oozing from his mouth, accompanied by a doctor.

Debate has raged over the motivation for the punch, but Dwyer says, 'The Pontypool Front Row were renowned scrummagers. Maybe he wanted to see how they could handle the tough stuff.'

Because the 'phantom punch', as the press described the hit on Price, was not seen by the referee, Finnane was not punished. But he never played Test rugby again.

Rugby league's greatest phantom punch occurred in the 1988 Grand Final between Canterbury and Balmain. Great Britain's Ellery Hanley, playing for Balmain, was felled at a critical point in the match and left the field with the assistance of trainers, his brain and legs as wobbly as jelly. The force and location of the hit were as mysterious as the Muhammed Ali punch that knocked out Sonny Liston.

Canterbury won the match and the subsequent debate focused on the source of Hanley's concussion. It was even suggested he knocked himself out when his head hit an exposed sprinkler. But the most educated guess was that Canterbury five-eighth Terry Lamb hit him late. The Bulldogs' Punchy Nelson tended to endorse this view with his quip, 'Ellery likes celery but hasn't got the stomach for Lamb.'

Seventeen years later, when Foxtel began replaying old grand finals, the referee of the 1988 decider, Mick Stone, sat down to watch it, intent on monitoring any action involving Hanley and Lamb.

Late in the first half, he observed Hanley offloading the ball, with Lamb coming in over the top, crashing him into the ground. Stone says he picked up his telephone and called the touch judge, Mick Ryan, who was responsible for monitoring incidents in back play on the side of the field where the illegality occurred.

'I said to Mick, "I think we have a problem,"' Stone recalled saying.

Ryan, who was also watching, agreed. 'It looks terrible.'

'I knew something had happened,' Stone said, 'because Balmain tried to bring Hanley on in the second half. I saw him on the sidelines but he looked white. They couldn't get his legs working.'

Blocker Roach, Balmain's prop in '88 before suspension robbed him of a place in the grand final team, said of the late hit, 'You'd get 12 weeks for it today.'

Sometimes the wrong player suffers retribution for a late blow. In 1962 Wests and St George played the second of three successive grand finals. Magpie fullback Ken Bray opened up the Dragons' captain-coach, Norm Provan, who was so concussed he could not communicate with his own players at half-time. Veteran prop Bill Wilson assumed the role of captain and began stalking around the dressing room, repeatedly ordering the furious Dragons not to retaliate. They believed Wests' tough, young second-rower, Jim Cody, was the culprit, but Wilson persisted with his 'no retribution' instruction.

'We'll fall into their hands if we retaliate,' Wilson insisted. However, Wilson walked over to half George Evans and ordered him to build a little mound for the kick-off, with the object of kicking the ball high and short, in the direction of the Western Suburbs' second row. The ball travelled on cue to Wests' Chow Hayes and Cody turned his back to cover him.

'Wilson knocked Jim into next week,' Chow recalls. 'I don't know why they thought it was Jim who had hit Provan. Jim was just a young bloke.'

Referee Jack Bradley sent Wilson off, but it didn't stop the Dragons prevailing 9–6.

Brawls are rare in modern football because of the watchful eye of TV, the costly nature of the punishment handed down by an image-conscious judiciary, together with the speed of the modern game.

Given the big-money contracts and the continuous nature of play in all codes, any player who stops to join a brawl risks hurting himself in the pocket and his team in the action. All codes encourage players to feign injury in order to gain penalties, a practice which does not sit comfortably with past toughmen, whose mantra was never to show hurt. Egregious diving is problematic because it falls into a grey area where intent is difficult to define.

Brawling in ice hockey became so endemic, the sport risked a black eye in the US. Now, however, acting has reached a point where it has been accused of being a 'shame game'. Some key men are said to play two positions – centre and prone. The National Hockey League has accused some players of crossing what they felicitously call an 'embarrassment line'.

Soccer is blighted by players re-enacting the death scene from *Othello*, or performing Greg Louganis Olympic gold-medal dives. The game has sport's biggest divas, athletes simultaneously vainglorious and nightmarish, part peacock, part Hitchcock.

The World Cup qualifier between Uruguay and Australia, played in Sydney in November 2005, featured players swooning on cue better than Scarlett O'Hara. Then Football Federation Australia board member John Singleton, a lover of rugby league, was prompted to say that the player who collapsed on the turf, as opposed to the one suspected of felling him, should be the one receiving the yellow card.

While delighted with Australia's victory, most agreed they had not seen so many faked injuries since the Vietnam War draft. Soccer's bandwagon was overflowing with Australian supporters during the national team's spirited play in the 2006 World Cup in Germany, but many jumped off, disgusted by an Italian player taking a dive in the final minute of play, earning a penalty that led to the 1–0 loss.

Rugby league people ridicule AFL's confrontations, where players shirt front each other and push and pull, where punches are rarely thrown, accusing it of resembling slapstick comedy. When this involves a large number of players, the AFL deem it a 'melee', an interesting term considering melee was the predecessor to soccer, an 11th century British game first played with the head of an enemy Danish soldier.

Similarly, Aussie Rules men have trouble with rugby league's tolerance of two players trading punches while their team-mates and the referee stand idly by, waiting for exhaustion to overtake them. The Melbourne hierarchy took to their favourite airwaves and Boswell columnists to protest when TV images were shown of Brisbane's Gorden Tallis and Penrith's Ben Ross exchanging blows, with the referee not intervening.

Before most big games, Tallis worked himself into such a rage, his deep-set eyes seemed to have melted into his skull. His style was shockingly abrupt – a rattlesnake's quickness with the impact of a beer bottle over the head. But he is also remarkably candid, and AFL jaws really dropped when he explained at a Melbourne lunch the motivation behind his assault on Ross.

The lunch celebrated the Storm's hundredth home game, and Tallis, then retired and an NRL board member, sat with Melbourne's leading AFL writer, the *Herald Sun*'s Mike Sheahan. Sheahan's mouth fell open when Tallis explained why he zoomed in on Ross as a target. Most assumed the attack originated from some past problem in Queensland where they both grew up, or something said on the field. No, Gorden explained, he was losing respect and needed to regain it at Ross's expense.

'I was losing respect from the young blokes coming through, so I picked out a big target,' he said. 'Ross was a young State of Origin player, and I picked on him because I wanted to show everyone I could still handle the biggest and best coming through.'

Sheahan was aghast and even more so when Tallis told him he had informed coach Bennett of his plan. Former Storm executive director John Ribot watched the interplay, highly amused, in the company of Jimmy Barnes.

'Do you mean it was premeditated?' asked Mike, his mouth forming a giant O.

But the plain-speaking Tallis did operate within a code of honour. He picked on the biggest player, not the smallest; his attack was open, not a cheap shot; and in the flurry of blows, no-one was badly hurt. Furthermore, Tallis didn't have to repeat his attack. As Ribot said, 'It kept him alive for another six months. The message was clear – stay away from me.'

*

Bad Boys and Brawls

It's hard to get anyone on the record to elaborate about AFL's most vicious modern brawl: 'Lethal' Leigh Matthews, then playing for Hawthorn, shattered the jaw of Geelong's Neville Bruns, inciting an all-in brawl at Princes Park in 1985. As in the stillness after a violent storm has blown its last breath, there was the wreckage: Matthews was charged by the police with assault and deregistered by the AFL for a month.

Matthews, judged one of AFL's greatest players and a four-time premiership coach with Collingwood and Brisbane, is outspoken on most issues, but the Bruns incident is a no-go zone with him.

Parkin, who normally is to chatter what a machine gun is to ammunition, elects to be almost silent on the topic. 'He hates mention of the Neville Bruns affair,' Parkin, a former coach of Matthews, says. 'It troubles him. He won't talk about it. I think he explained it once as a response to Bruns getting someone else.'

Bruns has never forgiven Matthews.

The Kangaroos' Wayne Carey was the best centre half-forward of the 1990s and West Coast's Glenn Jakovich was the best centre half-back, meaning their match-ups were the best of the decade. Their confrontations were rarely malicious but always immensely physical.

Constant interchange today has lessened the likelihood of a duel between two players igniting a wild brawl, but, because players are rested when they return to the fray, the physicality of contests has increased. Rotation, in addition to coaches insisting players kick to non-contested positions, dilutes the one-on-one duels, leading many commentators to believe Aussie Rules is becoming more and more like soccer.

Except for the full-forward and fullback, AFL players can have as many as six different opponents during a match. With 16 players per team leaving the field an average of three times, sixty rotations a match is not uncommon.

Rugby league has limited interchange, imposing a ceiling of 12 replacements. The 80-minute player is therefore highly prized, and he is not likely to risk his value by engaging in activity that places him in the sin bin. But it can be argued that cleaning up the brawls has swept the dirt under the carpet, driven the violence underground.

I first became aware of this possibility in 1980 when visiting the United States on a 'Coach of the Year' trip. While in Buffalo, the home of the Bills, I met their coach, Chuck Knox, a friend of rugby league's top coach, Jack Gibson. I don't know what aspects of my reputation had preceded me, but Knox linked me up with one of his wild men. The pair of us adjourned to a Buffalo hotel where drinks were on the house and we proceeded to sink endless shots.

Towards the end of the evening, the American player, short but barrel-chested with Popeye-type forearms, said, 'I do things on the field that coach wants me to.' If you compare him with the military, he was in special operations, the force that do the dirty work under cover of darkness. He made it clear he was not popular with opposition players and, given he had no team-mates with him that particular evening, I suspected some of his colleagues feared him as well. While American football has all but eliminated 'cheap shots', has it driven the dirty work underground? The code is powerless to do anything about the violence in 'the pile', the jumble of bodies in a mass tackle or a turnover.

Sports Illustrated's 31 January 2005 issue quotes nine NFL players describing the degradation of the pile. Philadelphia Eagles linebacker Ike Reese says, 'When we played the Patriots last year [Eagles running back] Brian Westbrook fumbled a punt, and we were all down there scrambling for it. [Patriots linebacker] Mike Vrabel had my testicles in his hand and he was squeezing them. Where the football ends up depends on who has the strongest will or the strongest hands. Guys reach inside the face mask to gouge your eyes. But the biggest thing is the grabbing of the testicles. It is crazy.'

San Diego Chargers linebacker Ben Leber concurs. 'I don't know if people really want to know what goes on down there: basically anything you can't get away with on the field, you can get away with under that pile. Nobody can see you. The go-to spots are the eyes and the family jewels. If anybody grabs your family jewels, you are going to let go. In the pile you hear some screams of pain, but you don't know where it's coming from – unless it's you.'

'There's a lot more opportunity in rugby union for violence because you've got more bodies, rucks, mauls, breakdowns, scrums,' Nathan Grey says. 'I watch Super 14 games on TV and see captains speaking to the referee, and I know what they are saying. The refs and linesman can't see everything and there is a lot they miss. The captains are telling them there has been a lot of illegal play going on and warning them that if he doesn't do anything about it, his players will retaliate. Good captains can keep a lid on things.

'In the World Cup final in 1999, Australia versus France in Cardiff, there were a number of incidents in the rucks, and it got to the stage John Eales went to the ref and told him if he didn't do something, his players would take matters into their own hands. Any brain explosions you see in rugby now, you can put down to the same thing – reacting to something which has gone unpunished.

'I was on the end of a severe raking by South African hooker Naka Drotske. I fell on the wrong side of the ball and he raked me, tearing my jersey and shorts. When I got up he waved his finger at me, saying, "You must not slow down our ball." I certainly didn't do it again.

'The biggest brawl I was involved in was as a member of an invitational side playing the touring Argentina team in Darwin in 1996. It started on the halfway line and ended up working its way to the try line where the crowd was. There was no video of the match. I sat down with the opposition Argentinian five-eighth, and we had a quick chat about being happy not to be involved. The crowd, mainly family and friends of the Northern Territory players, broke it up.'

I spoke to Grey later at a cafe in North Sydney, the day he flew back to Japan where he is playing. 'Last week I watched two blokes in a Super 14 game continue scuffling after the play had shifted away, with the referee saying to play on,' he recalled. 'They were both about 30 metres behind play and, as they fought, you could see them say, "We're not going to have any impact on the game here. Let's join the play," and they both jogged back onside together.

'The game is so fast and there are too many negatives having a fight. The only big stinks you see today are at scrums. The game's too fast. The guys are too rooted.'

BAD BOYS AND BETTING

One Friday night at the *Herald*'s old Broadway building, my phone rang and a beery voice said, 'Glad you're there, Roy. Want you to settle a bet.' The wager involved an ancient South Sydney game and concerned a certain long-range goal. The correct answer was Rabbitoh fullback George Longbottom.

I gave the answer and the punter said loudly, 'Good on ya, Roy. I knew it was Clive Churchill. My mate said he'd pay the $100 on your say so.' I protested, politely saying he must have misheard me. 'Yeah, that's right, Roy. Clive Churchill. I can remember the goal like it was yesterday.'

Whereupon I said, 'Listen, you arsehole, you're dudding your mate. It was George Longbottom, not Churchill.'

There was the sound of a busy pub in the background and a moaning mate, but the caller maintained his pitch, speaking over my protests, carrying on with the conversation as if I was totally in agreement. 'That's right, Roy. Clive Churchill. Knew you'd know. Bye, mate.'

On another occasion the phone rang and a different guy offered me a tip in a midweek race. Being only a sporadic punter, I ignored it, not even checking the race results. A few days later, the guy called with another tip, forcing me to check the previous one and discover his horse had come home first.

So I passed the second tip on to the racing writers, who activated their phone accounts and sent the copy boy scurrying to the TAB. By the time the third tip arrived, I was an investor.

It wasn't long before any ring from my phone had the racing writers sprinting to my desk. Within days it seemed they had formed a permanent circle around me, mouthing their disappointment when the phone rang on a football call, someone whispering softly to the others, 'It's just the NSW League.'

Finally, I asked the mystery punter to identify himself.

'You did a favour for me once,' he said. When I persisted, he mentioned the final match of 1978, a battle for the minor premiership between Wests and Cronulla, played at the Sharks' home ground.

Perhaps he was the Wests supporter I hauled from the stormwater canal at the back of the ground, after returning to the car park from the nearby Sharks Leagues Club where we had celebrated.

Heavy rain had fallen while we were inside the club, and when my long-term driver and I walked to the car, we heard groans coming from a canal. We dragged a near drowned Magpie supporter out of the swiftly moving water, piled him into the back seat and wrapped him in a blanket. By the time we reached Auburn, he appeared okay, and we left him at the railway station, near the police station. In retrospect, that may not have been the best place to deposit him.

The phone calls with the tips had come about five years after the rescue, suggesting my man had taken some time to put himself within access to hot racing information. And just as mysteriously –

at the time the racing writers were considering careers as professional punters – the calls suddenly stopped. I could only assume the mysterious man was in the boob, or a permanent watery grave.

When the phone next rang on a gambling matter, it was in the *Herald*'s new building, a glass and concrete tower in Sussex Street. The caller wanted to pass along information on what he believed to be a sting in a match between Manly and Souths at Brookvale Oval on 27 April 2003.

He insisted a mate had forewarned him that a Manly goal would be the game's 'first scoring play' on the TAB, an option that paid the relatively lucrative $6, far more than the usual $2 paid when a try is the first points scored. Insofar as Manly five-eighth Ben Walker kicked the goal – after 86 seconds – following a breach of the rules by his brother Chris, the South Sydney fullback, the story warranted investigating.

Furthermore, the caller claimed his mate had information that another Walker brother, the Brisbane-based Luke 'Skywalker' Walker, was aware of the sting. It seems the night before the match, the Australian women's touch football team was in Brisbane for a training camp. They attended a bar where one of the girls, the partner of the caller's mate, chatted with Skywalker.

The caller suggested I contact his mate, a high school teacher on the mid-North Coast of NSW. The school teacher confirmed the story, telling me his girl had given him advance knowledge that Manly's Walker would be the first scorer, via a penalty goal, in the match. Could I speak to the girl? I asked the school teacher.

No, she was in Japan with the Australian team. However, she was a teacher at the same school and he gave me the day when she would be back in class.

When I did make contact, the girl was furious. She made it very clear her boyfriend had no right to speak on her behalf. In fact, I gained the distinct impression they were no longer an item.

The original caller said Skywalker was keen to impress her, and the boyfriend confirmed this, indicating he had no regard for the brothers. It's possible, therefore, the whole thing was an act of vengeance against a footballer hitting on a bloke's girlfriend. Ben Walker certainly sounded appalled when I contacted him shortly after the match, days before I made contact with the female touch footballer.

'That is ludicrous,' he said. 'Fair dinkum, it's a joke. I find that outrageous.' Asked if he remembered the incident where Manly was awarded the first penalty of the match and he kicked a goal, Ben said, 'I do remember it. I told him [brother Chris] to settle down when he went off at the referee, otherwise it was going to be a long day. As it turned out, it was.' Manly won 28–20 and Ben kicked eight goals, two coming from infringements by his brother.

Asked what had allegedly upset Chris, Ben said, 'I remember him going off at the referee, but I can't recall what he was complaining about.'

The game was played on one of Sydney's wettest weekends on record. By a twist of programming fate, Channel Nine was locked in to cover the battle of the two struggling clubs, having been forced to choose the match five weeks in advance. Only 8178 fans attended in defiance of the torrential rain.

Souths won the toss and referee Matt Cecchin signalled time-on. The Rabbitohs elected to kick off, certainly not the tactic if the team wants Manly to kick the first goal, but the correct strategy in wet conditions.

The Sea Eagles fielded Souths' kick and carried the ball up field for four tackles before Ben Walker booted it into the Rabbitohs' quarter. Chris Walker, Souths' high-profile State of Origin recruit, went for a run from dummy half, but the ball squirted free as he was met by three Sea Eagles.

Three tackles later, with only 86 seconds of the match gone and the action closer to the posts, Cecchin blew his whistle and called out Chris Walker and Souths captain, Bryan Fletcher. Channel Nine commentator Peter Sterling told viewers, 'Well, this is very interesting. It seems as if Chris Walker may have said something.'

Despite not being involved in the play since turning the ball over, Chris Walker approached Cecchin, asking, 'Why don't you just do your job?'

Cecchin replied, 'Do you want to play a player short? Your job is to play football.' He then turned to Fletcher and explained, 'I've had a mouthful for three consecutive tackles. I've put up with it, but for only so long.'

Cecchin then awarded a penalty to Manly for Chris Walker's backchatting. Ben Walker kicked a penalty goal; Manly took a 2–nil lead and punters who had invested on a Manly goal as 'first point scoring play' collected $6 for every $1 invested with the TAB.

After hearing rumours of a plunge on the first points scored in the match and fielding media enquiries, the NRL requested the NSW Department of Gaming and Racing to investigate. The department in turn asked the NSW TAB to check its records.

Two days later, the department concluded its investigation into the round seven match, saying via a spokesperson, there was 'no evidence of any improper betting activity'. The TAB has a world-class automated monitoring system that records the account, location and time of every bet made. A seach revealed betting on the 'first point scoring play' option throughout NSW agencies came to a total of only 'several hundred dollars' and was dispersed across a number of agencies. The department also said 'the majority of bets were less than $20' and the highest was $100.

Records of licensed sports bookmakers in NSW were also inspected as part of the investigation. Despite the rumour emanating from Queensland, records of money wagered in other states was not pursued, although the NRL claimed to have done so.

The league issued a statement, saying it was 'satisfied that there has been no evidence presented to support these rumours'.

The Walker brothers went on to make history in their own different ways. Ben scored the first ever golden point in an extra-time victory over Parramatta. Twenty-four hours later, Chris made headlines when he transferred to the Roosters, turning his back on a $300,000 contract from Souths to accept a $40,000 deal.

Chris Walker's move to the Roosters raised eyebrows. He claimed he wanted to play with a semifinal bound team, despite the Roosters only being able to pay him rookie money because of salary cap constraints. He was released by the Roosters at the end of 2005 and took an incentive contract with the Storm.

Mastering the salary cap has never been a problem for inventive businessmen, particularly in a league where clubs go from insolvency to invincibility, from naught to juggernaut, in 12 months.

One story, perhaps apocryphal, concerns a club keen to acquire midseason backup in a certain vulnerable position. A player from an opposition club was invited to play a game of golf with a wealthy director. The bet was $100,000 on the outcome. As they approached the 9th hole (no point wasting time on 18 holes), the director three-putted and the footballer was $100,000 richer, demonstrating his gratitude by successfully appealing to leave his current club.

In the days before legalised betting, footballers and punters didn't have the myriad of wagering options, such as first scorer or points margins, or the plethora of opportunities that will come with interactive digital TV.

Brownlow medallist and commentator Gerard Healy remembers a major plunge his fellow Swans took on an interstate game in the early 1990s when betting on football was ignored by administrators. 'NSW played Victoria at the SCG ... Anyone who had flown over the NSW–Victorian border was eligible for NSW,' he says of the game, chosen on very dubious State of Origin lines. 'I was selected for NSW but I was a Victorian and wasn't about to swap allegiances. I considered it hypocritical and so did Greg "Diesel" Williams.'

Both withdrew with 'injuries'.

'It wasn't Victoria's strongest team because none of the boys wanted to be there,' he says. 'But the NSW guys were playing for history. The Daniher brothers were playing together for NSW and [John] Longmire and [Wayne] Carey were 19-year-olds. We had seen the NSW boys train through the week and noticed their great camaraderie. The betting was 10-1 NSW and, as far as the bookies were concerned, Victoria couldn't get beaten.

'It was a shocking night weatherwise with the ground very heavy. All the Swans were on NSW because we knew everyone in the team was up and it was a fair chance it would piss down. We kept getting weather forecasts on the half hour, and they all indicated it would belt down. It did. Almost everyone at the Swans plunged.

'Even at half-time, NSW was 4-1. The blokes kept putting more money on because we knew the southerly buster was coming. It was one of the great stings.'

Money was clearly a motivating factor in the Swans' victories when they backed their team. 'David Bolton put our bets on,' Healy said. 'He'd take the hat around as a way of bringing the blokes together. Rarely did we have a plunge and not get the money.'

Another champion Swan, Tony Lockett, was embroiled in a greyhound scam, although it involved the siring of the animals rather than betting on them. Five greyhound breeders took civil action against Lockett for allegedly duping them into believing his top dog, Malawi's Prince, sired pups for them. DNA tests established the breeders' dogs were serviced by an inferior dog called Black Pirate at Lockett's property near Cranbourne in outer

Melbourne. Although Lockett was the studmaster, he was busy playing with the Swans and was merely charged with signing misleading documents.

His friend and trainer, Darren McDonald, took the heat for the substitution racket. The matter was settled out of court.

Wests were expected to finish last in 1978, having won the wooden spoon the previous year. The odds on making the top five, offered by a bookmaker at Flemington Market, were 200-1.

The Magpies duly won the minor premiership and some of the players, such as Dallas Donnelly, made more from the bet than they did from their playing contract. The bookmaker took some time to pay but beseeched any Wests player appearing on TV to declare the bet had not been settled, basically to save him from losing his house to his backers. The following year he offered 12-1 odds for making the top five, and Wests again collected, this time with Sydney journalists as co-investors.

Even before then, 'doubles' represented an option for teams to gamble, particularly in exhibition games. This was a fundraiser by the home club where a prize was paid for the first scorers from both teams.

A former international second-rower remembers travelling to Papua New Guinea and playing a game at Goroka in the highlands.

The international's team was ahead 20–nil at half-time and discussion focused on the double. They pooled their tickets and discovered they had a live one: a double with the number of the first scorer from the visiting team linked to a little winger from Goroka.

'Fair dinkum,' says the second-rower. 'We took twenty minutes trying to feed the little winger the ball so he could score, but somebody would drop the ball or the play would go the other way.

Finally, he made a break down the sideline and we all stood back cheering to ourselves. But he passed the ball back infield to the centre who scored.'

The winning double would have only been worth 'drinking silver' to the visitors, small change compared to the big investments and variety of betting opportunities today.

Similarly, an unknown man offered Wests a keg if the Magpies did not beat a Northern Territory team by ten points in an end-of-season promotional match at Darwin in which Arthur Beetson made a guest appearance for the home side.

A Top End defender was incredulous when a Wests player ran from dummy half on his own line, engaged him and then slammed the ball into his stomach. It took some time for the Northern Territory player to grasp both the ball and the opportunity before he lumbered forward for a try.

After the match, with Wests winning by less than ten points, the man who had offered the keg had vanished.

A peculiar morality surrounds gambling on sport. It is absolutely taboo not to try in sport, meaning a bet against your own team is the greatest of all sins. To profit from not trying is anathema to the athlete and the coach. But even when a team backs itself, doesn't it raise ethical questions, or expose the participants to a conflict of interest? Healy and Williams both withdrew from the NSW team, pushing out the odds on the Blues and, aware of the general malaise of the Vics, backed NSW.

Did the Wests players try hard enough in the Darwin match by not seeking to win by a massive margin in the searing heat of that October night? Were the journalists complicit in joining Wests players in a bet and not writing about it for fear the publicity would undermine their chances of being paid? Suppose a team backs itself one week in order to generate team morale but not the next. Does it imply the effort was less than total in the non-wagering week?

Sports simply respond to these ethical conundrums by banning their athletes from gambling on their own sport. However, the point about the Goroka and Darwin stories is that even when the entire team seeks to engineer a try for the opposition, it is extremely difficult. Everybody must be in the sting, increasing the possibility of discovery.

One coach, long since retired, still lies awake at nights thinking about his now deceased captain. 'I think he was betting against us,' the coach said. 'We got beaten by Balmain by a fair bit and he was marking [winger] Larry Corowa. It's obvious when Corowa is in the team – you'd kick deep if the ball is going to his side. I told the team to kick it deep, but he was captain and told them to kick it short to his wing.

'Larry Corowa caught it and scored. But he kept doing it. I said to him at half-time, "What's going on here?" But I never got an answer. He and his wife were a bit aloof from the rest of us. They lived away from the area in a wealthy suburb. He kept his secrets pretty well.'

It's easier to organise a result in soccer, particularly with a corruptible goalkeeper. A Columbian defender, Andrés Escobar, was murdered when he returned from the 1994 World Cup after scoring an own goal, although police suggested the killing was also related to road rage.

In May 2006 Socceroo Archie Thompson was summoned to attend an enquiry by the Belgian Football Association into match-fixing involving his former club, Lierse. The manager of Lierse, Paul Put, admitted fixing two matches and was dismissed, as were a number of Lierse players. Thompson denied any involvement, arguing he was one of the top goal scorers in the Belgian league when the match-fixing occurred.

Bad Boys and Betting

The 2006 World Cup in Germany was marred by allegations of a match-fixing racket in Italy. Sepp Blatter, the German chief of FIFA, denounced it as the worst scandal in the sport's history. Shortly after Australia lost 1–0 to Italy in a round of 16 match, following a dive by an Italian player, a manager of Juventus attempted suicide by jumping from a building. Commentators noted it was the second dive by an Italian in a week.

Unresolved in many minds is a first grade match between South Sydney and Western Suburbs in 1994. Souths lost in an upset, and a Channel Seven current affairs program, *Real Life*, went to air on 13 September that year with imputations that some of the Rabbitohs had thrown the match.

The broadcast identified three players by pictures – Craig Field, Jacin Sinclair and Tyran Smith – and suggested they had fraudulently fixed the result and bet against themselves. The three players sued Channel Seven for defamation, but the case had still not been determined by the courts when broadcaster Alan Jones, then the football manager for Souths, wrote a letter in February 1999 to Seven's owner, Kerry Stokes, seeking settlement.

Jones claimed the three players had received hate mail, abusive phone calls, death threats and their own fans had hurled abuse at them. He pointed out he had formally requested the then police commissioner, Tony Lauer, to conduct a full investigation. A written report of the investigation, according to Jones, revealed no evidence to sustain the allegations. He suggested $80,000 per player would remedy the players' angst. Seven had offered $15,000. It is understood a settlement was finally reached with terms not disclosed, but that 1994 match still resonates with many good judges.

Also unresolved is the 1978 NSWRL finals series. On the eve of the final round, only Wests and Cronulla, who played each other, were safely in the top five. Four clubs – Manly, Canterbury, Parramatta and Easts – were on a tightrope. Manly were drawn to play Easts.

Referee Greg Hartley, who had been officiating in reserve grade for most of the season, was recalled to adjudicate the Sea Eagles versus Roosters match. In his book, *Big Artie*, Beetson, who was then captain-coach of the Roosters, refers to a mate who was 'contemplating a sizeable wager with a prominent Manly official'. Beetson writes that his advice to his mate, based on Hartley's appointment, was, 'I wouldn't back us with stones.' He felt that Hartley's refereeing suited Manly's style of play.

He also writes cryptically, 'The Sea Eagles went on to beat us 20–10, with at least one of our key blokes well off his game.'

The Sea Eagles defeated Wests in a final where Hartley disallowed two Wests tries. Manly went on to face Cronulla in the grand final. With the scores locked 11–11 near the end, Manly half Steve Martin fed the ball blatantly into the second row, and Cronulla kicker Steve Rogers, who had been on target with his kicks, walked over, assuming his team would be given a penalty.

But Hartley ignored the breach; the game was drawn and Manly won the replay.

I recall watching it in the ante room of the visitors' dressing area at the SCG. A northern beaches federal politician walked over to chat and remarked to me on the number of big-time Sydney gamblers in the room.

Hartley subsequently was invited away with the 1978 Kangaroos, as travelling referee, the first appointment of its type, and his fares were curiously paid from England. Rogers approached him on the tour and asked about the penalty not awarded.

'You wouldn't have wanted to win a grand final on a penalty,' was Hartley's response, according to Rogers.

The '78 series should have been thoroughly investigated by journalists at the time, considering one former Manly player walked into the offices of the now defunct *Sun* newspaper on the eve of the finals and advised everyone to back the Sea Eagles.

Bad Boys and Betting

Journalism, it is said, is the first draft of history. Sometimes it is the only draft. Gary Lester, who covered the '78 series, now admits he and his colleagues should have asked more questions.

The 1963 Grand Final still smoulders in the minds of Wests players. Not a reunion goes by without someone making an angry curse on the grave of referee Darcy Lawler.

It still haunts men like former second-rower Chow Hayes, whose team had beaten St George in all three games in 1963 and qualified first for the grand final. 'We should have let St George beat us in the major semi and let Darcy get his big win over before the grand final,' he says.

Instead, St George qualified via winning the preliminary final and, on a mud-soaked day, won the grand final 8–3, with Wests penalised 18–7. Dragons winger John King was tackled by Wests fullback Don Parish in the 65th minute but simply regained his feet and continued for a try. Wests players insist they hesitated when Lawler instructed King to play the ball.

'I was close enough to hear Darcy say "You play it", but King just got to his feet and kept going,' Chow says. Jack Gibson, who played prop for Wests that day, chased Lawler and abused him.

Wests players remember Lawler threatening to send him off, but Gibson replied, 'If you do, I'll give you up.' However, Gibson had already done so.

Gibson then worked at Thommo's Two-up School in inner Sydney with his mate Ron Taylor, the son of legendary owner Joe Taylor. He was therefore familiar with the flow of big money and had been told of a £600 ($1,200) wager on the Dragons by Lawler, then secretary manager of South Sydney Junior League Club, a poker machine palace frequented by Sydney's shady netherworld.

'You've got no chance,' one of the bookies told Gibson, making it clear his colleagues had backed St George and Lawler was in the bet with them. At the next training session, four days before the grand final, Gibson approached Wests secretary Bill Beaver, a kindly old soul who held a senior position in NSW Railways. But Beaver did nothing.

Gibson also confided in his Wests team-mate, Noel Kelly.

Kelly, gutted by the injustice, gained his own private hearing with Gibson's source days after the grand final. However, the source was a notorious liar, well-known for his '2KYs', the name of a Sydney radio station and rhyming slang for lies.

On one occasion a mate, disappointed to have backed a loser on the recommendation of the liar (who had subsequently backed the winner), challenged him. 'Don't you know I'm a liar?' was his defence.

It brings to mind the famous words of the American fight promoter, Bob Arum, who said, 'Yesterday I was lying. Today I'm telling the truth.' Or Bullfrog Moore: 'Never tell a lie unless it is absolutely necessary.' Professional gamblers are reminiscent of fishermen – the only time they tell the truth is when they call another fisherman a liar.

It's no surprise Beaver did nothing, considering his misguided faith in human nature and dedication to winning life membership from the NSWRL.

Fifteen years later, a record turnout for a Wests–Parramatta game at Lidcombe Oval forced officials to use an abandoned turnstile in order to clear the crowd queuing on the nearby road. When the gate attendance was announced, it clearly did not reflect the big crowd.

Someone congratulated Beaver, then treasurer, for finally hiding gate money in order to pay players black money, income free of taxation implications, a practice we believed was widespread around the league. Plus, the NSWRL extracted a fixed percentage of the gate, meaning any ruse to reduce income to an organisation Wests believed was working against the club was welcome.

But Beaver explained that the crowd counter on the abandoned turnstile was not working and, while the attendance figure was therefore inaccurate, the NSWRL would still receive their rightful percentage. Nor would there be a fund for illicit payments to players.

Wests were occasionally the beneficiary of dubious refereeing.

The Magpies beat Souths in the 1952 Grand Final when the stars from both teams were en route to England and France for the Kangaroo tour. One Souths star who remained behind, skipper Jack Rayner, then a serving NSW policeman, has never forgiven the referee, George Bishop, for what he believes was corrupt decision making. Bishop announced his retirement after the match. Rayner and Bishop both lived in the same Sydney suburb of Maroubra, but the honest copper never spoke to him again.

Former Souths and Manly winger Tom Mooney, now licensee of six pubs in northern NSW, says of Rabbitoh reunions, 'Every time Jack talks, he mentions the rort of 1952.'

Rugby league author Ian Heads recalls attending the funeral of Easts legendary prop Ray Stehr, when a little Runyonesque character approached him with 'a good story'. 'I'm the bloke who put the 400 quid on for George Bishop in the '52 Grand Final,' the little man told Heads.

Aware information on gambling is often salted with gossip and innuendo, Heads was hesitant. 'He spoke out of the corner of his mouth, but he had a ring of authority about him. He said he'd call me and did so about a year later. I arranged to meet him at the Waverley TAB. I spent three years waiting for him and all I found at the TAB were a few losers.'

Huge money was wagered on rugby league during St George's 11 successive premierships. On the eve of one grand final, there was a kidnap plot by big bookies to get John Raper, Graeme Langlands and Reg Gasnier out of the team and secrete them away for a weekend. One insider, when I checked the story with him for this book, made it clear some of the crooks were still alive and he wanted to stay the same way.

'I didn't know of it,' Raper says. 'If I had I would have been scared. I'm not surprised given the amount of money in SP (starting price) betting in those days. But I was in the police force at the time and that would have deterred them. I was the pin-up boy in the police. I was a favourite of commissioner Colin John Delaney.

'Plus Bumper [Farrell, a former Newtown prop and senior detective] was around. The cops would have blasted the city apart. It would have made it hard for the SPs. They would have raided [prominent bookies] George Freeman and Lenny McPherson and destroyed their business. They worked in with the police, and if they heard about it, they wouldn't have agreed it could proceed.'

Jack Gibson's reputation in the game as a coach can never be compromised, but it's interesting to reflect on the fact that he may not have been allowed to coach in the United States, a country whose football code he admires enormously.

US officials take a hard line with sports betting, and players are not permitted to even associate with known gamblers. Famous quarterback Joe Namath was once ordered by NFL Commissioner Pete Rozelle to surrender a financial interest in a New York nightclub because it was the haunt of notorious bookies.

Ice hockey icon Wayne 'The Great One' Gretzky came under intense scrutiny when his wife, former actress Janet Jones, admitted laying hundreds of thousands of dollars on sporting bets. At the same time, the assistant coach of the Phoenix Coyotes, the team Gretzky co-owns, was charged with money laundering, fraud and conspiracy after an investigation found he was involved with organised crime figures.

Rugby league, built on the income from Sydney's poker machine palaces, can't be so moralistic. Gibson long ago accommodated his own ethical position with gambling, one he explained patiently and painstakingly to my brother Chris Masters, the *Four Corners* reporter who exposed gambling in rugby league in 1983. Basically, Gibson argued he never backed against a team he coached.

A story told by Gibson's lifelong friend, coaching colleague and punting partner, Ron Massey, demonstrates how Gibson could influence the fortunes of a team he did not coach and still achieve a good financial outcome.

In 1980, a year Gibson did not coach, Massey and Gibson ran a book on the rugby league season. The biggest bet they took was from the late Kerry Packer, who nominated three teams to finish atop the ladder. By the halfway mark of the season, Packer's three teams were gone, too far back to make the semifinals. It was, according to Massey, 'a bookmaker's dream. We couldn't lose.' His satisfaction indicated the massive wager by Australia's then second richest man.

In view of the totality of bets they laid, Easts loomed as their optimum financial return. About this time, Easts reserve grade coach, Ron Coote, was in the doldrums. His team wasn't playing well and he needed coaching assistance. He called Massey, with whom he had a great relationship from the Roosters' premiership seasons of 1974–75. Massey has a rare capacity to watch a match live or on video and make judgements on a team's effort and ability.

Massey agreed to an arrangement to meet Coote at his Maroubra home for viewing sessions. However, on one occasion the video player broke down and they were forced to adjourn to Easts' training headquarters at the old Sports Ground (now the site of Aussie Stadium) and watch the tape on the Roosters' machine.

Bozo Fulton was coaching Easts first grade and, observing Massey assisting Coote, asked him to look at tape of *his* team. It was Bozo's second approach to Massey, having asked for video assistance at the beginning of the season.

But Massey, quite reasonably, expected to be paid, an arrangement rejected by club boss Ron Jones, who argued Massey had fulfilled the role gratis while with Gibson at the Roosters in the mid-1970s. A further Massey suggestion that Bozo pay him from his own salary also fell, predictably, on deaf ears.

Following the second approach, Massey agreed to help Fulton.

The arrangement continued until Arthur Beetson, then playing for Parramatta and doing some private training at Easts Leagues Club, spied the pair emerging from a lift. Beetson, still seething from the fact that Fulton succeeded him as coach of Easts, seized upon the opportunity in his newspaper column to credit Massey, whom he called 'The Turtle', with the Roosters' return to form.

Gibson, a Beetson ally, read the column and asked Massey why he was assisting Fulton. 'Easts is our best result,' Massey said, reminding his old friend of the book they had taken on the season. 'I'm helping us.'

However, Gibson then laid a massive wager against Easts. 'What are you going to do now?' Gibson asked Massey.

'I won't be helping Easts,' Massey replied.

Canterbury, the eventual premiers, became their best result. 'We'd already backed Canterbury to win, and they became an even bigger winner when Jack laid Easts,' Massey says.

Around this time, Fulton called Massey to confirm a mutual time to watch the video. 'I won't be helping,' he told Fulton. 'It's a money thing and you understand money more than anyone.'

Gibson was also central to the biggest administrative scandal in Australian sport: the resignation of ARL executive chairman Kevin Humphreys following Chris Masters's landmark ABC *Four Corners* program, *The Big League*.

In 1977 Humphreys was charged with defrauding the licensed Balmain Leagues Club, where he was chief executive, of $50,519 for his own use. Charges were dismissed that year, although rumours persisted that the state's senior magistrate, Murray Farquhar, had advised another magistrate to find in favour of Humphreys. In 1983, following Chris's program and a subsequent Royal Commission, Humphreys was retried, found guilty and fined $4,000.

The Royal Commission, chaired by Sir Laurence Street, a former lieutenant governor of NSW, was one of the most significant chapters in the state's judicial history. Premier Neville Wran stood down temporarily while the commission's investigations proceeded on an allegation, ultimately found to be unsubstantiated, that he assisted Humphreys to avoid prosecution for fraud. Farquhar, who had retired from the bench in 1979, was sentenced to four years' jail for attempting to pervert the course of justice.

The Big League was Chris's first program for the long-running current affairs show, and he initially set out to expose payola in sport – broadcasters receiving secret commissions to promote certain sports on TV. He found evidence of a proposed payment for promoting basketball.

The proposition was put by Barry Ross, the sideline commentator for Rex Mossop, who called Channel Seven's Sunday match of the round. Ross explained the system to the basketball chiefs. They responded by having him charged with soliciting a bribe. Ross took the entire blame for the payola and, even though the charge sheet mentioned the involvement of another person, he was found guilty (although no conviction was recorded, an outcome allowed under NSW law). Ross subsequently faded from the media.

This was a time when the second-best match was televised by the ABC on Saturdays. Because Mossop took some time deciding the match of the round, the ABC had to wait, often until Tuesday, before it could choose the No. 2 match. Teams would often go to training unaware whether they were playing in four or five days' time, unlike today where the times of matches are scheduled five weeks in advance.

While Chris investigated this story, he stumbled across the allegation that Humphreys escaped prosecution on the 1977 case because of Wran's interference with the appointment of a magistrate to hear his case. Chris deliberately kept me out of his enquiries, aware I would be accused of being a major source. After all, rugby league is a sport where the only whistleblowers allowed are the referees. Another of my coaching colleagues agreed to meet Chris but remained ludicrously hidden from view behind a huge oak tree in a suburban park.

Gibson had no such misgivings.

He had lent Humphreys $32,000 to settle his debt with Balmain Leagues Club on the condition the league chief not gamble again. Gibson's high regard for the administration of American football took another compromising ethical twist: it would be anathema to the NFL for a coach to lend money to settle the gambling debts of its chief officer.

Because Gibson had close connections with Sydney gambling interests, it didn't take long for him to learn Humphreys was back on the punt soon after his bailout. Gibson told Chris on camera that Humphreys was gambling again and had lost his support.

At this time *Four Corners* went to air on a Saturday night, and I recall the reaction of many league officials the following day when I took St George to Penrith. Some were cool, others chilly, all implying I had contributed to 'giving Kevin up'. The criticism of Gibson must have been manifoldly worse, yet, significantly, never to his face.

Humphreys on the other hand showed no bitterness, never once mentioning my relationship with Chris in any of the discussions we ever had. In fact, Wran was equally non-vengeful, saying to me once, 'We should never be held responsible for the sins of our fathers, or, in your case, your brother.'

Many, including prominent Sydney businessman John Singleton, consider Humphreys to be the most gifted sports administrator they have ever met. His clever pioneering of what has become rugby league's crown jewel, State of Origin football, despite the opposition of Sydney clubs, was classic political manipulation.

He has that same combination of unabashed enthusiasm, street intelligence and unshakeable self-confidence that marked Pete Rose, the US baseballer barred for life from his sport and its Hall of Fame for gambling. Both had the Aristotelian 'fatal flaw'. Rose set stellar records as a player and a manager and could have become one of the greatest names in his sport.

In his autobiography, *My Prison Without Bars*, Rose wrote that during one three-week gambling splurge he wrote 11 cheques, each for $8,000, to a bookie in New York. Apart from the $88,000, he also lost another $100,000. 'I was just following the same competitive instincts I had as a ball player. Sports had taught me how to bounce back after a loss.'

In the case of both Rose and Humphreys, the bets were not so much a means to add to an income as they were lubricants to a competitive nature.

Humphreys admits being a poor punter. While he always had two of the three ingredients to make a gambler – money, guts and brains – he says, 'I'm the world's worst punter. The most I've ever won is $2,400.' He was also willing to admit his problem when Singleton organised a fundraising lunch for him. The former league boss, who had ignominiously resigned 15 years earlier, was suffering prostate cancer and needed money to fight the disease. He was at financial ground zero, living in rented accommodation at Ashfield and with the threat of having his car repossessed. A condition of the fundraiser was that Humphreys admit his addiction publicly. Singleton asked me to write the story in the *Herald*.

We met at a city restaurant, and he said of the disease invading his body and the addiction that had destroyed his career, 'The biggest cancer is the other one. If I get over it, I'll be right.'

He has a plastic shoulder and an artificial knee and walked with a slight limp from the constant pain in his hip, a legacy of his earlier career as a Balmain prop forward. Yet he says the hardest steps he's taken have been to join Gamblers Anonymous.

'I got all the literature, read it thoroughly and went to my first branch meeting at a suburb not far away,' he told me. 'I parked the car a couple of streets away and walked up this narrow lane to a church hall. The first thing I saw was two blokes in deep discussion. One of them was a bloke I tipped out of Balmain Leagues Club years ago for whacking his wife. I stopped in my tracks and went home.'

Humphreys's relationship with his own wife, Joan, is one of the great love stories. Since the day they were married, they have had a plaque in their kitchen that reads, 'Lord help me to remember that nothing is going to happen to me today that you and I together can't handle.'

While the plaque refers to a heavenly companion, Humphreys equates it with Joan. 'She is the greatest thing . . .' The words trail off, as if anything else would be superfluous.

Rumours of his gambling on the roulette table in English casinos were manifold, but he swears he made only one bet – £50 on a number which is the date of his wedding anniversary. The wheel stopped on the number.

The luncheon Singo planned was to be held at the Sydney Football Stadium, but bookings were so great that it was transferred to the casino, not an appropriate venue, but one with the biggest seating area in the city at the time.

When Humphreys and Joan walked into the gathering of 700 or more, everyone stood and clapped. A delicate sadness fell over the barn-like room and tears welled in Humphreys's eyes as he walked to his table. The dormant power was there in the still square shoulders, as was the gentlemanly charm from another era when he ensured his wife was comfortably seated, yet he could not disguise the honour he felt.

Broadcaster Alan Jones summed up the prevailing mood that the punishment outweighed the crime when he said, 'In many ways it is a bit of purgation for us all. We've been too long in the crucifixion and too late with the redemption.'

The luncheon raised $160,000, which allowed Humphreys the top medical treatment for his full recovery. He also beat the gambling bug, or certainly appeared to have done when I sat with him and Singo at one of his favourite haunts, the Haberfield Rowers Club. A punter approached the table with information on a hot tip and, while Singo rolled it over in his Pentium-quick mind, Humphreys made a quiet aside to himself, 'Been there, done that.'

The trade-off to a life away from the punt seems to be an increasing youthfulness. Perhaps it is personal vengeance on what may be perceived to be an unfair world – a world that included a barb from Rupert Murdoch, during the Super League war, that he had spent time in jail. Humphreys, too poor to defend himself in a defamation action against one of the most powerful media companies in the world, was forced to cop it.

Nor does he have a harsh word for Gibson's need to bring him to account, nor any apparent regrets that he failed to fulfil his administrative gifts. Samuel Taylor Coleridge's words seem apposite, 'By what I have effected, am I to be judged by my fellow men; what I could have done is a question for my own conscience.'

He has an elephant-like memory for initiatives he promulgated and a fanatical alertness, quickly seizing on fallacious argument.

He remains fiercely protective of the code, saying, 'Anything which has happened in my life is my fault, not the game's fault.' He has strong views on legalised gambling, which, ironically, mirror Gibson's opposition to the legalisation of illicit drugs.

Like the push to legalise drugs, sanctioned gambling appeals to those who believe the solution to anything difficult to eradicate through law enforcement is to make it legal. This view overlooks the fact that illegal operators rush in behind the legalised gambling and eat up a fair slice of the anticipated tax revenue pie.

Humphreys moved swiftly when faced with a fait accompli by a NSW Government that invited him to the launch of FootyTAB without having first consulted with the NSWRL, which he headed. He threatened to schedule a last-minute change of games unless his code received a share of the revenue gambled on it.

While sports now ban their players and officials from gambling on their own events, this purity of purpose may be more related to finance than ethics. Sport takes the view of gambling that it 'gets all the pain and none of the gain'. In other words, sport is forced to deal with the allegations of match-fixing, while receiving none of the wagering revenue their events generate.

Although cricket administrators were horrified following revelations of bribery scandals in South Africa and India, with links to Australia and the consequent high volumes of money wagered, it was never certain whether they were concerned about the damage to the integrity of the game, or the revenue they were forgoing.

In a sport where its highest post – the captain of the national team – is often compared in status to Prime Minister, the current skipper, Ricky Ponting, is known as 'Punter'.

Rugby league was brutally honest when Australia's biggest bookmakers suspended betting on matches in 2006 because of doubt over injury to Newcastle's Andrew Johns. The bookies complained that they set their generous start to Newcastle's opponent when

Johns was fit and reduced the margin when it was assumed he was out injured.

Even when it was revealed that Johns was a partner in six racehorses with a brothel owner who had gambled against Johns's team, the NRL simply said, 'Bad luck. We don't get a commission.'

The NRL did conduct an enquiry when they found that the brothel owner, Eddie Hayson, was in contact with many NRL players and jockeys and had been picking up the tab for those who used prostitutes at his up-market Sydney establishment, Stiletto.

Bookies accused Hayson of having inside knowledge following a huge betting plunge against Johns's team, the Newcastle Knights, in a game where the champion halfback was a late withdrawal. Hayson denied receiving inside information; Johns denied speaking to him about his fitness and the NRL took no action. Johns even rang NRL chief David Gallop, telling him, 'You know I would do nothing to hurt the game.'

The code's administrators have had little sympathy for bookies after copping all the blame following a plunge on North Sydney's David Fairleigh to win the Rothmans Medal, the equivalent of AFL's Brownlow. Such was the weight of money on the Bears' second-rower, TAB and Sportsbook betting on the event was suspended.

The smart money was right: Fairleigh did win the medal. The game shielded the sponsor from blame, despite the tobacco giant being the source of the leak.

The then director of referees, Mick Stone, whose responsibility it was to lock referees' votes per round in sealed envelopes in a safe, reveals, 'With two rounds left, the TV station televising the count wanted to prepare graphics of potential winners. So I sent the sealed envelopes by armed guard to the sponsor, who prepared the information for the TV network. Because Fairleigh was so far ahead, someone knew he couldn't lose with two rounds left. They got the money on after the votes left my office. It was hardly a fair go on the bookies.'

The rise of Betfair widens gambling opportunities to encompass betting on losers as well. Betfair, a joint venture between a licensed British online betting exchange and the Packer empire, frightens most sports, although the AFL has signed on as a commercial partner for some of the revenue it expects to generate. The professional sports, including cricket, have formed a coalition to lobby for a share of government revenue and access to gambling records, but they are powerless to investigate the records of illegal operators, who handle most of the big money gambled.

Because the professional era frees players from the obligation of a job, they have considerable spare time. This adds to the lethal cocktail of high salaries and a plethora of wagering options.

'I would hate to be a young person today, having whatever gambling bug I had at age 25,' Humphreys says, 'particularly because of the proliferation of gambling outlets.'

Many go straight from school to become full-time footballers, meaning they miss the counselling available, via families, to young men when they open their first pay packet. Order is not a natural gift of youth, particularly among young footballers. In this context, order doesn't mean the drive to train and learn, or the willingness to make sacrifices for the team – football players have that in the extreme. They lack the order obtained from having priorities set, from being independent of a player manager to pay things like car insurance, from knowing when to take a tip and when to stop. Many haven't had their Copernican revelation yet. They still think the universe revolves around them.

Nearly half of NRL players polled in an annual survey conducted by *Rugby League Week* in 2005 admitted knowing a player with a gambling addiction. (NRL chief executive David

Gallop questioned the methodology of the survey, pointing out that they could all be referring to the same player!)

A counsellor from Wesley Mission, Reverend Chester Carter, described the increase in gambling amongst NRL players as 'dramatic' and linked it with long-term problems he had identified in the armed services. Describing the military as 'obviously another high-risk lifestyle', Reverend Carter says, 'These blokes [NRL players and armed servicemen] have a real need for adrenaline; they find it through gambling.'

Reverend Carter, who counselled big-name NRL players and officials, warned the problem threatened to spiral out of control following a significant increase in addiction in the past three years. 'There's no doubt a gambling culture exists in league,' he said. 'I know of several players who are secretly leading a double life. Blokes have lost cars, houses, relationships, contemplated suicide ... It can be fatal.'

Just days after the poll was conducted, Sharks halfback Michael Sullivan stunned fans by confessing publicly to a gambling addiction on horse racing and market shares that had cost him $100,000 and forced him to play in England where the favourable exchange rate allowed him to settle his debts in Australia.

'Gambling is definitely a massive problem for a lot of us,' one representative player revealed to the magazine. 'You take it up because it is a great way of simulating that adrenaline rush you get from winning games. That's why a lot of players get stuck into the pokies when they're out injured.'

But poker machines also make everything go away. They make you forget.

A Broncos player, who wished to remain anonymous, was quoted as saying, 'There's a lot of blokes getting a lot of money who haven't had jobs before, so they don't know the value of money. There's a lot of gambling going on and it's happening at every club. It comes down to the individual; it's not the game's responsibility.'

Gallop did not abrogate the league's responsibility, saying, 'If they are suggesting it is a problem, it certainly is a social problem from which we are not immune. We've got specific courses through our education and welfare committee that we've run over the last few years dealing with the issue.'

The NRL did take action in 2002 when an understrength Dragons team backed themselves to beat the Warriors in Auckland. The Dragons were 5-1 because their stars were missing and everyone invested $50 each. The winnings were to be used to fund an end-of-season trip to an exotic location in the United States, but the NRL, learning of the bet, fined the Dragons $10,000, consigning the team to the Gold Coast for their holiday.

The *Rugby League Week* survey, based on confidential responses from 100 elite players, revealed gambling replaced sex, alcohol and drugs as the code's biggest off-field problem.

It was bad news for fans who expect athletes to be role models.

But why should a person who can run fast, kick accurately, hit a cricket ball or dunk a basketball necessarily be someone to be admired, emulated or even listened to, considering none of his skills have much value away from the playing arena?

Games aren't like life, no matter what the motivational experts say. The appeal of sport is that it is wonderfully *unlike* life in that games have specific beginnings and endings, exact rules, prescribed boundaries, referees, judges, penalties, half-times and, when time expires, losers and winners.

People who work on an assembly line don't end the shift neatly divided into winners and losers. They know how the shift will end, unlike a sporting contest where no-one can be certain of the outcome. Maybe because most working lives are vague and mundane, glamorous sports figures and celebrities are expected to be our role models.

NRL director and former Broncos star Gorden Tallis expressed the incongruity best when he argued with a group of sports journalists before a dinner one evening. In reference to Princess Mary, who married the Crown Prince of Denmark after meeting him in a Sydney pub during the 2000 Olympics, Tallis asked, 'Because she is now a member of a royal family, does that make her a good role model?'

Tallis had a point: was an attractive real estate agent from Tasmania best equipped to be the standard bearer for Danish women? 'Where in the school curriculum is the subject called "Being a Role Model"?' he wondered.

Great athletes are not like most people because they almost always have tunnel vision. They perform best when acting instinctively, by-passing the brain completely. In fact, too much time to think is an athlete's mortal enemy. Great footballers are a lot like children – self-centred, naive, fiercely competitive. Their success is the outcome of relatively simple events: a ball steered between the posts, a tackle made near the corner post, a goal gliding into the corner of the net.

In fact, they fall the hardest at precisely those moments when the simplicity of their calling collides with the complexity of the grown-up world: when they are caught by the breathalyser, dudded by corrupt managers, identified having sex with someone else's partner.

It follows that the public wants its heroes to stay out of trouble. For a relentless media, ostensibly serving the public, the absence of vice in a big-name footballer has become more important than the presence of virtue. The media justify this vigilance on players' private lives in terms of the public's right to know. Often, it is the journalist's need to tell.

'We need never fear an objective appraisal of our heroes,' Thomas Reeves wrote in *A Question of Character*, an analysis of John F.

Kennedy and the lore that surrounds the former US President. 'Truth is ultimately more enlightening and satisfying than myth.'

Indeed it is when you compare the truth concerning the gambling activities of two big stars in the NRL and AFL with the myriad of murky myths concerning former Broncos star Allan Langer. Langer, a well-known punter, was ludicrously rumoured to retire because police apprehended him driving a getaway car after a robbery in northern NSW.

Shortly after the *Rugby League Week* survey that referred to a State of Origin star who had lost two houses to gambling, Auckland captain Steve Price was subsequently identified in *The Daily Telegraph* as the player.

Price, former captain of the Bulldogs and public face of the club during the media trials on salary cap breaches and sexual assault allegations, was quoted as suffering a private hell with poker machine addiction. However, a phone call to him in Auckland revealed the problem had been hyped.

'I probably lost $20,000 over ten years,' he told me. 'The headline in the story said I risked losing my wife and three kids, but it never got to that stage. I recognised I had a problem and Canterbury helped me by banning me from playing poker machines. I also arranged to have an additional signatory to a cheque. Going to an ATM was too easy.

'It all culminated in the time my wife and kids went away and I lost $1,500–$2,000 on the pokies over five days. I felt so depressed over losing that much, because whenever I admitted to my wife, Jo, that I'd lost $100, she'd say we could have spent the money on the kids.

'The worst thing about the publicity was when my mum went to the bowling club in Toowoomba and put five dollars in a poker machine. A lady walked by and said, "Now I know where your son got it from." She was shattered.'

While Price managed a problem that was exaggerated in the media, there is a chilling corollary to it. 'The worst thing is that, since then I've come across [NRL] guys who are really bad [gamblers],' he said. 'They have a chuckle with me, saying, "You're the one who got all the publicity, but we're the ones with the real problem." They recognise it is a major problem, but they still keep gambling. It's scary for them.'

A measure of the amount some highly paid stars gamble is the $10,000 Wallaby Wendell Sailor invested with a Vanuatu bookie to break even after a day's punting. Sailor borrowed Price's phone to make the bet.

'I've invested $10 and he's bet $10,000, and it got up by a nose hair,' Price said. 'Afterwards I'm thinking *holy shit*, and Wendell is just sitting there, relieved he's got $20,000 back to finish square on the day.'

Sailor is one of the few big punters in rugby union, according to Nathan Grey. Maybe union still hasn't adjusted from the days players were given such meagre spending money on tours, card games were banned lest one player lose all his allowance.

'The biggest punter is [Waratahs] Morgan Turinui, but he's very good,' Grey says. 'When Makybe Diva won her second Melbourne Cup, he backed the first four placegetters. We were training at Coffs Harbour at the time and the manager organised a TV in the change room. Players are standing around with a fist full of $1 TAB tickets, and I'm sitting next to Morgan and he says, "I think I've got the quinella, trifecta and quadrella." He jumped for joy and everyone was excited for him.'

But sadness met the story of AFL star David Schwarz, published in Melbourne's *Herald Sun* three weeks after the Price story. Schwarz admitted to being virtually penniless when he retired in 2002 with a 15-year gambling addiction.

'I lost $20,000 in a day,' he is quoted as saying, the same amount Wendell made in one punt. 'Then you go home and get up the next day and chase, trying to get it back. It's that never-ending circle of chasing your tail and trying to find money to get it back.

'I won $300,000 in three weeks. I bought a house, but I had to sell the house because I couldn't afford to keep the repayments going. When you punt, some days you are flushed and you've got thousands in your pocket, and the next day you can't afford to pay 49 cents in your parking meter.'

Schwarz, once a superstar with Melbourne before a triple knee reconstruction, said his addiction was so consuming, friends would tell him the results of race meetings at half-time of games. 'I was horribly addicted,' he told the newspaper. 'It consumed my life. It's a disease, a real disease, as serious as drugs and alcohol.'

Although earning $400,000 a year, he made so many drawings on his football salary, he ended the season receiving a cheque for $20,000.

'I got hooked on the pokies; I got hooked on bloody blackjack; I got hooked on roulette; I got hooked on the horses, the trots, dogs, everything.

'But not footy. The thing about footy is I'm not sure if betting on footy can affect the result of a match. But you can bet on possessions, bet on player versus player. And if you knew a player was in the backline or got a tagging role, or it's Mitchell versus Stevens — that can be manipulated. But you're just asking for trouble if you're betting on the footy.'

It's difficult to believe a player so addicted to gambling would not punt on something where he had the most knowledge, but no-one has come forward to dispute Schwarz's admissions.

As Healy says of today's players, 'They're not allowed to bet, even on themselves. They all have a lash but do it through friends –

who wins the Brownlow, team betting in some small way. Margin betting means things can be manipulated. I don't think you could ever get a team to lie down. For the sake of winning $200 to do something ridiculous is something a player would not consider.'

While Healy is not a regular punter, many of his colleagues in the football media are. In rugby league, the major commentators are fierce punters and there is an ever-present risk it influences their call. The Man of the Match in State of Origin games was once chosen by the TV commentators. To guard against criticism that the commentators selected the winner and then backed him, the ARL asked the national selectors to choose the award.

Their bosses are equally switched on to gambling.

When Channel Nine lost the AFL rights contract to a Seven/Ten consortium, the misery at the Packer compound could have been related to the fact AFL was the only sporting organisation to sign an agreement with Betfair.

The looming spectre in sport is punters sitting at home with split digital screens, betting via the remote on matches in progress, with players staring up at the big screen at stadiums, watching the goal they kicked turn some punters into princes and others to paupers.

It is a long way from the day Brisbane's Allan Langer went to the coin toss for choice of ends with $50 in his sock to bet with the opposition captain on who would win the toss. Even longer ago are South Melbourne captain Ron Clegg and Richmond's Don 'Mopsy' Fraser, who played with the football program stuffed in their socks. In those days, the program also included race meetings, and the results of races were shown on the scoreboard.

When play moved away from Clegg and Mopsy, they would compare the result on the scoreboard with the form in their socks, according to Lindsay Fox, the former St Kilda truckie turned multi-millionaire. Theirs was a world, far from the information age, when gossip travelled at warp speed, probably just as quickly as it does today by email.

'My wife, Paula, left her bag in the car in the main street with the door unlocked,' Fox recalls. 'Somebody stole the bag and I got a phone call from Cleggy to say he had the bag. If I came down to The Argo pub in South Yarra and bought him a beer, he'd give me the bag back.' Lindsay knew that a rich man entering The Argo was equivalent to a fat man walking into a cannibal convention and asking, 'Anybody know how I can lose all this weight?'

But he went just the same.

'Two blokes were standing with Cleggy at the bar, and they give me the bag and I buy them a beer,' he says. 'When I get home, Paula and I look in the bag. The purse is gone, but there is a note in the bag. It reads, "This Fox is a mean old fox. Give your wife more money."'

Some wives spend gambling money their sportsmen husbands haven't earned, the subject of a delightful story told by former champion jockey, now trainer, Ron Quinton. It's a tale that again demonstrates the unfairness of sport, but the curious way it makes amends.

'It was the second running of the Magic Millions race on the Gold Coast in 1988,' Quinton says. 'I was on Molokai Prince and [jockey] John Marshall had this thing called Prince Regent. It was a pretty normally run race and in the straight my horse hit the front. Marshall's horse challenged inside the last three-quarters of a furlong. He ran up and headed me and made slight contact.

'I stopped riding immediately, put the whip down and made use of the contact, albeit being very light. It's what I'd been taught to do in the circumstances. Subsequently – and in some quarters controversially – the protest was upheld. Back at the hotel where we were staying, the wives were sitting around the pool, listening to the race on the radio. There was no TV coverage in those days.

'They heard the race as Marshall first, Quinton second. My wife, Margaret, said to Marshall's wife, Debbie, that second place at least paid for our expenses. Debbie is very happy, so she buys champagne for everyone. None of the girls knew about the protest and the final result. We all came home separately from the track and go to our rooms.

'When I walk in, Margaret says "Bad luck," and I say, "What are you talking about? I won on a protest." So she is very happy. Meanwhile Marshall walks into his room and Debbie is happy, and he's got a glum face and explains he lost on protest.

'My room was happy and his was sad, so I decided to give his room a ring. There were no mobile phones in those days. I told him we were all going to dinner and he should come. I said, "Shit happens." He declined, saying, "No, I won't worry." I told him not to begrudge me the win because the big races were coming up and he and [trainer] Bart Cummings had all the best horses.

'As it turns out, they did clean up, winning most of the Group 1 races.'

BAD BOYS AND BOARDROOM BATTLES

Fans complain that sport is now merely business. They feel justified when some bad boy of business, sponsoring sport to legitimise his activities, is exposed as an Enronesque wheeler-dealer.

Jailed felon Brad Cooper was vice president of Collingwood, courtesy of a $250,000 sponsorship from HIH Insurance, until both the company and the businessman drowned in a sea of red ink.

The Canterbury Bulldogs protest that all their salary cap problems began when they embraced Sydney businessman Al Constantinidis, a man former Prime Minister Paul Keating famously fell out with over investment in a piggery. Big Al initially beguiled the Bulldogs board, despite Keating's quoting a Greek archbishop who told him no-one should be fooled by the fact Constantinidis looked 'like a giant altar boy'. However, as events transpired, Big Al was merely the conduit for the illicit payments.

The football codes aren't saturated with scoundrels like professional boxing, but they do seem to be caught at the crossroads. Football is too much of a business to be a sport in the minds of the assistant stationmasters and plumbers who ran football clubs in the 1960s. To them, i's, not coms, were dotted.

Football is too much of a sport to be a business, according to millionaires like Peter Holmes à Court, who now owns South Sydney, the club once called 'The Pride of the League'. Businessmen speak the language of sport. Snap the ostentatious braces of most chief executive officers of public companies and a sports metaphor falls out. Bosses want 'team players'; directors 'go into bat' for each other or 'put the boot in'; an idea comes from 'left field'; companies play 'hard ball' in order to ensure the market isn't 'a level playing field'. The words 'blue chip' now refer almost universally to an athlete, not stock in a well-performing company.

Young chief executives resemble male sport stars with their huge salaries and win-at-all-costs attitude. When the Swans' Barry Hall travelled to Melbourne to answer a tribunal charge, he did so on the executive jet of a business friend.

Entertainers and sports stars have swapped positions with businessmen. The old Australian business establishment has retreated into football. The Roosters' board is nicknamed 'Millionaires Row', with chairman Nick Politis, who made his money in cars; Mark Bouris, who started Wizard Home Loans; Peter 'Talky' Newton, who trades in mining shares; David Gyngell, the former boss of Channel Nine; and Mark McInnes, the managing director of retail giant David Jones. For these men, money is a way of keeping score, while Roosters players score in order to make money.

Football players wear suits to games, while advertising executives wear up-market sneakers to work. The best example of the elevation of the new sport and entertainment elite is Oscar-winning actor Russell Crowe reading the eulogy of Australia's richest man, Kerry Packer, in the company of South Sydney footballers and Australian cricketers.

Crowe's fealty to his footballers must have been tested when he had caterers provide a barbecue for South Sydney players after a training session at Erskinville Oval. One player picked up a fillet steak, wrapped it around his penis and handed it to 'Master and Commander' who, according to one observer, 'copped it sweet'. Crowe acquired the nickname 'Mixed Grill', because he was the only one to have a sausage with his steak.

Bill Veeck, one-time owner of the Chicago White Sox, once famously said, 'I have discovered in 20 years of moving around a ballpark, that knowledge of the game is usually in inverse proportion to the price of the seats.' Perhaps this explains why the one sport that can call upon Australia's wealthiest businessmen and cleverest corporate lawyers – rugby union – has the most amateurish boards of all the football codes. Perhaps TS Eliot had rugby union directors in mind when he wrote in his play *The Cocktail Party* that 'half of the harm that is done in this world is due to people who want to feel important'.

John O'Neill, now chief executive of Football Federation Australia (the renamed Soccer Australia), is a lawyer whose first big job was chief executive of State Bank (NSW). The truth is the luck of the sportsman landed him the job. The incumbent was Nick Whitlam, son of former Prime Minister Gough Whitlam.

Nick, who had already signalled his departure, went on a tour of the ancient building just after office hours one weeknight and found O'Neill was the only one there. Whitlam rewarded this diligence, promoting O'Neill rapidly, eventually recommending him for his own post. O'Neill was merely killing time that night until rugby training started. He was coach of a Sydney University lower grade team and found it more convenient to remain in the office than cross the Harbour Bridge twice.

But the amateurish mechanics of this appointment paled compared to another that occurred at O'Neill's next job, chief executive of the Australian Rugby Union.

'I had been head of the State Bank for eight years and been headhunted for the rugby job,' he told me one day as we sat in his FFA office. He had just returned from Leipzig, Germany, where the 2006 World Cup soccer draw had been held, the first draw including Australia in 32 years. 'I was to start on October 8, 1995, a Monday, but on the preceding Friday, Phil Harry, the president, asked me to observe an ARU Council meeting.

'Under the old constitution, the governing body had 14 grey, faceless men – five from NSW, three from Queensland and one each from the smaller states. Plus there were life members, representatives of the schools, referees, armed services – all the affiliated bodies. They met on the top floor of the Mount Street, North Sydney [ARU] office. I'd come in like a shiny new pin, with my shoes polished and nicely dressed. Leo Williams was the chairman. The big decision of the day was the appointment of the Wallaby coach. We'd just had the World Cup [in South Africa] and the wounds were very raw. There were three candidates: Bob Dwyer, John Connolly and the dark horse, Greg Smith. This meeting decided every position from coach down to baggage master. It was a ludicrous way to run sport.

'The preceding couple of weeks I had been taken out to dinner, and the subject of the coach was raised. I'd been told Connolly was a shoe-in. Dwyer was regarded as treacherous [following the near sell-out to World Rugby Corporation] and Smith didn't have the form. Connolly from Queensland was even money favourite. The whole room was divided on party lines.

'The night before the meeting, they had all been to dinner and the vote trading had taken place, the politics of rugby being played out. The election went to secret ballot. The result was declared and Greg Smith was the coach. The three Queenslanders, led by Dick McGruther, uttered some colourful language and stormed out. There was some serious finger pointing in the direction of the smaller states, particularly the representative of South Australia.

'He was seriously under suspicion for selling his vote. I sat there dumbstruck. Having left the genteel world of banking, watching this high farce play out, I was determined my first job was to change the constitution and change the ARU to an unlisted public company.

'There were some very big cheesy grins from the NSW forces. The NSW powerbrokers – [corporate undertaker] Ian Ferrier in particular – didn't want Dwyer and couldn't bring themselves to vote for Connolly. They voted for Smith, but I suspect their intention was he be a short-term coach until Rod Macqueen was ready.' (Redemption in rugby moves at a glacial pace. More than ten years after being passed over, 'Knuckles' Connolly was finally appointed Wallaby coach following the sacking of Eddie Jones.)

'The postscript to the story,' O'Neill continued, 'is a month later I was at a [ARU] finance committee meeting, and I found the budget had allocated $50,000 to the South Australian RU for their international sevens tournament. I asked, "What's that 50 grand for?"' O'Neill's question had the same answer as 'What's in the sausages?' 'I was told, "Don't ask."'

When McGruther became chairman, growing disillusionment with O'Neill put McGruther under pressure. 'Dick was my Great Protector,' O'Neill said of a united campaign by NSW, Queensland and the ACT to get rid of him over his outspoken views. McGruther didn't mind expressing a few opinions of his own, including complaining about a second-rate team England had sent to Australia. It was the biggest sell-out since Gallipoli, according to McGruther, who the English press subsequently called 'the biggest dick since Turpin'.

'They had to get rid of one of us and it was going to be me, but it was unaffordable to pay me out,' O'Neill admitted. 'They had all come to Canberra for a board meeting and a Test match, and the mood was foul. NSW moved a no-confidence motion in Dick, and all but myself and [another representative] voted for it. They took me to task and I told them turkeys don't vote for Christmas. Everyone went back to the hotel, spending the afternoon in huddles, getting primed for the Test match.

'McGruther became a man on a mission. If anyone came within ten feet of him, he was going to knock their block off. Everyone went scurrying down the corridors when he appeared, except Steve Williams – six foot eight inches tall, 15 years his junior. McGruther gave him a gobful outside the men's urinal.

'Williams said to McGruther, "What do you want me to do about it?" Dick looked at the big, strapping former second-rower, still as fit as when he played for the Wallabies, and said, "Nothing today."'

Tension built after the Test match, with the New Zealand officials joining in, the chairman accusing O'Neill of deserting McGruther.

'I lost it when he said that,' O'Neill confessed. 'He was poking his finger in my chest and vice versa. It was the most volatile night ever. Electric. Blood everywhere. McGruther was blacklisted from the free ticket list at Test matches because they were scared he'd job someone. I left him on the list until the new chairman sidled up to me one day and said he thought it would be a good idea to take him off.'

Queensland officials tend to be the most volatile, even at Reds selection meetings. Big, craggy-faced, cigarette smoking former Wallaby prop Stan Pilecki landed a punch on one of his fellow selectors following a difference of opinion. These meetings were more open than many councils of the code's head body, the International Rugby Board.

Former ARU deputy chairman Ross Turnbull recalls a particularly tense IRB meeting held at a manor outside London, close to a

RAF fighter-bomber base. 'The meeting was held to celebrate the centenary of rugby, and as we lay in bed on the Sunday morning, you could hear the planes taking off to bomb Libya. Then, when we went down to breakfast, news of a New Zealand rebel tour arriving in South Africa had broken. South Africa still had a representative on the board, Dr Danie Craven, even though they were banned from playing international rugby.'

To borrow the line from former US President Lyndon Johnson, the IRB thought it better to have South Africa 'inside the tent pissing out, than outside the tent pissing in'. But news of the rebel tour threatened to drench the code, and all eyes turned to two old war horses – Dr Craven and the New Zealand chairman, Cec Blazey.

Turnbull says, 'They eyed each other off and then both denied any knowledge of the tour. They lived in communities where any whisper would be heard within seconds, yet they knew nothing.'

O'Neill adroitly manipulated the competing egos on the IRB to win Australia the role of sole host of the 2003 World Cup and then proceeded to organise the best tournament the code has seen. But ARU chairman Bob Tuckey and his successor, Sydney businessman Dilip Kumar, forced his resignation and O'Neill's Irish hatred will never allow him to forgive them. When Kumar, a Sri Lankan-born car dealer, was ousted in a Queensland led coup, O'Neill sent a voice message to me from Germany.

'What goes around, comes around,' he said, offering me the opportunity to quote him in the *Herald*. 'What a coincidence it is, that almost two years to the day they decided they no longer wanted me, they now had a chairman resign. The boards of sporting bodies really need to be more transparent and need to be more accountable why these things happen.'

Back in his FFA office, O'Neill elaborated, pointing to the handcuffs big business applies to prevent CEOs from moving to a rival company. 'Imagine the boss of Woolworths being allowed by his board to move over to head Coles?' he said.

He has subsequently pieced together the jigsaw puzzle of his own sacking.

'David Crombie, now president of the QRU, is a very reputable bloke,' he says of the Queensland millionaire agribusinessman, who was an ARU director during O'Neill's term but now holds the ceremonial position of state president. 'I asked him one day, "My departure never went to board, did it?" Crombie said no. The NSW group wanted me out, but Tuckey selectively dealt with each one separately. There were three options: extend my contract, leave me in the post for a year as a lame duck or let me go.

'Tuckey was nervous. "What do you want to do?" he asked. I said stay on for a few years. He indicated that wasn't an option, so I said, "You've got the three options. Extend?" He said no. I asked if this was unanimous and he said yes. I asked was there a reason and he said, "We're looking for a different style." I said, "That's it?" He said yep.

'That left two options. I said the lame duck wasn't good for either of us, so let's agree on an early termination. Within two hours the lawyers had agreed to early termination. I asked, "Is the board across this?" and Tuckey said yes. I went to the board meeting and Tuckey asked me to leave it to the end. He said, "We'll keep it short and sweet."

'The end of the meeting came and he said, "As you know, John has asked to move on early and we wish him the best." Crombie's face was one of enormous surprise, and the others all had their heads down. I made a heartfelt farewell speech and left the room. I can't recall anyone shaking my hand, except Crombie walking into my office afterwards. He said, "What was that all about?"

They didn't know I had an offer from Frank Lowy [chairman of the then named Soccer Australia] in my back pocket.'

O'Neill then behaved like a man executing a plan he'd downloaded into his Machiavellian mind for such an occasion. 'After taking some holidays, I saw Tuckey and told him about the soccer position and he said, "You didn't tell me about that when we negotiated your departure." I said, "I didn't have to." It was my entitlement. Tuckey said that if he knew I was going to work for one of the competitors, he would have acted differently.'

Tuckey said that O'Neill should have put them on notice, unaware O'Neill had already gazumped him with a typically cunning manoeuvre.

'I told him that, since returning to work, I had informed everyone, on ARU letterhead, where I was going and the letters had already gone out. I reminded him that, under the agreement, which expired on February 27, I was still the CEO of the ARU.'

O'Neill, trained in law, had therefore acted within the strict letter of it, if not its spirit.

Furthermore, while rugby slumbered in the euphoria of the successful World Cup, O'Neill used the vapours of these indignities as fuel. He busied himself with his new code, sacking a coach and appointing one who would steer Australia to soccer's World Cup, the biggest sporting event on the world stage.

He also guaranteed Australia's future in the sport by taking it out of the weak Oceania division and into the Asian confederation, inaugurated the A-League competition and even changed soccer's name to the one with which most of the world identifies – football.

He is a first-class performer in the boardroom and media, elusive with directors while appearing candid and always knows when to become 'a highly placed source'. Who knows where the ambitious, capable O'Neill, on a salary of $1 million a year, will move next and whether his independent management style will draw him into conflict with Lowy, Australia's second richest man and one accustomed to having his own way. Their egos collided in Germany over who would secure Australia's next World Cup coach, and O'Neill, whose contract had ended, was in no hurry to start negotiations on a new term.

When Australia qualified for the 2006 World Cup, my first thoughts were for Eddie Thomson, a coach with whom O'Neill would have related. Thomson, a former top grade player in Scotland, was close to Lowy, who hired him to coach the Jewish club Sydney Hakoah.

St George, which I was coaching at the time, and Eddie's team would often train together, the pair of us wickedly conspiring to organise training drills to expose the weaknesses of our own players. Eddie would arrange for his most timid player to tackle the Dragons' fierce Tongan John Fifita while I'd put a lumbering prop in goal to catch soccer balls. Afterwards, we'd drink buckets of beer, go home, burn a steak and chat.

After coaching the Socceroos, Olyroos and then working in Japan, Eddie suffered a brain disease, retired to his eastern suburbs Sydney home and died in 2003. He loved Australia and, with wife Pauline, drove around our island continent, an achingly apt example of the SAD generation: See Australia and Die.

We had dinner at the Bellevue Hotel in Paddington shortly before his death, and he challenged his inevitable fate by having one small glass of white wine, knowing it would kick in badly the following day.

The Bellevue boasts the fare loved by men in their 50s and 60s – bangers and mash, crumbed cutlets, corned silverside and cabbage. When Suzie Carleton, former wife of the late *60 Minutes*'s Richard Carleton, owned it, the pub was a popular haunt of ALP powerbrokers. The regulars who drink there, including Ken 'The

Sergeant' Bowditch (the retired NSW police detective who conducted the NRL enquiry into sexual assault allegations against the Bulldogs), are not known for their political correctness. When Paul Keating was campaigning for his 'unwinnable' election, Suzie approached Bowditch and his mates, pleading with them not to say anything disrespectful to the visiting Member for Bankstown.

Not that Keating was unfamiliar with the lowest strata of Australian idiom. According to former Federal Sports Minister John Brown, Keating once attended Junee RSL Club, which had booked two top shows at much expense to the management – Les Girls and black American singer Lovelace Watkins.

The mob didn't appreciate Les Girls, jeering and booing, and the general noise level hadn't diminished after Lovelace began his gig. The club manager interjected to bring the unruly audience to attention, booming over the club's sound system, 'Listen, if youze don't give the coon a go, I'll bring back the poofters.'

The Bellevue's idiom is more refined, with pre-lunch Sunday drinks called 'choir practice'.

It was important that I had dinner with Eddie, because I had let him down badly at the Bellevue a couple of months earlier. We'd arranged to meet at 6 pm and I had another meeting at 8. When Eddie hadn't arrived by 6.45, I phoned his home and he apologised, explaining his ailment caused him to mix up times. So we only had about three quarters of an hour before I had to go, and I felt so bad leaving him there, sitting sallow, sad and all alone, staring into a soft drink.

It was Eddie who led the push to have soccer played in the Australian summer, rather than compete with the major football codes. He managed to tiptoe through the long minefield of the sport's ethnic rivalry, both on the pitch and at code headquarters, only for him to die before stability and World Cup qualification came.

Sydney businessman Ian Knop, who was chairman of Soccer Australia prior to the federal government-imposed Lowy takeover, can attest to the bitterness between the factions. 'One board meeting in Sydney, I had a difference of opinion with Perth-based Paul Afkos and Adelaide's Les Avory,' he told me, a reference to the impasse between the old rump of Soccer Australia, who sought to retain both their power and their blazers, and Knop, an instrument of reform. 'Afkos said he had a good mind to give me a thrashing and Avory told him, "When you're finished, I'd like to follow." So I said, "Why don't we do it now? Why bother going outside? So I'll start with you [Afkos], then him, will I?" They shut up. They knew I meant it. But the worst thing is I meant it. I wanted to hit them.

'Then I felt ashamed. I felt sick. I felt dirty. I've never said anything like that in my adult, corporate life. I thought when you reach that level, you've got to get out. Two days later, I resigned.'

Although Knop and Afkos were both closely connected with the Liberal Party, their political affiliation meant nothing at the soccer board table.

Incidentally, two political opponents once found a soccer crowd even more intimidating than anything they had faced in their respective party rooms. When Neville Wran and Jeff Kennett retired as premiers, they subsequently became soccer officials. One night, while attending a major match in Melbourne, a spectator brawl threatened to invade the VIP area. Wran pointed to a rear high, wire fence and told Kennett in his raspy way, 'Jeffrey, this is every man for himself. I'm 20 years older than you, but I bet I can get over that bloody fence before you.'

*

Eddie's early relationship with Lowy was a precursor to the American and English models where teams are owned by multinational corporations or billionaires who made their fortunes elsewhere. The new bosses tend to approach the club, or 'franchise' as it is called in America, like they would any other business. A season is defined in terms of targets and goals, some more realistic than others.

Rupert Murdoch's News Ltd, which owns three NRL clubs, has not demonstrated the impatience of some of the owners of American baseball and football clubs, who tend to favour instant gratification over growth. However, News Ltd did enjoy early success with the Melbourne Storm, who won a premiership in its second year, and there were rumblings in corridors of Holt Street, Sydney, when their Cowboys made mistakes in their preparation for the 2005 Grand Final.

The boards of all clubs are taking greater heed of the voice of the fans. The beer-fuelled chants from the hill, the rants, the yak attack of sports talkback radio and the calls for action on internet message boards are no longer so breezily dismissed in the boardrooms.

I often think about how Jack Gibson would perform in today's corporate era. At Christmas 2005, he asked his long-time friend Ron Massey, 'Ronny, do you think we could get back into coaching?'

Massey, 76 and hobbling badly, replied, 'No, Jack. I'm not going back.'

Jack thought for some time and said, 'I can handle the training, provided I don't have to go to games on Sundays.'

Massey, always one to bring a discussion to a conclusion with a pungent observation, said, 'You've revolutionised coaching in many ways, but that would be your biggest innovation – being the first coach not to turn up to a match.'

Maybe Jack, who occupied a Pharaonic perch, would have taken the new owners and boards head on. After all, as Massey recalls, Jack stood up to Kerry Packer, the benefactor of the Roosters, and to the club boss, Ron Jones.

'Jack and I were sitting together and the phone rang and it was Ron Jones. Jack motioned for me to pick up the other phone and I heard Ron say, "Kerry and I have been talking and we think this should be the team." Jack listened to their team and said that's terrific. Then he said it wouldn't be the one running out on the paddock and hung up.

'It happened during 1975 [a premiership year], after we'd lost a couple of games. The next weekend, we beat [star-studded] Manly at Manly.'

Nor did Massey demonstrate he was intimidated by powerful businessmen. While chief executive of Cronulla in the early 1990s he attended a conference of club bosses at Wollongong. Packer was the guest speaker, shortly after he died the first time, falling off a polo pony following a heart attack. AFL chief executive John Quayle organised two questions for Packer – one from Parramatta boss Denis Fitzgerald and another from Massey.

Fitzgerald prepared a two-page question on the viability of pay TV, delivering his long preamble before asking Packer, 'Has it any future in Australia?'

Packer, who enjoyed embarrassing anyone with the temerity to ask him a question, gave a three-word answer. 'No. Next question.'

Massey came next with a question about the future of form guides for midweek race meetings appearing in newspapers, predicting the TAB would sponsor this with generous advertising. Again Packer was incorrect, saying he didn't think the proposal was viable.

Massey, never one to be humbled, stood up again and told a story, which had as its unstated but obvious message that both men weighed in excess of 16 stone.

'I was up at Jack's farm, riding a horse named Velvet,' he began, his voice so deep it seemed to rumble up from somewhere near the earth's core. 'The big old mare lay down with its four legs in the air. Fair dinkum, I thought I'd killed it. So I went away and came back with a can of petrol and thought I'd burn it before Jack got home. When I walk into the paddock, the horse jumps up and says, "Not you again."'

When the laughter subsided, Massey directed his question to Packer, 'What did your horse say to you when it tipped you off?'

A nervous silence followed. No-one said a word. Embarrassment began to sweep over the gathering. Then Packer began to laugh, and everyone dutifully followed.

Massey told me these stories while we sat in his home in Sydney's southern suburbs, a glass of water each and a $90 Christmas cake especially imported from a Texas bakery that his sweet tooth had identified on one of his coaching trips to the United States with Jack.

'Did I ever tell you the smartest thing Jack ever did as a coach?' he asked, unsure whether I was aware, as a past St George coach, of Jack's battles with selectors at the same club a decade earlier. 'It was how we got [second-rower] Peter Fitzgerald into the team.'

But the meandering story began with Jack's troublesome back and the old coach's legendary refusal to disguise it. 'Jack did his back in in 1971, and I drove him to the eastern suburbs hospital where they put him in traction. It was the worst trip I have ever had. He bellowed like a stuck pig every time I braked and yelled every time I pulled up at the lights. He missed the game at the weekend, and there were no videos, no film of the game.

'In the game, [Brian] Chicka Norton had run 50 yards and scored a try in the far corner of the old Sports Ground. Before that, Chicka had not been playing well. Jack wanted him out of the team and wanted Peter Fitzgerald, a tackling machine, in. But when we went to St George, we inherited their selectors and Jack always had a problem with selectors. He was always outvoted by the four selectors when it came to getting Peter Fitzgerald in the team.

'So he gets out of hospital and is determined to get Peter Fitzgerald in. When he mentioned his name, all he got was, "Oh Jack, you should have seen the try Chicka Norton scored." But he couldn't see it. There was no video. He had to come up with a scheme at the selectors' meeting.

'There were two players at St George who were head and shoulders above everyone – Graeme Langlands and Billy Smith. So we start at the fullback and Jack says, "I'm not happy with Langlands. I want to give the young bloke in second grade a go." The four selectors say, "Oh Jack, you can't leave Langlands out." And Jack is outvoted.

'Then it goes through the rest of the backs and comes down to Billy Smith at half. Jack says, "I want Mark Shulman in." And he's outvoted again.

'Then it comes to Chicka Norton and Peter Fitzgerald, and they all say, "I wish you had seen that try Chicka scored." And Jack says, "I wish I'd seen the friggin' try too."

'They argued and Jack said, "I'm the coach. I'm the one who has to bear the responsibility of a loss. I gave you your way with Langlands and Smith, don't I get my way with anybody?"'

Massey began chuckling at the memory, before saying of the duped selectors, 'They said, "All right, Jack, you've got Peter Fitzgerald in your team."'

Massey, aware St George selectors might communicate selection secrets to the players, warned Gibson he should immediately inform Langlands and Smith of the deception. Not that Gibson hid his disappointment with Chicka from Chicka.

ARL chief executive Geoff Carr was then a winger with the Dragons and remembers Gibson's address to the team following the selectors' meeting. It had been a memorable game for Carr. He had scored three tries in the final 20 minutes and hoped to win 2SM commentator Frank Hyde's Seiko watch as player of the match, but Chicka's try had impressed Frank more.

Carr challenges Massey's memory on only two points: the match was at the SCG and Chicka ran 80 metres. He recalls Gibson telling Norton, 'That was a great try, but you only made four tackles and you are a front-rower. If I want someone to run 80 metres to score a try, I'll get him [pointing to Carr] to do it.'

Nor did Jack win all battles with officials. He was only sacked once – as coach of Souths.

'The president of the club had a go at the players after they'd lost one Sunday,' Massey recalled. 'Jack ordered him out of the dressing room. That was the beginning of the end.'

One coach who didn't so much battle with the boardroom as ignore them was Tom Raudonikis. Before transferring back to Sydney to coach Wests and NSW, he moved around the Brisbane clubs, including coaching Brothers where he once brought an actual ox's heart to training and demonstrated his love of blood by smearing it over himself.

Tom knew the Brothers' board intended to replace him with another coach, Ross Strudwick, but they didn't have the courage to tell him. As the club's end-of-season dinner loomed and with no word from the officials, Tom phoned me for help in preparing a farewell speech. 'I want a really classy one with Shakespeare stuff, which makes those bastards on the board squirm,' he said.

Knowing Tom's first school after the Cowra migrant camp was the local convent and aware that Brothers is a Catholic club, I led off with the virtues the nuns had taught – loyalty, honesty and love your neighbour. The speech then moved to Shakespeare's *Julius Caesar*, with Tommy pointing to the particular director who had stabbed him in the back, saying, 'Et tu, Brute?'

As I dictated the speech to Tom over the phone from Sydney that Saturday afternoon, he wrote it down and began practising it. Then he drove to Brisbane airport to collect Henry Foster, a young Aboriginal halfback from Penrith who was to collect the Brothers' player of the year trophy at the dinner.

On the journey to the city, Tom tried his speech out on Henry, who allowed him only a couple of sentences before saying, 'You're fuckin' kiddin', Tom.'

Worried he'd have trouble remembering it all, Tom rang again in a mild panic and asked if he could read the speech. I encouraged him to, saying it demonstrated thought and preparation and would impress the audience. He seemed relieved, saying he would stuff the speech down the front of his pants and retrieve it if necessary.

'But you've got to promise me one thing before you speak,' I told him. 'Only have three schooners!'

About 3 am the phone in my Sydney home rang. It was a jubilant Tommy. It seemed the audience reacted in stages, like a rocket travelling into space. First there was stunned silence at the Brutus line, then laughter, followed by incredible clapping.

'The players and their wives got up on the tables and stood there cheering,' he said. The directors sat there looking like mongrel dogs. And you know what? I had the speech down the front of my strides and didn't have to pull it out.' Then there was a longer pause, one that conveyed something more than words ever could.

'I have a confession to make,' the former altar boy said. 'I had six schooners.'

Tom's dress sense didn't endear him to directors. When he moved to coach Ipswich, which included the Walters brothers and Allan Langer, the club president gave him a $300 voucher for the local menswear store. 'Don't they think I dress proper?' an indignant Tom asked me by phone.

His grooming hadn't improved when he moved to Sydney and took charge of the Blues. He once appeared on stage at a sponsors' function where then NSWRL chief executive Neil Whittaker observed he wasn't wearing socks. An assistant was ordered to add socks to Tom's wardrobe. When told he was about to become the beneficiary of a week's supply of black socks, honest Tom admitted, 'I don't wear no underpants either.'

Raudonikis and the carefully attired Gibson were polar opposites as coaches, not only in their fashion sense. Gibson was part pedagogue, part demagogue, moulding men and championing the virtues of discipline, pride and responsibility. He was the first coach to argue that a bloke who was an idiot through the week was not likely to be different on Sundays.

'If you dress a mug up in a tuxedo and put him in a Rolls Royce and you open the door of the car, what have you got?' he asked, with the answer clearly being 'a mug'. The Swans' Paul Roos espoused the same philosophy with his 'no dickheads' policy, ridding the club of disruptive personnel.

'Jack pushed that principle in the 70s,' Massey says. 'People would ring him regarding some problem child and they'd say, "He'll play well for you." Jack would say, "I'd rather he play for someone else." The problem children are a big problem in the game now, particularly with the binge drinking.'

Raudonikis culled the difficult ones by different means, giving them an opportunity, but when they showed a lack of moral courage, he eyeballed and outed them. Today's coach cuts a vastly different figure. They have an army of assistants, even full-time 'leadership coaches', to instil teamwork and modify the behaviour of the egomaniacs. Whereas there were two full-time employees when I coached St George and none at Wests, the number of coaching and training assistants almost exceeds the playing group at some clubs today. Parramatta's 2005 photo of its three teams has

104 players and 71 officials; the first grade photo has 25 players and 24 officials.

An assistant coach can spend his working life as a No. 2 man, moving around the clubs, never getting a top job, content to be a video-watcher and skills coach, a bleary-eyed lifer free from the media glare.

'After the first death there is no other,' Dylan Thomas wrote, but he didn't know about football coaches. Some have as many chances of nirvana as a Hindu soul, with the opportunity to move from life to life, learning, yearning and earning as they go. Some clairvoyants see dead people, coaches see the next job opportunity.

Before a ball had been kicked in the 2006 NRL season, four clubs had already indicated they would have new coaches for the 2007 season, with three of them appointing head coaches at other clubs. By May 2006 one of them had gone, with Brian Smith finding his position at Parramatta untenable following a series of withering losses. Smith, signed to coach Newcastle in 2007, headed to Bradford in England to see out the rest of the season as assistant coach.

The boards of the major football codes in Australia have, overall, shown a tolerance with coaches, sacking them only after a reasonable tenure of failure. There are long-termers like the Broncos' Wayne Bennett and Kevin Sheedy at AFL club Essendon who, when they retire, will sound like Robert Duvall in *Apocalypse Now*, wistfully describing the victorious smell of napalm in the morning. Maybe that is why they hold on so long, fearing the emptiness of retirement – the 'quiet desperation' in our lives that the American philosopher Thoreau talked about, when there is no prospect of a creative, meaningful future.

If the life span of coaches has increased, salaries have gone up just as dramatically. They are getting more pay and less job satisfaction, making some inured to a loss, rationalising the defeat in terms of some statistic seemingly outside their control, content to turn up at the office at 8 am.

To be fair, they are beset by pressures their forebears did not endure. The salary cap means a club cannot make a top talent happy via the cheque book, forcing the coach to treat his star halfback like a Ming vase. Even then, they are betrayed by underachieving players with gross, usually guaranteed, contracts.

If a coach shows loyalty to stars who have lost their shine and grown old, he is criticised for delaying the club's overhaul. But how do you cut the veterans who bleed for you, who do everything to bring you a title?

The internet means fans have more knowledge of the internal machinations of the club and the means to exert pressure on nervous boards with their unrealistic expectations. The power of coaches has also been undermined by the rise of player managers with whom the player often has a closer relationship and to whom he demonstrates more loyalty. This means today's footballer, often cosseted from the time he shows a glimmer of talent, makes more money than his coach and is flanked by apologists and sycophants.

The ethical lines with these agents are very blurry, although the football codes have attempted to introduce workable registration systems. If the player manager has a disproportionate number of players at one club on his books and makes a dubious investment with their monies, as occurred with agent George Mimis at St George Illawarra, it has the capacity to destabilise the club.

Australia will eventually move to the American model where the contemporary coach is a man under seige. The US baseball or football coach, even the venerable, at some clubs is little more than a well-paid temp who has to be prepared to return the keys of the sponsor's car whenever the boss's name appears on his mobile phone.

Former AFL coach Tony Jewell remembers being sacked by trucking magnate Lindsay Fox, who was brought in to revive St Kilda when the club fell into administration. Jewell admits leaking his impending resignation to a reporter and Fox summoning him, demanding he leave immediately because 'there had been too many leaks to the media'.

'He looked at me through those big, green eyes,' Jewell recalls, adding Fox was 'the only bloke at St Kilda I was frightened of'. Jewell walked out the door, thought about the money he was owed, gave additional thought to the fact that St Kilda was broke and strode back into the office. He asked Fox when he would be paid and was told in good time. Jewell then said, 'Unless I get it by noon tomorrow, I will be going to the press and exposing all the shit administration in this place.'

'You'll get your money by noon tomorrow,' Fox replied.

Asked to validate the meeting during a visit to his Toorak mansion, Fox smiled and declared it accurate. The meeting lasted longer than the one Fox had with his fellow directors when he was made chairman on the condition he stay for five years and resurrect the club's finances.

Fox had played for St Kilda for four years until, as he says, 'I asked the coach, Allan Jeans, "What's my future here?" And he said, "You don't have one."' Eighteen years later the club invited him back when its debts were believed to be $250,000.

'I brought in an auditor and they did a search and gave me a report showing the club was $1.6 million in debt,' Fox said. 'I addressed the seven directors and said I wanted each one to write me a cheque for $230,000 or resign immediately. They all resigned. It was the biggest, quickest exit of a board ever. A five minute job, but it probably avoided the first bankruptcy in AFL history.' You could almost hear the chuckle inside his words.

Fox's palace includes a garage of cars bigger than a standard house – including a Mercedes once driven by one of Hitler's generals. Further signs of opulence abound, such as African statues, a grand piano, giant Mediterranean vases, antique furniture and two McCubbin paintings, one a massive 1910 canvas of an Australian bush scene. But there are also mementos of a loving family, with photos of children and grandchilden filling every polished wooden table and his wife's tomato garden at the base of delicately pruned crab apple trees.

Lindsay, who enjoys introducing himself to the establishment with 'I'm just a simple truckie', also has a life-size oil painting of himself in hunting pinks. After he enjoys the viewer's reaction, he lets on that it is really some unidentified Englishman with the original face painted over with Lindsay's.

I sat with him years ago on the board of the Australian Sports Commission, the funding and policy arm of the federal government, and he hasn't changed, being devoid of pretence. He remains St Kilda's No. 1 ticket holder, dismissing his generous donations with a vague, 'I'm always called on to be involved.'

When it comes to boardroom brawls at one of rugby league's most successful clubs, the Bulldogs, the words of US senator Trent Lott come to mind. Lott once said that keeping a party of senators together was akin to 'loading bullfrogs into a wheelbarrow'.

The Bulldogs have won more premierships than any club since they broke through in 1980, and many of their key players have moved to the club's administration, leading to conflicts that undermine their capacity to harvest the real fruits of the game – lifelong team friendships. Canterbury touts itself as the 'family club', yet for much of the last quarter century it has been more like a bunch of squabbling siblings in the back seat of the family station wagon on a long, hot drive.

The bonds that tie South Sydney's four premiership teams from the late 1960s and early 1970s are unlikely to be replicated at Belmore.

Some of the Rabbitohs have bought adjoining properties on the NSW South Coast in order to spend their retirement years together.

Four months before he died of cancer, former Rabbitoh prop John O'Neill was anxious to ride a horse in company with his grandchildren on his property. Team-mate George Piggins lifted him onto the horse and, shocked at the weight loss of his front row partner, turned his head aside to disguise his tears.

The horse threw O'Neill and, as Piggins recalls, 'I drove him back to Sydney and he's got six broken ribs and liver cancer and there's not a tear on his face, and all he's saying is, "Gee, this is hurting."'

When O'Neill finally succumbed on 9 August 1999, the same day of the year that his fabled coach, Clive Churchill, passed away in 1985, further adding to the sacred numerology of the Rabbitohs, it was Piggins who told the world. 'A lovely bloke has died,' was the simple epithet offered from the O'Neill family home.

By contrast, at times there has been as much chance of peace in the Middle East as achieving lasting unity at Belmore. The three Mortimer brothers and three Hughes brothers, all members of the 1980 team, no longer attend past players' functions, a result, not of conflict with each other, but anger with the administration of president Dr George Peponis, their 1980 premiership captain.

Halfback Steve Mortimer, winner of four premierships, became Bulldog chief executive when the club was looking for a cleanskin legend to help redeem its image after the salary cap scandal. Steve appointed his brother Peter to the board, but he resigned when Steve was sacked for dismissing Garry Hughes in the wake of the Coffs Harbour sexual assault allegations. Garry won an out-of-court settlement for wrongful dismissal that, together with Steve's payout, cost Canterbury $750,000.

The Hughes trio are nephews of the late club patriarch Bullfrog Moore, whose daughter married Steve Folkes, the Bulldogs coach.

Bullfrog was a man so adroit at talking out of both sides of his mouth that he could probably eat miso soup and play the saxophone at the same time. He had a 'hee hee' laugh that sounded like the jingle of money.

Bullfrog held the club together, although Steve Mortimer identifies the nepotism he fostered as the root of the conflict. When it was evident Steve would become a superstar as a player, Moore would invite him to join a post-match Sunday night dinner group in the club's Chinese restaurant, a gathering that included Moore's nephews and sons-in-law, including premiership player and later coach Chris Anderson. Mortimer asked whether his own brothers could also join the group and, when told no, politely declined the invitation.

More than twenty years later, when Mortimer was appointed CEO, he gathered the football staff together and one of his old enemies opened proceedings with a question: 'Who fucking appointed you?' Mortimer responded with some vitriol of his own, but the message was clear – he was never going to change the club's culture.

Nepotism appeared to be part of the Bulldogs' salary cap scandal. The club's executive president at the time, Gary McIntyre, wanted to install his son, David, a lawyer, as chief financial officer of all the Bulldogs' operations, including an ill-fated partnership with Liverpool Council to build a new stadium called Oasis.

One impediment was the incumbent chief executive of the football club, Bob Hagan. McIntyre Snr wrote Hagan a letter, detailing excess spending on players, including $1 million in illicit payments via the Oasis project, clearly identified as salary cap breaches. The letter was delivered to Hagan in Auckland where the Bulldogs were playing the Warriors and was guaranteed to enter the public domain, but McIntyre Snr, also a lawyer, reasoned that any salary cap breach would be punishable by a fine.

The NRL salary cap rules specify a one point loss for every $50,000 to a maximum of four premiership points, to be deducted the following year. However, the fine print also allows the NRL to impose an additional penalty at its own discretion for a breach of 'exceptional circumstance'. McIntyre was willing to pay a $500,000 fine, not a burden on an organisation which then made $12 million profit annually, but he never believed the team would be stripped of 37 premiership points.

Such is rugby league's culture of mateship, the Bulldogs board believed NRL chief executive David Gallop would be lenient. After all, Gallop was employed by News Ltd when it began Super League and Canterbury was its prize signing. Furthermore, Gallop had always been given the best seat in the Bulldogs' corporate box whenever he attended a home game.

But McIntyre did not read Gallop's resolve, his respect for law, his reading of an appalled public's reaction to the cheating, his immunity to duchessing and, most importantly, his determination to seize the opportunity to demonstrate to a less-than-convinced rugby league world that he was a strong man.

In fact, aware the *Herald* was breaking the salary cap scandal the following day, Gallop went to the Bulldogs' box for their Friday night game. It was there he took mobile phone calls from the *Herald*, surrounded by nervous Bulldogs officials. But the newspaper retained all documentation, leaked by Constantinidis in order to save Hagan and gain revenge for his own sacking by McIntyre. All Gallop had was the Bulldogs' subsequent admissions. He had to bluff his way through the interviews with McIntyre and colleagues and ignore threats to take the NRL to court, aware it would strangle the code for more than a year.

Finally, Gallop and his board brokered a punishment where, in addition to being kicked out of the 2002 semifinals and fined $1 million, the Bulldogs would not take legal action. At the end of a harrowing time, when a guard was placed on 24-hour duty outside his home, Gallop, in an emotion-choked voice, announced the punishment at a news conference. The former in-house lawyer, once perceived to be a man of the hourly wage, had become the man of the hour.

The facility to appear and declaim impressively on TV is crucial for any public person. It's an attribute of new leadership in our time. Just as two centuries ago the ability to ride a horse and wield a sword were attributes of leadership, nowadays it is performance in front of the cameras. It is said that 'no man is a hero to his valet', and TV has become a valet, following sport's executives and politicians to their cars after door-stop interviews, waiting for a slip-up.

The salary cap saga infuriated Canterbury fans, because their definition of cheating accorded with that espoused by Charlie Francis, the coach of drug-tainted world 100-metre record holder Ben Johnson. 'It's only cheating if no-one else is doing it,' Francis said. Canterbury fans believed most clubs were rorting the salary cap. Having seen their club go from league leaders to wooden spooners, they descended from uttermost to guttermost in their retaliation. Although the *Herald* stories about the Bulldog salary cap rorts were written by a small team of journalists, including me, I had been involved in some memorable battles against the club as a coach. Their fans, therefore, focused their vitriol on me, particularly after someone posted my mobile number on the internet. Their calls to me came mainly on Friday nights when they were driving around Sydney's Botany Bay strip after the match of the round.

When one caller threatened to rape my wife, I tricked him into identifying himself. His call had flashed up on my mobile as a private number, but his voice had the ring of one particularly persistent fan who had weeks earlier given me his mobile number. I immediately called him back on my mobile, identifiable to him. He didn't answer.

Because I was in Melbourne, I then called him on a landline, knowing he could not resist the temptation to answer an unrecognisable Victorian number. The same voice who had threatened my wife answered. I reported it to Belmore police. Nothing happened.

Another caller lulled me into a conversation, relating how, as a 15-year-old, he had met me and Ted Goodwin at Lidcombe when I coached Wests. Not wanting to be rude, I let him meander until he casually mentioned, as if it had been seamless with our earlier conversation, that we had committed an act of pedophilia on him. Fearing a set-up, I reported it to an executive editor at Fairfax. His first question filled me with revulsion: 'Has Goodwin got any form?' I spoke with pride of Goodwin, a model citizen who referees matches continuously through weekends. It took me three years to mention it to Ted and he was equally horrified.

The disgust and disenchantment many felt with the game, particularly so soon after the internecine Super League war, is reminiscent of a passage from Hemingway's *The Sun Also Rises* where Bill asks Mike, the dissolute spendthrift, how he went bankrupt. 'Two ways,' Mike replies. 'Gradually and then suddenly.'

The saga soiled more than the Bulldogs.

St George is druidically secretive on boardroom blues. However, there were some horrendous confrontations, usually involving long-term secretary 'Fearless' Frank Facer.

One committee man, the late Horrie Maher, had an annoying habit of waving his hand dismissively at anyone whose comment he disregarded. Once, Fearless was advancing an opinion and Maher, rising to his feet to speak, cut him off mid-sentence with his traditional demeaning gesture. Fearless, who had had a leg amputated, began the long struggle to his feet. His stump had a prosthesis and, having checked it was attached, he reached for his cane to stand. He began moving towards Maher. There was no doubt in anyone's mind that Fearless intended to strike him. The late Laurie Doust, then club manager and father of current Dragons' boss, Peter, stood up and blocked Facer's path, ordering him to settle down.

That physical confrontation didn't eventuate, unlike the occasion John 'Martin Place' O'Toole and Eric 'The Bosun' Cox, two directors of the NSW Leagues Club, burst from a boardroom, rolling around on the floor, wrestling and punching each other. The fight erupted when Cox alleged that O'Toole, so nicknamed because he was on occasion 'half-full by lunchtime', over the use of hire cars to take his wife shopping. It ended when another director, Ken Arthurson, heard the commotion and investigated.

'Thanks, Ken,' the navy-trained Cox told Arko, implying he could have been charged with murder, 'these hands are trained to kill.'

Today, board arguments are more likely to be settled by legal letter. Wests Tigers, a shaky joint venture of Wests and Balmain, witnessed a fiery board meeting shortly after their first premiership. It concerned a column I had written, saying Balmain were receiving a disproportionate share of the glory.

I quoted Wests president Kevin Hammond, and he was taken to task by director Benny Elias, a former great player with Balmain. The discussion became heated, with Elias calling Hammond a liar and Hammond directing a legal letter be sent to Elias. Still, the name-calling didn't make the newspapers, an indication Wests Tigers can be as discreet as the Dragons were during the leadership of Facer.

Fearless Facer enjoyed a beer, and on one end-of-season trip he misbehaved. The committee voted to bar him from the next trip.

The Dragons subsequently won another premiership and Fearless, assuming his past sins had been forgotten in the present euphoria, reported to Central Station for the Dragons' trip to Cairns.

The club's long-serving treasurer, Glynn Price, was seated in a carriage of the North Coast mail and reminded Fearless of the ban, citing the relevant committee minute. Facer was forced to pick up his case, walk back along the platform and return home. Yet Facer was allowed all the praise for steering the good ship St George during its eleven consecutive premierships. Good clubs don't care who gets the credit; poor clubs concern themselves with who cops the blame.

The Dragons remained a good club after Facer retired, only because strong men filled the void. When current leagues club boss Danny Robinson reported for his first day of work, he was greeted with a posse of TV cameras.

Billy Smith had played a trick on the committee at a celebratory lunch held at the Penfolds-sponsored Minchinbury Winery. Billy drove the team bus into a grove of trees, dived in a pond, ensured he had a lily pad on top of his head and walked into the lunch dripping wet, claiming he had drowned the bus.

Everyone was horrified, but after the ruse had been exposed, Billy whacked a Penfolds official who objected to his behaviour. He also wrote graffiti in the visitor's book. The following day Doust and Robinson sacked him from his leagues club job as a cellarman. The previous year, he had been dismissed from the football club for reporting to training intoxicated.

Smith was one of the Dragons' greatest players, yet the board moved swiftly to discipline him. Compare that to the board's latitude afforded to red-headed second-rower Lance Thompson, eventually released after years of misbehaviour. Doust Junior admitted that he did not sack Thompson when he twice reported to training drunk in the pre-season of 2004 because, 'I was new to the club and he had a strong power base.' This clearly reflected the change in differential between official and player. So Thompson continued to destabilise the club, right up to the eve of the club's final match for 2005 against Wests Tigers.

When Sydney Kings coach Brian Goorjian concluded his address to the Dragons at a Randwick hotel during the finals campaign, he immediately asked the St George Illawarra coaching staff, 'Who's the redhead?'

Thompson's body language annoyed the basketball coach, whose team has won the last three NBL titles. While Goorjian spoke of the team ethos, sacrificing individual egos for the collective good, leadership and the pressure of finals, Thompson shuffled in his seat, loudly crunched a yoghurt container, anything to convey the message that he wasn't paying attention.

On the bus trip to Aussie Stadium to play Wests Tigers, Thompson sent two text messages to team-mate Justin Poore. One accused him of being soft, and the second threatened him when Poore turned around in his seat and looked in Thompson's direction.

At the club's annual presentation dinner at Sydney Town Hall, the club planned to make an award to Thompson in recognition of a milestone of games with the club, while simultaneously planning to serve him with a breach notice for his indiscretions. A director tipped Thompson off and he stormed from the function before the presentation was made.

Former captain Craig Young, an international and the club's recruitment officer (and ex-detective), tracked Thompson to a city hotel. 'I couldn't reason with him,' said Young of his inability to penetrate Thompson's self-obsessed psyche. 'He kept talking about "my fans". Nobody owns fans.'

In Thompson's many barbs at the Dragons' coaching staff and management after his walk out, he promoted himself as a self-sacrificial local junior who believed the club is everything.

Thompson's declaration 'I'm a professional' didn't sit well with his treatment of others. He complained to Nathan Brown after the coach did not promote him as a potential Kangaroo when quoted in a newspaper. The club eventually paid Thompson out, and he joined neighbours Cronulla where he exacted some revenge by scoring the opening try in a match against the Dragons.

The Dragons' tolerance with him is a parable of the changing power relationships between a club board and its players. The late and venerable American baseball coach Casey Stengel said the key to managing a club was keeping the ten players who hated you away from the rest of the club. That rule no longer applies. Today, the ones who hate the coach tend to win most of the time.

Because the major source of a club's income is TV rights fees, footballers are little different from any other class of elite worker that has sprung up during the information age. Footballers now join that wide range of occupations that rely on expanding technology — merchant bankers, entertainers, share brokers, webpage designers. Called 'the new social elite' by the late cultural critic Christopher Lasch, this group includes just about everybody whose livelihood 'rests not so much on the ownership of property as on the manipulation of information and professional expertise'.

For Ron Barassi, the worlds of business and sport bizarrely intersected at Hobart's Constitution Dock. He began telling me a story about an occasion when he did a breakfast gig with entertainer/former footballer Sam Kekovich and bankrupt businessman/former Carlton president John Elliott in the Tasmanian capital.

'Don't write this,' he said as I took notes of our conversation in a St Kilda cafe. So I stopped, and he chewed on another thought and said, 'No, write it. [Elliott] could have been Prime Minister.' He shook his head repeatedly of the former Fosters boss who, having escaped a penalty for foreign exchange dealings, challenged his prosecutors in the courts and was eventually brought down by his hubris. 'All the ability in the world. Could have been anything. Arrogance. I hate seeing talent of any kind wasted.'

Of Kekovich, whom he sacked at North Melbourne, Barassi says, 'We have great relations now.'

After the breakfast function, Elliott and Kekovich proceeded to the wharf area for an early lunch, inviting Barassi. 'I told them I had something to do,' Barassi said, obviously seeking to avoid a long, lunchless luncheon. 'I told them I'd get there about 2 pm, and I did and they invited me to join them in a glass of red. I had another glass and, when I emptied it, I asked the waiter to bring a bottle of the same to compensate for what I'd had.

'When it was time to leave for the airport, I asked for the bill for my bottle. I could sense they were watching me, but fortunately I have a poker face and they couldn't tell my reaction. But I was horrified when I saw the bill. $132 for one bottle! That's the price of the red they drink.'

BAD BOYS AND THE BEYOND

A handwritten letter I received a year after I retired from coaching had an unusual request. It asked me to quiz the men of the small NSW timber and farming town of Bombala on the murder of Bill Donnelly, a 56-year-old father of five.

The letter was written by Donnelly's youngest daughter with the encouragement of his widow, Beulah. Bill, or 'Womby' as he was nicknamed, was a victim of the 'Darlo Drop', the practice of throwing men out of cheap Kings Cross hotels after they have been robbed, usually with the cooperation of a prostitute.

Womby belonged to a group of Bombala men known as 'The Warhorse Syndicate', a collection of long-retired rugby league players and followers who bought horses in Melbourne Cup calcuttas and visited Sydney for the grand final. They regularly booked into the Manhattan Hotel at Kings Cross, ate in Chinatown, went to the races, visited the brothels and, of course, attended the big game.

Donnelly's last grand final was the last one at the Sydney Cricket Ground, the 1987 decider when Manly beat Canberra, the club that included Raider Paul Elliott, whose father, Tony, was Womby's partner in a building business. Six weeks later, during the Melbourne Cup carnival, Donnelly inexplicably returned to Kings Cross, booked into the Manhattan Hotel, checked out and then went to the Barclay Hotel. At 4 am on 9 November he was found dead in the street from internal injuries.

None of the Warhorse Syndicate would say anything. A wall of silence rose up around the Bombala husbands.

Beulah and her daughters believed there was a link between Womby's visit to Sydney for the grand final and his subsequent death. They were aware how he died and even suspected a prostitute was involved.

'Dad would come back from the Sydney grand finals and say he had a jump,' one of the daughters told me. 'We would tell him he was a silly old bugger and leave it at that. But we knew his nickname of Womby [Wombat] came from "eats, roots and leaves".

But the Donnelly family was perplexed why he left Bombala early in the morning of Monday 2 November, telling no-one, leaving only a note for his eldest daughter, saying he had gone to an eye specialist. He did not make contact with any family or friends for a week.

The letter asked me to infiltrate the Warhorse Syndicate, who they believed knew the answers to these mysteries. I had been to Bombala twice before – to assist Brian Lawrence, the captain-coach of the local team, prepare it for the grand final in 1976 and then later to help present the Clayton Cup for it being NSW's best-performed country team.

The first visit to Bombala was uneventful, except for a kangaroo jumping out in front of my car on a foggy bend on a Tantawanglo mountain back road, smashing the bonnet. The second trip, with Wests players Dallas Donnelly, Tom Raudonikis and Peter Young, was memorable, both for the Clayton Cup victory celebration and the early morning drive to Cooma airport, 89 kilometres to the north.

Dallas upset the female owner of the motel where we stayed, ordering two breakfasts and eating neither because he woke up late and we had to rush to catch the plane. Youngie was already upset, having stained his trousers and his ego at the after party.

The men of the town had adjourned to the river bank, where the challenge was to pick up a thick, sawn log and roll it up onto your shoulders. Peter had a reasonable mantelpiece for shoulders and hay baler's hands, but he failed.

A young shearer with a sinewy frame, one of those skinny blokes who roll their own cigarettes, drink a stubby for breakfast and rarely eat, addressed the log. He did a half-squat, rolled it up to his thighs and then jerked it onto the back of his neck. Youngie had another go and failed again, forever staining the brand-new pair of trousers he had purchased from a Hong Kong tailor during an end-of-season trip.

The driver of the car bound for Cooma was a Raudonikis devotee. He had gladly accepted responsibility for taking us to the airport, even shunning the victory dinner in order to appreciate every minute with his hero sitting beside him in the front of the car. I was sandwiched in the back seat between the two props

The earthy and girthy Dallas, with his fire hydrant thighs, occupied most of the back seat, but there was no way the driver would allow anyone but Tommy beside him as he stole adoring glances during the trip. His idolatry changed by the town of Nimmitabel, one of the coldest places on earth, rivalling Patagonia for its winds. It is said the Nimmitabel pub, when owned by the Paton family, never closed and no-one was ever evicted.

Tom first began breaking wind in order to make Dallas sick, causing the driver to wind down the window a mere fraction. After all, it *was* Tommy's fart. When Raudonikis wiped snot on the scowling Buddha in the back, the driver showed mild distress, swallowing quickly. But when 'The Kraut', as Tommy was also known, began digging deep into his loins, he finally lost a fan. The driver continued the journey in sullen silence, as if an expensive marble bust of a hero had smashed on the floor.

So there I was 12 years later, travelling back along the same road, having caught a flight to Cooma in answer to the letter from Beulah's daughter. The mid-winter, early evening flight had also been memorable.

I sat in the aisle seat next to an incredibly attractive young woman, who began the trip with her head turned towards the night sky. But she finally told me her story. She had broken up with her long-standing boyfriend after catching him cheating. She was having a few days in the snow country to forget. She wanted revenge. His greatest love was his sports car.

Her jealousy was so lethal that she asked me about draining cars of brake fluid. I discouraged her but described how brake fluid did horrible things to duco. She smiled, closed her eyes and fell asleep with the look of a woman who knew what she had to do. It's a sin that still sits on the top of my eyelids some nights.

The young woman passed on more about her life than the mill-workers offered about Womby. I remember sitting one lunchtime huddled around a potbellied stove at the Bombala mill while Womby's best friend cooked a piece of steak in a frying pan, expertly slicing off pieces of onion to join it.

I remember feeling incredibly hungry, both for a slice of steak and a piece of information. He gave nothing.

My former captain at St George, Craig Young, a detective, had given me access to the Kings Cross cops, who provided details of their investigation into Womby. I relayed the information to Womby's mate, hoping it would elicit a trade back. Some of it he already knew – three days before Bill left Bombala, the family enjoyed a combined birthday party for Beulah and one of her grand-daughters.

The day before, Bill put Beulah on a bus to Melbourne, where she planned to spend Melbourne Cup week with his brother and wife. His last words were, 'See you 5 pm Saturday, honey.'

Bill then visited Bombala RSL Club that morning and the hotel in the evening, drinking with his eldest son and his two closest friends, giving no indication of his plans. He cashed a cheque for $2,000, which was not unusual. He liked a full wallet.

Elliott, his partner in the building business, called in at his home on the Monday morning and, seeing the note to Womby's daughter about the eye specialist, was surprised he had not been informed. No eye specialist in southern NSW saw Donnelly that day. Police were able to trace most of Womby's movements, but he used aliases and they admit some days are blanks.

He signed into Goulburn RSL under the name W. Roberts and used the address of a relative in Yass. He left his car at Goulburn Railway Station, with the keys in the ignition, something he never did. His whereabouts on the day of the Melbourne Cup, 1987, are a mystery, but he booked into the Manhattan Hotel in King's Cross the following day, using a different name and the Yass address.

Because the Manhattan was double-booked, he checked into the Barclay and paid until 9 November, the day he was found dead in the laneway. He spent most of his time at the Aquatic Club and the Mansions Hotel where PubTAB and Sky Channel suited a bushie with a love of beer and the races. Police say he continually shouted girls who entered the hotel, again not out of character according to his daughters, who say he regularly bought drinks for them and their friends. However, police believe his practice of flashing a money-filled wallet would not have been missed by prostitutes or their pimps.

Some aspects of his behaviour were bizarre – he bought a fawn panama hat with a brown band and was seen to tip it regularly, encouraging pub patrons to call him Panama Bill. Beulah says he rarely wore a hat and never tipped it when he did.

Police believe that a street prostitute and her minder – a big, athletic ex-prisoner – entered the Barclay and, avoiding the lift that can be seen by a mirror from the front desk, went by stairs to Donnelly's room on the third floor. They believe the girl lured Donnelly from the room, perhaps to the nearby showers, where the minder frogmarched him to the window.

Donnelly had one handkerchief stuffed down his throat, another tied around his mouth and was probably held out the window while the minder demanded money. After a week of wanton spending, there would have been little of the $2,000 left. Donnelly may have struggled, but he eventually fell and died.

One witness, a British reporter for an adventure magazine, heard a muffled 'No! No!' and a woman scream. The reporter arrived in the back lane to find Donnelly still alive. He died soon afterwards.

Uniformed police were on the scene within minutes and reported hearing banging from inside the Barclay's ground floor rear fire escape door. They raced to the front of the hotel and met the girl and the minder leaving. When questioned, the two claimed they had entered the hotel for a heroin fix in the ground floor toilet. A cursory search of the couple found no money, and they were released. A check of the hotel toilet found no needle. Also unexplained is the $19 found in Donnelly's wallet in his back pocket. In his hotel room, police found a cigarette butt in the ashtray and chewing gum. Donnelly neither smoked nor chewed gum.

The hotel night clerk remembers the couple entering the hotel and has a sound recollection of the minder, who was a guest a week earlier. The clerk swears they were the only ones to enter, other than guests collecting their keys. A check of the guest record revealed that only one person had given his correct address. Most guests used names like D. Duck and gave Darwin and Townsville addresses. Even the witness, fearing he would be murdered, fled the country after a TV reporter broke a police embargo that he be neither interviewed nor identified.

The prostitute further claimed the couple tried to leave by the bolted rear door when they heard the shouting. The minder, in a separate interview, told police they entered the hotel to steal a TV and tried to take it out the back door. However, there were no television sets on the ground floor.

While investigating Bill's death for the Donnelly girls, I visited the hotel accompanied by an old school friend and author, Bob Ellis. Ellis was terrified to even enter the building, but more so when I insisted we test the theory that it was possible to climb the stairs unseen by the desk clerk.

We checked the third floor corridor, then entered the shower room. When I suggested we enter the basement, Ellis shot from the building like a frightened forest creature fleeing a fire. I met him later at a coffee shop where he had composed himself.

Bob offered comparisons with his father, Keith, once a womanising commercial traveller. Ellis expounded the theory that the geographic imperative moves old men irresistibly to be elsewhere, with another name, doing unfamiliar things and, as with British poet Masefield's call to the sea, they yield to it and wind up out of their depth. They become lost among the barbarians, in physical danger and, unacquainted with the siren call of the Sinful City, they lack the strength or savvy to deliver themselves from it.

The police had a more pedestrian explanation. 'Billy was a victim of the Darlo Drop. It was a rip-off gone wrong,' a Kings Cross detective said. Still, the police conceded an increasing incidence of elderly men from the country coming to grievous ends at the Cross. These men, in memory of Donnelly, were called 'Billys'.

Womby's few furtive days of secret life in another city overtook and destroyed him. To bushies on a football trip, the Cross deceives and relaxes. Amid the neon lights and nudity, buskers and spruikers, there are enigmas – the Country Women's Association had a building sitting between the Manhattan and the Aquatic Club.

Bombala buzzed with rumour. Suicide was a popular theory. Police discounted it because of the witness's report about screams and protestations, and Beulah rejected money as a motive. 'He left a very small superannuation-type insurance policy, and I'm still working as a cleaner at the old people's home,' she told me.

Another theory around the town was that Donnelly arranged with professionals to kill him to avoid family embarrassment of suicide. But that would have required a large sum of money. Beulah was the family accountant. To defend herself against these rumours, she checked all records and even visited the Bombala TAB to determine if he had won a large sum recently.

The more likely explanation was that Bill was derailed by worry over his eye and the pain. Two weeks before Beulah went to Melbourne, he was ill and she volunteered to cancel her trip. On his last day in Bombala, he told friends at the bar he was sick of being 'mucked about by local doctors' over his eye, and he also bent over on one occasion, crippled by pain.

I had one last piece of information I kept up my sleeve for Womby's mate at the mill – one tasty morsel that might make him reveal something. The prostitute left Sydney shortly after the murder and resettled in Canberra. The minder went to jail on another charge. When police visited the prostitute nine months after the murder, she was pregnant and living in a de facto relationship. The detectives noted that she listened quietly, while smoking and chewing gum. As they left her lounge room, one of the detectives saw her take her gum from her mouth and put it in the ashtray, beside the cigarette butts.

But none of this had any impact on Donnelly's mate, who said, 'I know people say I am holding something back, but if I knew Womby's killers, I'd fix them myself. He and I were very close, and I reckon if he'd planned to leave Bombala, he would have told me.'

So I had nothing from the men of Bombala to tell Beulah when I went to visit her. We sat in the lounge room of the big family home, with its high ceilings, log fire, carpeted floor and doilies underneath every framed photograph and vase. Her words still make me feel inadequate. 'I thought the men might tell you something, Roy,' she said, not hiding her disappointment. 'If there was another woman involved, it would set my mind at rest. I wake up in the middle of the night and go through his clothes, looking for a letter, a receipt, anything that might give a clue.'

She seemed unwilling to accept the more likely explanation – Bill, an athletic ex-boxer, distracted by pain and at the shadow line of old age, with just medical cause or not, was looking down the drooping barrel of his imminent impotence and went off for one last bender that went wrong.

Two years earlier, I spoke to another bereaved Donnelly in another town in NSW. I didn't think anything could assuage the grief Rocky Donnelly, father of Dallas, felt the day I visited the family home in Gunnedah following the funeral of the big front-rower, avoiding the pub full of footballers who had flown into town on a chartered DC3. Dallas drowned in the surf at Byron Bay eight years after the infamous game against Manly at Lidcombe Oval (detailed in an earlier chapter).

The Donnelly home in Gunnedah was a scene of unrelieved sorrow. Rocky met me at the front gate and we walked though the carport, built to house the new Daihatsu he bought to replace his comfortable-as-an-old-shoe Wolseley. Over in the right-hand corner was the Wolseley, sitting on blocks, near what was once a fence. Rocky's brother, Ray, lived in the house next door, and the fence had been pulled down for access. It took Rocky years to sell the Wolseley. The old beast had carried Dallas and his mates to Coolangatta once for a holiday, and perhaps Rocky hoped one day the car would talk.

We turned hard left and walked along a narrow concrete path running parallel to the back of the house and past an old rainwater tank near the back door. Rocky then steered me to the rear of the backyard where, on the right, an aviary-like structure, converted into a chook pen, was covered by grapevine. In the left corner was a partially sheared-off water tank used to store uncut wood for the combustion stove. Rocky invited me to sit on a chopping block, next to a shed packed with chopped wood. Nearby was Gloria's delight, a vegetable garden, still boasting the fruits of the summer.

He rolled another block out of the old tank, sat down and asked me to re-create the events of that May day in 1978 when I confronted Dallas in the dressing room at Lidcombe.

It was all that could distract the grief-stricken Rocky.

Rocky had seen the match on TV, of course, with Dallas charging Randall in the opening minute. So I told the entire story, which ended with Wests winning easily, and Rocky smiled softly, as if he had been handed a little gift.

For him, life was no storybook. He saw it as page after page of sinkholes and small jewels, a volume of survival without a back cover to foretell the ending. When I finally left the home, Dallas's mother, Gloria, who kept herself busy making chicken sandwiches, farewelled me with only four words: 'You loved my son.'

Years later, when John Gray told me of the happenings after one scrum in that game, I wished Rocky had been alive so the humour of it could have cheered him. 'A scrum collapsed and Bruce Gibbs was there as well,' Gray told me. '[Gibbs's] gut was bigger. Dallas flopped on me. He pinned me. My head was on the ground and my eyes were skyward, but his gut enveloped my face. I was gurgling and gasping for breath. I couldn't speak. I couldn't turn my head. When I tried to break away, Dallas's gut kept coming into my mouth. I was in a panic. No-one was getting up. Dallas knew he had me. My arms were pinned. Every time I attempted to breathe, all I got was a mouthful of fat.

'I was anticipating getting near his navel and hoped I'd find a litle bit of space but couldn't. I tried to bite him but the volume was too much. Eventually, his great gut must have released an air pocket and it created a bit of space near his navel, and I finally gulped in some air.'

Ian 'Herbie' Freeman, a Wests forward, has a similar story about the suffocating gut of Dallas. A native of Cooma, where he is now a corrections officer at the local jail, Herbie says, 'Dallas and [girlfriend] Tanya were invited to my wedding in December '83. There were about 200 guests, and the reception was at the local bowling club. All the local footballers invited wanted to have a drink with Dallas, who ended up in two shouts. Everyone was crowded around him, and he was drinking schooners of Tooheys Old, keeping up with both shouts. There are some good drinkers in Cooma and Dallas was drinking two to their one.

'We had a band close to the stage, and near midnight Dallas got up to present me with a present from the Wests boys. It was a black-and-white, knitted cock sock about ten inches long. He presented it to me at the microphone, and then he went on and on and was staggering a bit. The MC was the president of the Cooma Rugby League Club, a local publican whom nobody liked much. He went up to escort Dallas off the stage. He thought Dallas might kick over the band's instruments.'

Herbie switches to present tense, as many do when telling familiar stories. 'Well, Dallas stumbles over and takes the president down with him. The president is a little bloke, only about nine stone and five-five. Dallas falls all over the top of him, lands on top and stays down. All you could see were these two hands wiggling out from underneath Dallas and these muffled sounds from the president. We knew he was under there somewhere, but you couldn't see him. He was smothered.

'We tried to get Dallas off but he was semi-conscious. He must have had 30 schooners. Everyone in the town still talks about it. The president ended up breaking his leg. But nobody worried because he wasn't that popular.'

By contrast, Dallas was immensely popular.

'The following day, Dallas was back on the drink again,' Herbie continues. 'When the drinkers at the other pubs heard Dallas was at this particular pub, a different one to the one owned by the president, they all flocked there. Dallas jumped the bar and started pouring drinks for everyone. The publican was too scared to do anything. It was his biggest crowd ever, and he didn't want to upset them or Dallas.'

Wherever I go, two decades after his death, I am asked more questions about him than any other player. People are still fascinated by Dallas, a walking contradiction, a man with dancer's feet and a sumo's belly, the bright grin and the wicked glare. Some Australians have passed into the role of cultural mythology, as if reality can't contain their wild stories. It's the same with American legends, like Wild Bill Hickok and even Jimmy Hoffa, the gangster supposedly buried in the cement of Giants Stadium in New Jersey.

Maybe this is why Oscar Wilde once observed, 'The Americans are certainly hero worshippers and always take their heroes from the criminal classes.' He could equally have been referring to Australia and our deification of Ned Kelly. Martin Pike, the Brisbane Lions player, has a tattoo of Ned Kelly on his back. People like Dallas and Ned sit on the narrow margin between fact and fiction, good and bad. But people recognise their regard for the downtrodden. Dallas radiated a sincerity that still leaves friends wistful at the mention of his name.

Stories of Dallas and food and drink are legion. When we returned from the Bombala trip, we adjourned to the Railway Hotel, Lidcombe, Dallas's haunt. I scolded him for not eating, and he immediately ordered food to keep me happy. But it was a silver foil container of mashed potato, a miniature Mount Vesuvius, salted and peppered at its peak, enough to line his ample stomach.

One cold, rainy winter night, we were about to leave Wests Leagues Club at Ashfield when we were stopped by the police at the door. The club car park was adjacent to a garage, and somebody had tipped off the police that noted criminal Darcy Dugan intended to rob the garage. The police were in position and we couldn't reach our cars.

A lone hot dog seller stood inside the foyer, avoiding the lashing rain. 'You might as well go home, lad,' I told the boy. 'There's only about five people left in the club.' But the hot dog boy wasn't moving.

'One of them in there is Dallas and he always orders seven,' the kid said.

Yet another incident occurred on an end-of-season trip to the Philippines. We visited Angeles City, the bar town near the then US air force and naval bases of Subic Bay. Wests had given me some money to feed the lads when I believed it necessary, and I ordered about 50 skewers of barbecued meat. When the food quickly ran out and some hadn't eaten, I challenged the waitress, accusing her of robbing us.

'No, no,' she said, pointing to Dallas. 'That big fat man eat 20.'

Who knows what gurgled around inside that giant gut of Dallas? He exacted revenge on Raudonikis with some of Tommy's own medicine one day as we drove through Strathfield's wide streets with their median strips filled with garden beds.

Dallas, sitting in the back seat, broke wind of such pungency that it may have wilted the flowers. Tommy tried to speak, but he feared the poisonous air would enter his mouth. Words of protest started to come out, but were double-clutched, regrouped in his throat and then boycotted all together. Tommy couldn't drive and have his head sticking out the window simultaneously, so he mounted the median strip and came to a halt near the garden bed to stop and smell the roses, literally.

It was ten minutes before the cloud passed, and Dallas remained in the back seat the entire time, wallowing in his gas.

Dallas suffered from epilepsy. His fits frightened anyone who witnessed them for the first time. The players cruelly called them 'Crowlies', after the Crowle Home, an inner west school for the handicapped.

Once, during a training camp at Nelsons Bay, he fitted – moaning, frothing at the mouth and in spasms, as if he had been electrocuted. It occurred in a classroom where referee Laurie Bruyers was holding a lecture on the season's new rules.

New recruit to the club Ted Goodwin of Maori ancestry, fearing Dallas had been seized by devils, fled the room. Dallas also suffered a fit in the presence of American tourists on a plane returning from the Philippines. They were so terrified, they rushed to the front of the plane, almost causing it to nosedive.

It was widely rumoured Dallas's papers were marked NTA – Never to Tour Again – because he coathangered a motorcyclist rushing a pedestrian strip while on the Sydney team's visit to Auckland. I suspect the truth is that the manager of the tour, Bosun Cox, had witnessed one of Dallas's fits and did not want to pass on the responsibility to another team manager.

When Dallas returned from England, after playing in London, he told me he had not had an epileptic fit in two years. Perhaps it was the constant vigilance of his girlfriend, Tanya, or the cooler climate meant that he did not sweat as much. After all, we believed his fits came because he forgot to take his tablets or, as the players said, 'All the piss he drank washed the chemicals out.'

He returned to Australia, having secured an appointment as captain-coach of the appropriately named Byron Bay Devils. He stayed in Sydney for a time with a pencil-thin former Wests winger, Wayne Bennett, who told me Dallas went on the wagon in preparation for his new job, spending his days at the TAB, dressed in a kaftan, drinking iced water and lime. Dallas in a kaftan evokes images of those giant thighs moving around under that loose cotton, like children hiding in the curtains.

He came to see me before leaving Sydney on the overnight train for Byron Bay, collecting a book on coaching drills that I used at St George. He took Bennett along as his reserve grade coach and trainer.

A couple of weekends after settling into a unit in Byron Bay, Tanya was forced to return to the Central Coast home of her family to attend a long-delayed but minor court matter. Only a few days earlier, Dallas's former captain at Wests, Warren Boland, had passed through Byron Bay.

Boland says, 'After I moved to Queensland in mid-1985, I used to go back over the border, ostensibly to surf but really to get out of Joh's state for a day. To go to a state that was sane. I had friends at Lennox Head, and I was driving back through Byron Bay about 8.30 pm and realised Dallas had just come back from London. I was driving past the Great Northern Hotel and saw this silhouette in the doorway. This great big gut. I pulled over and there was Dallas with a schooner in his hand. We only chatted for five minutes, but I told him I would come back and see him soon.

'I made the arrangements and two weeks later, on a Saturday, I drove down to meet him at either his house, or, if he was not there, the beach. I went straight to the beach and to the lookout at the kiosk to see if I could see him. There was nothing unusual. Then I went to his unit, knocked on the door and this whippet-skinny bloke from Wests days [Wayne Bennett] he was sharing the unit with came to the door. "He's dead," was all he said.'

Dallas had gone for a surf with the young daughter of the local football club president. Maybe, with Tanya away, he had forgotten to take his tablets, or the fierce heat dehydrated him. It seems he fitted there in the surf, only 50 metres from the shore, rolling and heaving and taking in giant lungfuls of sea water. The girl thought it was just horseplay, and the apocryphal story persists that a woman, walking along the beach, refused to let her son go into the ocean. 'Dallas is using it,' she allegedly said.

He was dead before the young girl could drag him to shore. No-one in Byron Bay, other than Bennett, who was in the surf club house, knew of the epilepsy.

Sometimes at Wests reunions, it's mentioned that Boland could have saved Dallas if he had arrived in Byron Bay an hour earlier. Because Boland was often late, it's sometimes assumed in the retelling that he was again late on this day.

'It did happen an hour earlier,' Boland says, 'but I never felt guilty about it, as though I was late or anything. I felt cheated because we were really going to catch up. I was going to spend the weekend with him. The irony is he was such a strong swimmer.' Dallas had been a NSW country freestyle/butterfly champion as a schoolboy and had the strength to swim to Julian Rocks, the outcrop off the bay.

In November 2005 I stayed at Byron Bay for a week and asked to be shown the precise point where Dallas drowned. It was about 50 metres to the right of the surf club as you look out to Julian

Rocks, not far from where local publican and former Souths and Manly player Tom Mooney plays gorilla ball – a game played with a giant medicine ball and volleyball rules, just the exertion needed to keep middle-aged drinkers remotely fit.

I stood on the beach, thinking about Dallas and gorilla ball and even Lord Byron, who once swam the Dardanelles. Byron Bay is actually named after the poet's uncle, who sailed on the *Endeavour* with Captain Cook. Many of the town's streets bear the names of poets.

Rex Hunt, the former VFL footballer and star of a TV fishing show, who was exposed in May 2006 for having a decade-long affair with a woman he paid $1,000 a week, had his infamous altercation with Byron Bay youth on Jonson Street, named after the poet Ben. It happened while I was in Byron Bay, Rex labelling the town 'more dangerous than Bali' after he and his family collided with local youth on the narrow footpath. Rex suffered lacerations to his bald skull, but a popular version of events is that the damage was inflicted by his daughter-in-law, who took off a high-heeled shoe, climbed on the back of one of the teenage locals in the melee and began striking him, hitting Rex instead.

Dallas never had trouble like that. He had a Pied Piper effect on kids and even adults. He gathered around him deaf mutes, ink-black isolates, the lame.

Once, while in a coaching camp at Narrabeen as an examiner, I stopped at the Sweet Fanny Adams Bar, a popular nightspot. Dallas was out the front with two friends, but no taxi would convey them back to Lidcombe. So I secreted them into a vacant lodge at Narrabeen and forgot about it until a phone call two days later. Frank 'The Deacon' Johnson, a former Kangaroo hooker who ran the courses, prided himself on the high marks rugby league traditionally received from the Narrabeen superintendent for cleanliness, care of facilities and so on. It was a badge of honour to the Deacon that rugby league camps scored higher than soccer, netball, rugby union and so on.

The Deacon was distraught. 'The superintendent said the netball girls witnessed three men pissing their initials in the sand from the verandah of one of the lodges,' the Deacon told me. 'One of them was deaf, another was a giant black man named Sambo and the third one was Dallas Donnelly. Do you know anything about this?'

Dallas and Fanny Adams was a lethal mix. After one game at Brookvale, Dallas adjourned to the bar and was so legless that he became a victim of Phil Franks, who was furious Dallas had punched his mate, Manly captain Max Krilich, during the match. Phil unleashed a thundering right and Dallas fell like a chimney stack that had been dynamited, crumbling all the way to the floor, in sections, like a slow-motion picture. Yet this punch has never haunted Franks like the one he did not throw.

Franks has lived for 40 years with the whispered accusation he struck and killed team-mate George Piper outside a Balmain club. Piper, then 29, a wharf labourer who played for Penrith, slipped and fell outside the Codocks Club and died three days later on 22 September 1968.

Franks recalls of the incident, 'George got dropped at Penrith and had the shits. We were both playing there. It was a Thursday. He didn't turn up to training, and he'd pissed off from work at the Docks and went to the pub.

'I had [team-mates] Bob Mara, Laurie Fagan, Dennis Tutty with me. All of us except George had been to training. He had been dropped [to reserve grade] on the Tuesday night. We picked up Arthur Beetson on the way from Balmain training. I felt sorry for George. As we came out of the club, I put my arm around him. He was a cantankerous big bastard and he just opened up his big arms when I put my arm around, and he's gone crash and hit me on the jaw. His right elbow hit my jaw. He lost balance and fell over.

He was blind. We ran over and picked him up and put him in the car to take him to Balmain hospital. He had a big lump on the back of his head . . . like a golf ball. I went home and next morning woke up with a bottom tooth aching badly. It was going thump, thump, thump.

'I went to Balmain hospital and had my jaw X-rayed. They said it was sweet as a nut. I thought I'd go and see George and then get my tooth out afterwards. George was lying in bed, his feet hanging about three foot over the edge. I remember saying, "Couldn't they get you a bigger bed?" and he laughed. George was the best. I was there for an hour. Then I went to a dentist in Darling Street and he did an X-ray and found the tooth was broken at the roots. He wired it up and I went home.

'On the Sunday morning we had plans to go to [Balmain lock] Peter Provan's house and help him lay a concrete driveway. We were going to have a barbecue and a few beers afterwards. Beetson was to pick me up at my home in Lilyfield at 12. At 2 pm he hadn't arrived. At 2.30 pm he turned up as white as a ghost. He said, "You wouldn't believe it. George has just died."

'He fell out of that bed on the Saturday night and haemorrhaged. They found him on the floor beside the bed. They had relieved the pressure on his brain but hadn't removed the tube. Maybe there was a tumour there from football. They found it to be an accident.'

Franks's story accords with Beetson's recollection in his autobiography, a copy of which was sitting on a marble table in Frank's apartment – except for one detail. How would Penrith still be training late in September and selecting teams when the club's first semifinal appearance was 27 years later?

Franks opened the book at a leather bookmark, identifying where he was mentioned – the only pages of any recent book he could remember reading. He checked the date of Piper's death in the book and decided Arthur was wrong. When I phoned him later, after validating the date with newspaper clippings, he admitted he had been thinking about it and decided the group had travelled to Penrith to collect their cheques for the season.

Piper, he decided, must have been told earlier that Penrith weren't re-signing him and chose not to go, drowning his sorrows instead. But everything else he said accorded with reports at the time.

'I went to the [Glebe] coroner's court,' Franks says. 'All the witnesses were there, including Tutty and company. It was deemed to be an accident. Laurie Fagan was very close to George. If there was any smell I did any wrong, they wouldn't be backing me up. But George's wife and his two kids . . . She turned on me. Everywhere I went in football, it followed me . . . I went to Norths the next year under Roy Francis . . .'

Today he lives in a $4 million apartment at The Rocks and works as a property developer. On the wall are framed pictures purchased at auctions, such as a photo of the Apollo II astronauts and the printed exchange between Neil Armstrong and the space craft, together with photos of his two sons as children, both later educated at St Joseph's College, Hunters Hill. He is museum neat, asking visitors to remove their shoes, and he provides scuffs to walk across the marble floors. He watched me carefully for any coffee drips on his comfortable white leather couches.

Fit, sinewy and balding, he still retains that latent combustibility. 'Everyone had their belief of what happened, but they weren't game to say it to me,' he said. 'It was a terrible time in my life. I'd get to a stage . . . People would say I was mad and I'd think, *I'll give you mad*.'

Rugby league, he believes, operates on the 'give a dog a bad name' credo. He identifies with anyone whose past skulks alongside him, whose reputation enshrouds him. 'I feel sorry for poor

Hoppa,' he said of the former Manly bad boy. 'The Pringle [Balmain and Newtown lock] thing ... I was supposed to put a glass in his face at a Cremorne hotel. We were having a drink one night, and I got into a stink with Barry Norton [brother of former St George prop, Chicka]. I don't want to get into that ...'

There are gaps in Franks's story, like sections of road washed away in a storm. He withholds some details that would repave these gaps but quickly extends a hand and jerks you from one section of the road to another.

'The coppers have assassinated my character,' he said. 'It still goes on today. I've belted a few coppers in my day. I've got a few assaults on my record. I grew up in Surry Hills and Glebe; I had no education. I spent my youth in orphanages and reformatories. My mother was living on her own. I was just a wild bastard. I couldn't be controlled. My old man got two sheilas up the stick at the one time and married the other one. The other family didn't know I existed. It wasn't until 1987 I met my stepbrothers. I knew they were there, but they didn't know about me. My youth was misguided. I learnt from experience.

'Around the time of the Piper thing, a woman knocked on my door at Lilyfield. "Are you Phillip?" she said. "Come outside." We went to a car and there was a girl in the back seat with a belly full of arms and legs. She reckons it was my kid from a one-night stand out at Penrith. The girl came from Katoomba. I said it wasn't mine and the next thing I get a summons. I went though two court cases and both were dismissed.

'[Penrith team-mate] Mick Leary was a copper at Penrith Station, and he had to serve me with the summons. I told him to tell them he couldn't find me and he'd say, "How can I say that when we are playing together?" In the Penrith court someone said, "Can't you see the resemblance?" Everyone laughed. The baby was only months old. I didn't want to know about it. Years later I kept getting letters from Western Suburbs or Penrith, or anywhere I played, being redirected.'

Franks became a big story in the main Sydney papers in 2003 when Manly were in financial trouble and he produced a spurious rescue cheque for $1 million, the media dubbing him the 'unsavoury saviour'. Suddenly all those letters that were chasing him had a known address.

'One night Zorba [Manly media manager Peter Peters] was up in Brisbane and phoned me,' he recalled. 'He said he's got this bloke with him – a 38-year-old who reckons he is my son. I ended up taking him to England [2004 Kangaroo tour] with Chang [Graeme Langlands] and Laurie Moraschi and my eldest son, Paul. His name is Sean. I told him, "Don't call me dad and don't give me anything for Father's Day and we'll be sweet."

'I was going to get a DNA test, but what's the point? I'm satisfied he is my son. He assumed the name of his mother when she married. I said to him this is history repeating itself. Franks is not my name. O'Connor is. I took the name of my stepfather. I believe in life you are dealt cards, but it's how you *play* the cards that is important. You learn from your mistakes.

'I was in a boys' home with Neddy Smith. They reckon he said in his book he'd never been beaten in a fight. I knocked him out at Mt Penang [boys' home]. He was up to the old standover rort.'

Franks entered into a partnership with Beetson in the Big House, a heritage-order hotel in The Rocks. His problems with police led to licensing court problems and the partnership was dissolved.

'Coppers would ring Beetson and ask, "Is he there?" I'd tell them to leave their guns in the car. My philosophy is if you rob me, I'll rob you ten times. If you do business with me, be straight. Don't give me bullshit. I'm a strong believer in what goes round, comes round.

'People say I carry guns, that I'm a hit man. Ring Bozo [Bob Fulton]. I'd never had a gun in my hand in my life until I went pig shooting with him. He put one in my hand but I couldn't shoot pigs. I hate guns.'

The evening of the very day I met Franks in his apartment, I attended the Dally M awards at Sydney Town Hall. I joined a Penrith group, including long-term president Barry Walsh, Mick Leary, now the club's football manager, and their wives.

I related Phil's story of the pregnant girl and Leary's order to serve a summons. One of the wives remarked that Franks carried a gun, and I was quick to say that Phil had denied it earlier that day. The intake of breath from Walsh almost sucked all the oxygen from the room.

'He got dropped one night and walked up to Doug Hamilton, a selector and union official,' Walsh said. 'He puts a gun under Doug's chin and says, "I hear I've been dropped." Doug says, "You're back in the side." We banned him for ten years for that.'

I called Phil the next day and related the story. 'That's bullshit,' he said. 'If I got banned for ten years, North Sydney wouldn't have taken me the next season. Make sure you write in your book about the three tries I scored when I ran past Chang Langlands at North Sydney Oval.'

I spoke to him again the day Frenchman Zinedine Zidane was sent off in soccer's World Cup final for chest-butting an Italian player. It was widely assumed the Italian had made an offensive remark concerning Zidane's Algerian-born mother. Sledging players on the basis of sexual exploits with the mother/wife/sister/ even daughter of an opponent happens in all football codes. It certainly occurred at North Sydney Oval when Langlands and Franks were opposing fullbacks. Each time Franks passed Langlands, he made a comment about Chang's mum. But the great Langlands had the last laugh.

'He ran towards me with ten minutes to go,' Franks recalled. 'I tried to anticipate his gigantic sidestep, but he left me sprawled on the ground as he scored under the posts.'

Insult joined ignominy with Langlands's final remark to Franks: 'She said you're a dud fuck anyway.'

Controversy still follows Franks. In early 2006 I received an anonymous letter stating that Franks had been paid $300,000 from Manly Warringah Leagues Club for 'property development advice'.

'Who else would ever pay Phil Franks this sort of money for advice, unless he threatened them, of course?' the letter said. I put it to Franks, who was in Japan skiing at the time, and he agreed the money had been paid.

'Three years ago the Commonwealth Bank had a valuation of $4 million on the club and wouldn't give a loan,' Franks explained. 'I got a new valuer in and the assets increased to $10 million and are now at $20 million, and I've introduced some big name money to the club. The club offered me the $300,000 fee. I didn't ask for it.'

It would be easy to say Franks is handcuffed to an identity not of his own making, but it would also be incorrect. Still, there lurks within him an almost inaccessible softness. At recent Men of League balls, he has offered to pay the tickets and hire car costs of four former players with varying degrees of quadriplegia.

When I chatted with him in his apartment, he pointed to a blanket hanging over the furniture on the balcony and said, 'I was with Fran, my lady friend, and I thought I could see a big spider on the deck. I went out to the balcony and it was a bat hanging upside down, its claws through a cane chair. I took a banana out, but it panicked and flew against the glass wall. It was stuck there. I asked Fran to get the camera, but she was too mesmerised to take a photo. I got the blanket and covered the bat in it and released it over the railing. It flew away majestically, weaving its way through the tall buildings.'

I later asked him if it was a parable of his own life. Wouldn't he like to be released from a reputation he has shadow-boxed with all his life?

'Exactly,' he said. 'I can't get on a soap box and protest my innocence. The Piper thing has really hurt me.'

It was just as well Newtown wasn't one of Phil's five clubs, otherwise he would have joined a rogue's gallery, including former Penrith team-mate Les Mara, who played a season with the Bluebags/Jets. Mara is on the run from police, who suspect him of being involved in a cocaine importation ring.

Other Newtown players more known for appearing in police line-ups than team ones, and more accustomed to mug shots than team photos, are World Cup forward Gary Sullivan, jailed for armed robberies on the Gold Coast with his stepfather; Paul Heyward, who died from an AIDS-related illness after being released from a Bangkok jail where he served time for drug importation; Doug Kemister, who drove a car for Neddy Smith; and Chris Dawson, who was under investigation following the disappearance of his wife in 1982. Dawson, then a physical education teacher at a northern beaches high school, was having an affair with a 16-year-old student, the family babysitter, when his wife went missing. After a 20-year investigation, the DPP decided not to proceed and dropped charges against Dawson for lack of evidence.

AFL icon Gary Ablett, a player of godlike status in his code, was also associated with the death of a young woman. Following a drugs binge in a Melbourne hotel, the woman died, with Ablett panicking and fleeing the scene after the ambulance arrived. Other Melbourne legends have spent time in the slammer for embezzlement or drug trafficking but have been quickly rehabilitated and welcomed back. In a city where AFL is the secular religion, it's a short trip from icon to ex-con and back again.

Buddy Cain, who played for Souths and Wests, was a small-time law-breaker. He once robbed the home of Rabbitoh great Bob McCarthy, demonstrating a mix of stupidity and bravado beyond belief.

TV footage captures some of his brazen acts, starting from an early age. In the 1968 Grand Final, as referee Col Pearce blew full-time, a teenage Buddy is captured on film stealing the ball off the ball boy on the sideline of the SCG. Buddy punched the ball from under the arm of the ball boy, ran forward to scoop it in and then swept around in a semicircle to disappear amongst the onrush of excited Souths followers.

David Waite, who later coached Newcastle, St George Illawarra and Great Britain, played in the 1978 Wests team with Buddy. David tells a story I don't recall myself, but maybe the memory rejects some events. It seems I saw smoke coming from a cubicle in the change room at Lidcombe Oval. Concerned that someone would be smoking a cigarette so close to a game, I protested outside the door. My concern transmuted to horror when Buddy revealed it was marijuana. 'Don't knock it till you try it, Roy,' Buddy allegedly said.

A crowd favourite at Lidcombe, Buddy once stood Parramatta centre Mick Cronin up, sprinted past and then stopped, turned and gave the icon the bird. The media howled that Buddy had embarrassed the legend, demanding I take action. I disciplined him but only for showboating before he actually scored the try. His teammates sometimes resurrect it at Wests reunions, saying I didn't support him sufficiently. I certainly never resolved it and lack of resolution always sits uncomfortably.

After Buddy left Wests, he played football with an A-grade team in the South Sydney subdistrict. His father had died of a heart attack and, as the players gathered in a circle after training one night at Moore Park, Buddy announced, 'I'm going to see my father now.' He dropped dead on the spot.

Who knows how much subconscious warning footballers have of imminent death? Cameroon soccer captain Rigobert Song says of team-mate Marc-Vivien Foe, who died on the pitch during a World Cup match, 'At half-time his last words were, "Boys, even if it means dying on the pitch, we must win."'

One of Buddy's team-mates, Ron Broderick, gave ample warning of his travel to the great beyond, yet no-one apparently listened. Nicknamed 'the Wolfman' because he looked fearsome and was known to wail at the moon when drunk, Broderick moved to Auckland with his wife, who took an important job in a hospital. He hanged himself after an earlier, unsuccessful attempt.

More than twenty years earlier, I witnessed the wild jealousy he had over his future wife, then a theatre sister. It was the night before Wests' 1977 Under-23 Grand Final win. After training, we opted to discipline ourselves by having a milkshake at Zorro's Cafe, rather than the obligatory six beers at the Railway Hotel.

Wolfman sat in a booth, sullenly sipping a shake, when he suddenly bolted from the cafe. A male, dressed in the blue, cotton uniform of a nurse, took off down Joseph Street, Lidcombe, with Wolfman pursuing him. Wolfman steered him into an alley, by which time I caught the pair. The fellow was helpless as Wolfman's fists thundered into him, trapped with his back against a brick wall.

His only crime had been to make eyes at Wolfman's future wife. One misdirected blow and Wolfman would have broken his hand. When I told him to stop, warning him an injury would cost him a grand final appearance, he diverted his attack to the unfortunate's midriff. I'd seen those piston-like arms work when I progressed to coach first grade at Wests. Wolfman occasionally joined me in the top grade, although he was too slow to hold a regular position in the back line.

After one appearance, a loss, he pulled me aside at the Lidcombe Dancers Club – one of our itinerant social bases – and asked me whether he would be retained. Protocol demanded I shouldn't say anything, but I did worse and told him the anticipated team. This was a serious error of judgement. He walked to the other side of the bar and whacked one of the new team members, Tom Arbor. When we pulled them apart, Wolfman merely maintained that he was toughening up Arbor for his debut.

Club officials treated Wolfman as if he was an unexploded bomb. On an end-of-season trip to Coffs Harbour, he sat propped against one of the town's traffic lights, his feet along the median strip, howling at a full moon. A policeman called our hotel and ordered someone remove him. One of the officials walked out onto the pub veranda, witnessed the task that lay ahead and, stuttering with fear, told the copper, 'No, nnn . . . No, you move him.'

I delivered the eulogy at Broderick's funeral but was more than upstaged by his son, who recited a beautiful poem he had written.

A few years later I received a letter from the headmaster of the Regent's Park primary school Wolfman had attended. The principal wrote about a mother enrolling her grandchild and crying at the sight of a team photograph in his office. 'There he is,' she told her grandchild, sobbing softly. The teacher said the encounter was too emotional to intrude, but it nagged at him and he wondered whether I could enlighten him. He listed the names in the photo of the school's state championship-winning team.

One of them was Ron Broderick.

The statistics on suicide are general. The tragedy is always in the specifics. In January 2006, former Cronulla and St George five-eighth/centre Steve Rogers took an overdose of the medicine prescribed for the depression he suffered. He had returned early from a world trip won in an auction, but his wife of a couple of years flew to Queensland to visit family, leaving 'Sludge' to three days with his mates.

On his final day, around 2 pm, he visited a golf club in the Shire. He was refused drinks at 6.30 pm and moved to the club's smoking room, playing darts with his nephew. His nephew's partner ferried drinks to the pair until 8.30 pm, when they left the clubhouse. Sludge could become cantankerous and narky when intoxicated, but on this night, perhaps the cold air took him to a new emotion.

He began sobbing hysterically, great heaving cries, all captured on the golf club's security camera. It wasn't just the pain of the death of his first wife, or problems with his second. It was pain from all across the map of his life; the stellar past that seemed to have evaporated behind him was now dripping down his cheeks.

His nephew insisted on driving him to his waterfront unit where, after leaving notes for his wife and three children, Sludge took the overdose. When he realised what he had done, he began banging without answer on a neighbour's door, but who knows how many times his neighbour had sat up in the early hours, listening to Sludge's rants against a world he believed had treated him unfairly?

Phone messages to others, including son Mat, a Wallaby, went unanswered. In a final, desperate attempt for help, Sludge tried to dial 000 but, unable to find his reading glasses, punched in 888 instead. Mat says, 'I feel so sorry for those moments before everything went black for him ... what he was thinking, what he was trying to do. He left a message on my phone the day before everything happened. He said he loved me and wanted to talk to me, but I didn't get to it which is a shame.'

Former Kangaroo team-mate Ian Schubert best summarised the mood of the thousands who attended Sludge's funeral. 'I don't want to remember him for what I read in the paper,' Schubert said. 'I want to remember him for what he was on the field.'

Rogers was the most versatile player of his generation. Yet, during the two years I coached him at St George (1983–84), everything he did was instinctive. There was no point asking him how he did anything on the field any more than it was to ask Frank Sinatra how he summoned that voice. His attitude to rugby league was reminiscent of Duke Ellington's response when asked to define jazz. 'Man, if you've got to ask what it is, you'll never be where it's at.'

In attack, Rogers moved like the surgeon's knife – the glide, then the quick incision. In defence, he hit bigger opponents like a lifetime supply of bad news, a metaphor for how his death was received by the league community. F. Scott Fitzgerald once wrote, 'Show me a hero and I will write you a tragedy,' and this dark, peculiar idea has haunted me since the day I learned of Rogers's death.

Rugby union gave one of their most loved characters, George Pippos, publican and long-serving Queensland official, a great send-off when he died suddenly of a heart attack at age 61. A legendary character, Pippos was a member of a Goondiwindi syndicate that owned Gunsynd, the champion Cox Plate-winning racehorse. He was also Lord High Executioner on the ARU board, organising the vote against those whose use-by date had passed. He used colourful language to refer to NSW officials he deemed gutless – 'weak as custard and twice as yellow'. But it was his breathtaking political incorrectness for which he is best remembered.

Once on a visit to apartheid South Africa, he asked President de Klerk, 'How many white fellas?' Told the republic's white population was around 4 million, he then asked, 'How many black fellas?' Told it was around 28 million, Pippos responded, 'Jeez, you're fucked.'

When the QRU believed that it wasn't duchessing sponsors sufficiently, directors were allocated a corporate box at Brisbane's rugby headquarters to smooch the donors. Pippos was given the Telstra box but spent two hours complaining about telephone services to his pubs. The next home game, he was allocated the code's long-time loyal supplier of footwear. After studying the benevolent businessman carefully from a distance, George sauntered over and asked, 'You the shoe cunt?'

When Prime Minister John Howard was feted at a function, Pippos walked past the fawning group encircling him, poked his head in without spilling a drop of the four beers he was carrying and said, 'You're doing a fucking good job.'

Former Wallaby Peter Crittle's eulogy of Pippos is considered the code's best. 'Angelo George Pippos was a one-off, stand-alone, never-to-be-repeated, throw-away-the-mould, you-won't-see-this-again, gem of a man,' Crittle said towards the end. 'George was never a poet and, as far as I know, never read a poem in his life. But if one poet did sum up George's death, it was the great 17th century cleric, John Donne. In a superb parable, Donne said, "Any man's death diminishes me, because I am involved in mankind. Therefore, send not to know for whom the bell tolls; it tolls for thee."'

Increasingly in rugby league, ex-players, aware their death from cancer or some disease is imminent, allow mates to organise a farewell. It's an eminently sensible idea in the most pragmatic of sports, the honoree sitting there proudly while all the eulogies wash over him. I've attended a few and invariably the words of Martin Luther King Jr come to mind. 'Like everybody, I would like to live a long life,' King told a group of people he loved, sanitation workers in Memphis. 'Longevity has its place. But I'm not concerned about that now . . . I'm happy tonight.' King was killed the next day.

Bliss is also reflected in the face of the honoree at league functions. He rarely responds, allowing the planned speech in his head to give way to the message in his heart. The happy memories appear in grainier texture these days, flickering inside battered heads like silent movies. These occasions evoke memories that make us all feel somewhat wizened and sage, and just a bit sad. But they are also opportunities to think about chance and fate and talent and the role each plays in our lives. It makes us wonder if we would change many things in the past, even if we could. The motto of Western Suburbs Past Players' Association sums it all up. It is a quote from the poet WB Yeats: 'Think where man's glory most begins and ends, and say my glory was I had such friends.'

The Men of League Ball in 2005 witnessed a beautiful admission. Wally O'Connell and Keith 'Yappy' Holman, both 1948 Kangaroos, were called to the stage, and Wally confessed that something had stuck in his throat for over 50 years. Apparently they had played together in a trial for the tour, Wests' Holman as halfback to O'Connell, a five-eighth, then with Easts. O'Connell dropped almost every pass and the press assumed it was Holman's bad passes. Holman was accused of attempting to play his club five-eighth and great friend, Frank Stanmore, into the team.

O'Connell told the black tie gathering how he had allowed the media to write this unchallenged. 'I had a recurrence of an eye problem that day, Yappy,' O'Connell said, revealing he had been plagued throughout his career with a vision impairment. 'That's why I dropped the ball. I owe you an apology for that.'

Everything decent comes right in the end.

Drop Punts and Torpedoes
by Suzi Petkovski

Talking football is the ultimate participant sport. Most of us will never fly up there like Cazaly on the sacred turf of the MCG, but the footy industry provides endless fascination and speculation through commentary, interviews and chatter. Whether it's a withering blast from a coach, a sharp witticism from a commentator or a player's verbal clanger, football language can be as colourful, chaotic, brutal and uniquely Australian as the game itself.

This classic collection of quotes from players, coaches, umpires, commentators and fans is perfect for the diehard fan of the Australian game.

It's Only a Game
By John O'Neill

John O'Neill, one of the world's leading sports administrators, believes in 'pipedreams' – those radical ideas that show us what is possible. Having enjoyed a successful banking career, John always held rugby union close to his heart. Taking over as CEO of the ARU in 1995, John lead the game into its most successful and financially prosperous period. Australia won the World Cup in 1999 and hosted the 'best ever' tournament in 2003.

In a recruitment coup by Frank Lowy, he left the ARU in 2004 to lead Football Federation Australia. His Midas touch was again evident in the Socceroos' dramatic 2006 FIFA World Cup campaign that lifted an entire nation.

John O'Neill recounts the power struggles with the establishment and players, and the lighter moments on and off the field – all against the backdrop of a sports-mad country where the top of the pedestal is the perennial expectation.

Say it Out Loud
By Adam Sutton and Neil McMahon

When Heath Ledger finished reading the script for *Brokeback Mountain* – a film about a love affair between two American cowboys – he thought of his friend Adam Sutton, and told him, 'I've just read this script and it sounds a lot like you.' He was right: Adam's own life was reflected in many of the film's themes.

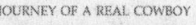

Brokeback Mountain went on to establish itself as a cultural landmark and its impact was felt far beyond the cinema: it was a human story, not a gay story, and audiences of every type responded around the world. Similarly, when Adam Sutton's story appeared on the front page of the *Sydney Morning Herald*, the response was immediate and extraordinary. 'Meet Heath's mate, the real gay cowboy,' the headline ran, and thousands did – setting a sales record for the paper, and prompting the TV program *Australian Story* to devote an episode to Adam's story.

By nature Adam is a masculine daredevil who survives on the strength of his boisterous character. He is 'the crazy bastard' – the maddest, bravest bloke in the room – who has faced tragedy, a prison stint, and five long years on the road, but who could not face himself. His extraordinary and unlikely journey from the world of cowboys, rodeos and stereotypes, to Hollywood and, finally, to self-acceptance, is a powerful reminder that sometimes truth is even stranger than Hollywood fiction.